KASPAR H

CW00832743

KASPAR HAUSER
The Struggle for the Spirit

*A contribution towards an understanding of
the nineteenth and twentieth centuries*

Peter Tradowsky

TEMPLE LODGE
London

Translated by John M. Wood

Temple Lodge Publishing
51 Queen Caroline Street
London W6 9QL

Published by Temple Lodge 1997

Originally published in German under the title *Kaspar Hauser oder das Ringen um den Geist* by Verlag am Goetheanum, Dornach, Switzerland, 1980

A catalogue record for this book is available from the British Library

ISBN 0 904693 89 9

Cover: Kaspar Hauser, 1830, by J.F.C. Kreul; layout by S. Gulbekian
Typeset by DP Photosetting, Aylesbury, Bucks
Printed and bound in Great Britain by Cromwell Press Limited, Broughton Gifford, Wiltshire

Contents

Publisher's Preface

Although the figure of Kaspar Hauser is well-known in German-speaking countries, in the rest of the world, apart from some notable exceptions—in particular the movement which has grown up around the work of Rudolf Steiner—he is generally not known at all. Thus the translation and publication of this book in English requires a few opening remarks.

Kaspar Hauser was discovered in 1828 on the streets of Nuremberg, Germany. Although he was 15 years old, he could only speak a few words, and could barely walk. It transpired, from his own account and from all available evidence, that he had been imprisoned since early childhood in a darkened space, within which he had not been able to stand or walk. During these years he had had no human contact to speak of.

Despite these great handicaps, Kaspar Hauser was able—with the friendly and kind guidance of a number of individuals—to begin a normal human development, and indeed started to display certain extraordinary qualities. But he was not allowed to develop. He was murdered in 1833, following an earlier assasination attempt.

The many riddles surrounding the life and death of Kaspar Hauser are dealt with in this work. However, Peter Tradowsky's main aim is to delve into the *occult* aspects of the Kaspar Hauser story. In doing this he draws primarily from the work of the educationalist, seer and philosopher Rudolf Steiner (1861–1925). Thus, the book assumes a certain knowledge of Rudolf Steiner's spiritual world-view (which he called Anthroposophy).

Although first published in German in 1980, this book remains a treasure of research for anybody interested in the mystery of Kaspar Hauser. It is being published in response to the serious deficiency of any substantial work on the theme in English.

While it was not planned as such, the publication of this

book happens to coincide with some recent attacks—of an 'exoteric' and 'esoteric' nature respectively—on the being of Kaspar Hauser. The former attack was launched by the German newspaper *Der Spiegel*, which printed a story on 25 November 1996 that claimed that genetic analysis of bloodstains from Kaspar Hauser's clothing proved that he was not the son of Stephanie de Beauharnais, and therefore not of royal descent. The attack of a more esoteric nature comes from within the anthroposophical movement and derives from articles published in *Das Goetheanum* (for example 'Das Rätsel der Geburt—Mysterium und Mystifikation um Kaspar Hauser' by Michael Klussmann, 22 December 1996) which uphold the view of the German writer Christoph Lindenberg that the typed record of notes of a key conversation between Count Poltzer-Hoditz and Rudolf Steiner (used extensively in this book) is a forgery. Although Tradowsky refers to these in his Foreword to the English edition (see p.xv), he answers the *Der Spiegel* attack in much greater detail in his article in *Das Goetheanum* of 15 December 1996). The authenticity of the notes of Polzer-Hoditz has been corroborated in a number of articles (see, for example, Thomas Meyer's piece in *Der Europäer*, February 1997).

Finally, the publishers would like to thank the many centres of the Camphill movement whose contributions have helped to support the publication of this book, and also the translator John Wood for his devoted work.

S.G., August 1997, London

Foreword

I have spoken about Kaspar Hauser in various towns in Germany during recent years. My first lecture was given within the Anthroposophical Society in Berlin in September 1970 under the heading: 'Kaspar Hauser and the myth of the future'. The direction was thereby set for the way in which I have since worked. My aim has been to allow Kaspar Hauser to be experienced not merely as a historical figure, but primarily as a spiritually inspired individuality bound up with the great future tasks of humanity.

The wish constantly expressed to me by many people that I should record the contents of these various lectures in writing, finally led to the composition of this book. In addition to that I felt ever more strongly my commitment to Kaspar Hauser to make the realized facts known to a larger circle of people. This work bears within it in more or less clear form the traces of its conception. The important questions were gradually approached from various sides in order to fathom their complexity. Out of this arises the repeated treatment of some of the central problems in different connections and from different points of view.

The more or less complete account of all previous findings makes it possible for the first time to compare all factors and illuminate them one against the other. So it may, for instance, be significant to throw light on all previous chapters by what we have just said. Yes, one could say that certain statements made in other parts of the book can only be more deeply understood with reference to the final chapter. Thus one thing qualifies and supports another.

The first chapter deals in rather greater detail with the classic witnesses of Kaspar Hauser's first appearance in Nuremberg. The account of this as comprehended by the different observers gives a more vivid impression owing to its very diversity. These indispensable sources of information about Kaspar Hauser are included here because, regrettably,

they are still far too little known. Every biographical and
historical account must start from them in order to acquire a
firm basis.

This book is intentionally directed towards the friends of
Kaspar Hauser. It is intended as a textbook for studying. In
many places questions have been raised which are intended to
lead further—they are a challenge to seek more deeply for the
solution of the riddle.

I have two reasons for avoiding confrontation with the
opponents, upon whom some light has been shed by this
exposition. In the first place we should think of Goethe's
saying: 'A wrong teaching cannot be refuted because it rests on
the assumption that the wrong is right, but the opposite may,
can and must be expressed again and again.'[1] In the second
place it would show disrespect towards the life's work of
Hermann Pies if one were to begin all over again to counter the
assertions and methods of those who wrote about Kaspar
Hauser—especially during the last century—in a personal or
even antagonistic way. Pies often exposed such antagonistic
methods for what they were. We owe it to him that he treated
and made available the actual and original reports and
observations. Later findings are reported in Appendix II,
where there is also a contribution concerning the unsolved
questions of the Kaspar Hauser investigation.

A certain amount of knowledge and understanding of
Rudolf Steiner's Anthroposophy is assumed to be possessed
by the readers of this account. Without Anthroposophy it
would be impossible to arrive at real conclusions concerning
the many questions surrounding Kaspar Hauser. This is very
properly based on the fact that Kaspar Hauser is a spiritual
phenomenon of a special kind and that Anthroposophy, as a
science of the spirit, is in a position to explain such a phenomenon scientifically. There is also the further point that
karmic connections exist between Rudolf Steiner and Kaspar
Hauser. Kaspar Hauser himself lives within the spiritual
stream of Rosicrucianism which leads to Anthroposophy.

Those friends of Kaspar Hauser who up till now have had
no contact with Anthroposophy may feel themselves obliged

to tread this path in their endeavours to find solutions to the riddles. In this way they will learn about Anthroposophy because the way to Anthroposophy can also be found through Kaspar Hauser.

All work done in connection with Kaspar Hauser will receive new aims and impulses out of what Rudolf Steiner tells us. For this reason all known sayings of his and some which have not previously been made known are recorded in Appendix I, as far as is possible in chronological order.

The work on the manuscript, which took me about three years to complete, was only possible through the intensive help given me by Sigrid Gräfe. She also carefully read through the manuscript. For her constant support and many helpful and elucidatory conversations I am truly grateful.

Out of given circumstances I should like to say in conclusion that the author alone bears responsibility for the contents of this book.

Peter Tradowsky
Berlin, Easter 1981

Foreword to the Second Edition

Soon after the publication of the first edition during Advent 1980, a second edition was called for. One gets the impression that the call to participate in the struggle for knowledge about the destiny and character of Kaspar Hauser has been heard and understood. From among the circle of the readers the opinion has been expressed that the appearance of this book has been felt and experienced as a spiritual need just at this time.

In consideration of the depressing destinies of Central Europe and the whole of mankind the question is often raised as to what can be done to help. Through understanding and experiencing the sufferings of the Kaspar Hauser individuality, as also that of the destiny of Central Europe and the spiritual connection between earth and cosmos, as we have tried to do here, the soul becomes activated, whereby the first step towards a transformation of these circumstances is achieved. In the Easter Event this earthly-cosmic condition has been created for all future times. The participating reader is looked for in the above sense.

Peter Tradowsky
Berlin, Easter 1981

Foreword to the Third Edition

The third edition of this book is dedicated to the 150th anniversary of Kaspar Hauser's death (17 December 1833). In connection with this anniversary Kaspar Hauser has stepped further into the limelight through a series of notices in the various media. As a result of this it has been shown what a great deal of uncertainty exists regarding the whole event of his appearance, as well as an almost inexplicable ignorance about it after decades of scientific investigation. A far-reaching symptom of this is the fact that Kaspar Hauser's descent from the House of Baden is still doubted today, even though all specialist investigators agree with Hermann Pies who wrote in the introduction to his documentation on Kaspar Hauser in 1966: 'Now I believe that I have obtained such irrefutable circumstantial evidence of Kaspar Hauser's princely descent from the House of Baden that there can hardly be anything more conclusive in the case of *successful* dynastic crimes'. One gets the impression that the struggle to understand Kaspar Hauser is just as difficult and essential for the twentieth century as it was for the nineteenth century. To honour, recognize and understand him is a spiritual task on which now as before the spirits are divided.

In order that all may be done to make the figure of Kaspar Hauser stand out in its true light, I have decided, together with Johannes Meyer, who has made himself responsible for the illustrations, to portray the life of Kaspar Hauser in words and pictures under the title: *Kaspar Hauser, Das Kind von Europa*

(Stuttgart 1983). This new work and the present volume support and complement one another.

After the printing of the second edition it was noticed that the Kaspar Hauser portrait was a detail of the famous Kreul picture which, through its inadequate reproduction, had gained a peculiar charm. This time the pastel drawing by Kreul has been reproduced in colour. This picture from Würzburg used to belong to Daumer. There is a second picture by Kreul, very similar to this one, which belonged to Feuerbach, which is now in private ownership. It can be regarded as a piece of luck that a colourful and more lively portrait of Kaspar Hauser has now made its appearance.

Peter Tradowsky
Berlin, Whitsuntide 1983

Foreword to the English Edition

The book presented here was published 17 years ago in Germany. It is obvious that after such a long time a revision of the whole work would be preferable, but in my present work situation this cannot be achieved. It is certainly true that the basic themes could be gone into in more depth and enlarged upon, but nevertheless they can also stand as they are on their own merit. In other words, changes would have been welcome, but are not essential.

Two aspects, which do not directly affect the main theme, require to be mentioned however. In the first place the identity of Kaspar Hauser as the heir to the throne of Baden has been brought into question. In the second place doubts have been raised about the authenticity of statements made by Rudolf Steiner which are published for the first time in the present book.

Der Spiegel (No. 48, 25 November 1996) roused a world-wide sensation with the cover story: 'Kaspar Hauser, the prince disenchanted. Genetic scientists solve a century old riddle', in which it is reported that an English and a German Institute for genetic research have independently established the fact that blood from the underpants which Kaspar Hauser was wearing at the time of his murder does not originate from a son of Stephanie de Beauharnais. With that the results of the serious Kaspar Hauser research of the nineteenth and twentieth centuries would be disproved. Research which has been carried out over 40 years by the most significant researcher, Hermann Pies, were summed up by him in 1966 in the following way: 'Now I believe that I have obtained such irrefutable circumstantial evidence of Kaspar Hauser's princely descent from the House of Baden that there can hardly be anything more conclusive in the case of *successful* dynastic crimes' (Hermann Pies, *Kaspar Hauser Dokumentation*, Ansbach 1966). So we should bear in mind that the facts discovered by a succession of researchers cannot be annulled by genetic analysis, as little as does the picture of Kaspar's character presented in this book depend upon his descent. Kaspar Hauser's imprisonment, his deeds and suffering, would not be changed through the event of some kind of change in his ancestry. The authors of *Der Spiegel*, however, would like to convey the unjustified and incorrect impression that by solving the question of identify the whole Kaspar Hauser problem would be solved in the truest sense of the word. For them he is ultimately only a 'half-wit bastard'. With that the whole underlying tendency is revealed. The object is to extinguish the spiritual picture of 'the Child of Europe'. Through that, however, the need and importance of getting a spiritual grasp of Kaspar Hauser's character, as we have tried to do in this book, is made all the more evident.

For all that, we must take a new line of research seriously and try to find out what is of value in it. For a start, doubt can be expressed as to whether the blood is really that of Kaspar Hauser. Furthermore we should confirm that no sources of error and failure lie in the methods of research. The scientists themselves admit that they are dealing with things which are 'close to the boundaries of proof'. That the fact of accepting a different identity for Kaspar Hauser is not easy is not due to the rejection of modern research, nor is it a clinging to out-of-date opinions, but it is the recognition of a fact which *Der Spiegel* simply fails to notice, namely, that the mystery is in no way solved thereby, but is made much more complicated. The opinion that Kaspar Hauser is the heir to the throne of Baden is supported by facts gathered by many researchers, not least of which is the fact that the behaviour and procedure of the state secret police and the Court of Baden give a very clear indication to any intelligent and open-minded person. Their course of action was determined by the premise that Kaspar Hauser was the heir to the throne of Baden. If this premise should prove to be wrong, the key question for future research into Kaspar Hauser would be: How could such a colossal mistake have been made? Why was it not noticed? Why was it impossible to give the truth convincingly? If one could have proved that Kaspar Hauser was not the heir to the throne, one could have spared oneself the trouble of a very risky state involvement. Apart from this key question others, such as the following, arise: How was it that Stephanie de Beauharnais could recognize her son by his likeness to his father when she saw him in the palace gardens at Ansbach, if this were not the case? And if it were not true, how is it possible that many contemporaries, familiar with the family, could take Kaspar Hauser to be the son of the Grand Duke of Baden—a process which can be repeated today on the strength of certain pictures which bear a striking resemblance to him? Finally, if Kaspar Hauser were not the heir to the throne, who then were his parents? How and why did he get into the hands of those who imprisoned him?

To the question of the authenticity of the notes by Count Ludwig Polzer-Hoditz, supplied by Paul Michaelis, the inheritor of his estate, and published in this book for the first time, let it be here shortly stated that justified doubt has been expressed concerning the responsible transmission of these texts. Thus, for instance, a meeting between Rudolf Steiner and Count Polzer-Hoditz did not take place in November 1916. Out of such and other observations the conclusion has been drawn that these notes are forgeries of Paul Michaelis. I cannot agree with this verdict, because there is nothing to show that the notes could not have been based on talks that Count Polzer-Hoditz had with Rudolf Steiner. In view of the fact that the original handwritten notes have gone astray, no conclusion can be drawn. Just as little, of course, can it be said that, under the present unstable conditions, it is possible to say that the notes given to us in this way are undoubted expressions of Rudolf Steiner's statements. The way must be sought to discriminate between forgery and genuineness by a study of the contents. In this way I have arrived at the conviction that the notes here published are essentially derived from Rudolf Steiner for the simple reason that I am unable to discover anyone else who could have produced such thoughts. But even if this should not be the case, the sayings would still have validity. Ultimately every reader must judge for himself if he finds these statements productive and sensible or not. Every statement must be judged on its own intrinsic merits; that is more important than reliance on some other authority. I should just like to mention that the notes of Count Polzer-Hoditz were given to me on account of the lectures I gave about Kaspar Hauser. They were not the source of my lectures, but they fitted into the framework of them without difficulty.

Since the reunion of Germany in 1990, the division of the country which is described in Chapter 3 '1944/45' might appear in a different light. This reunion, which is connected with the peaceful impulse of setting the East Europeans free, has also set East Germany free, but at the same time the apparent triumph of capitalism has brought unforeseeably devastating consequences for that country, as it has over the whole of Europe. I have expressed my opinion about these problems in my books: *Ere the Century Closes*, Camphill Books, 1995, and *Christ und Antichrist*, Dornach, 1996. In the first of these books deeper statements about Kaspar Hauser are to be found in the chapter: 'Kaspar Hauser, the Child of Europe, a picture of the Christ-Destiny'.

Peter Tradowsky
Berlin, Easter 1997

Introduction

In this book a picture is given of the history of the nineteenth and twentieth centuries, which in many details and in its entirety is very different from the picture which is usually given. The first way in which it differs is the view here taken and established that in the history of the nineteenth and twentieth centuries Kaspar Hauser forms a crux in which all important threads come together, but which, unfortunately, up till now has been left out of historical consideration. This situation has been brought about through the prevention of Kaspar Hauser's historical mission. To lessen the effects of this occurrence is the intention of this book. In this particular case knowledge simultaneously acquires the force of a deed.

The second thing by which the picture of the nineteenth and twentieth centuries has been radically changed—but also clarified—is the attempt to explain it directly in terms of the historical rhythm of 33 years, discovered by Rudolf Steiner through his spiritual investigation. This powerful force working into post-Christian evolution has had very little attention paid to it till now, nor has it seen much practical application. But it will come to light more and more that a true understanding of history will prove impossible without this insight. Deeply ingrained in historical consciousness—insofar as this still exists—is the thinking which runs along the track of linear-causal sequence. If these habits of thought are not overcome then the relationship of germ to fruit—the spirit-breath of history stretching throughout the generations—cannot be conveyed to mankind. We must overcome the great illusion which imagines that history can be understood by man without regard to the spirit. To represent history as a purely earthly series of events is unrealistic insofar as it does not take into account the spirit-ground of life in which—beyond human whim and apart from the ordinary consciousness—the development of man takes place in conjunction with the supersensible worlds. The comprehension of these real and effective connections is the true task, by the fulfilling of which the spirit is revealed and becomes effective. Consequently one will be enabled to understand and deal with history in a proper way. So long as we do not understand the spirit, which is actually at work in history—as illustrated by the 33-year rhythm—it will be no less a being than the demon who takes charge, who disguises the real issue.

To conquer or to lose the spirit, that is the real historical issue of the nineteenth and twentieth centuries. In the struggle for the spirit the real issue at stake is the 'to be or not to be' of an existence worthy of humanity.

My work has spiritual predecessors without whom it would be unthinkable. Georg Friedrich Daumer, Anselm Ritter von Feuerbach and Heinrich Fuhrmann[2] in the nineteenth century and Jakob Wassermann, Hermann Pies and Karl Heyer[3] in the twentieth century. The title of this book consciously takes its cue from the sub-title of Wassermann's novel: *Caspar Hauser oder die Trägheit des Herzens* [Caspar Hauser or the indolence of the heart], for to the aspect of the heart must be added that other aspect of knowledge, which portrays Kaspar Hauser at the centre of a struggle for the realization of the spirit.

It is my wish to refer here to the hundredth anniversary of Daumer's death in 1875, the recollection of which might be regarded as a spiritual obligation (born 5 March 1800 in Nuremberg, died 13 December 1875 in Würzburg). Whoever would seek access to the personality and history of Kaspar Hauser will always be led to Georg Friedrich Daumer. This will be particularly the case when one attempts to identify oneself with the living current which radiates outward from Kaspar Hauser and when one unites with the endeavours and struggles of those who have already laboured to elucidate the Kaspar Hauser destiny by their knowledge.

Daumer is not only important on account of being the teacher and friend of Kaspar Hauser. He is paramountly the unbiased observer-phenomenologist in the sense of Goethe who summons up the courage and strength to let appearances

speak to him, or at least to leave them as they are and faithfully record them. Still more important is the fact that during
his whole life he was a courageous and steadfast defender of
Kaspar Hauser in his historical uniqueness. It was characteristic of him that his last and summative work: *Kaspar Hauser*,[2]
which is hardly to be overestimated in value and is a bib-
liophilic rarity, was written to defend and protect the person
(of Kaspar Hauser) who had been persecuted and maligned in
Julius Meyer's book *Authentische Mitteilungen über Kaspar
Hauser*[4] [Authentic records of Kaspar Hauser]. The sense of
responsibility which Daumer felt towards Kaspar Hauser and
his belief that he was acting under higher authority are plainly
expressed in these words from the preface:

> It is in the sense of an *epilogue* to this subject that I am
> publishing this account. With it I believe that I have done all
> I could to fulfil my obligations in this direction; I am an old
> man and am seemingly rapidly approaching my end; in
> respect of my physical condition it is a wonder that I am still
> alive. In the meantime I believe I still possess sufficient
> spiritual strength to fulfil such a task as this and that I am
> equal to the conflict which lies before me; an old warrior like
> myself is still able on occasion to take up his sword again
> and test the strength of his arm even though he has already
> retired; a higher assistance will surely not be lacking to one
> who is *dedicated* and *committed* to the struggle. I affirm
> most solemnly that, as in the past, so now too, the truth is
> sacred to me and that I have never intentionally or know-
> ingly made any false statement in this my writing.[5]

In a certain sense we have to be grateful to Julius Meyer, the
son of the notoriously ill-famed teacher of Kaspar Hauser in
the Ansbach days, that necessitated the writing of Daumer's
book. Daumer, by the way, was convinced that Meyer published his book under the mistaken belief that he, Daumer,
was already dead. The deceased was Daumer's brother.[6]
Daumer is a person who, in the last third of the nineteenth
century, lived in the hope of seeing an end to the age of
materialism, awaiting and sensing the approach of a new age

of the spirit. He saw clearly that human evolution in the form
it then took was on the road to catastrophe if it continued in its
materialistic outlook. With an ardour hardly equalled by any
of his contemporaries Daumer longed for the beginning of a
new spiritual revelation, as it was to appear a few years later,
introduced by the young Rudolf Steiner at the beginning of the
Michael Age. One can only say that a soul such as Daumer's
would have rejoiced exceedingly if it could have experienced
the knowledge of the spiritual world and its inhabitants as
Rudolf Steiner gave it to mankind at the turn of the century
and into the beginning of the New Age of Light. A passage I
will quote for this reason sounds directly prophetic. The hope
of a so badly needed change in man's attitude of soul is clearly
expressed therein—a hope that cannot be so quickly realized
during the time to come, which will only be fulfilled after a
long spiritual battle:

> I cannot deal more fully with this subject here. But never-
> theless one can see that a spiritual ferment is taking place, of
> which the outcome is uncertain, but which seems to predict
> that a change is in progress which is not at all favourable to
> materialism. The diverse Spiritualism or Spiritism of our
> day which has this in general as its aim and purpose to put
> spirit and spiritual deeds before raw matter with its outer
> commitments and necessities, is what I have always wished
> for. It challenges the spiritual and moral world-supremacy
> of materialism in such a way that the latter is no longer able
> to pretend that it is the sole ruler and master of all things
> and that there will be far worse to fear from a future epoch
> to which the present one appears to build a bridge. World
> history is an ever-turning wheel; thrones topple as well in
> the political arena as in the realms of faith, thought and
> science; and many things bluster and show themselves off as
> if an immortal existence had been granted them whereas the
> feet of those who are to supplant them are already at the
> door.[7]

In connection with this mood of anticipation of the coming
spirituality is the saying of Rudolf Steiner in which he

characterizes Daumer as 'the last of the Rosicrucians'. In Daumer's work itself this point of view is not directly evident. But one is struck by the fact that what Daumer did for Kaspar Hauser was performed out of service to a higher authority. In his dedicatory poem Daumer lets the dead Kaspar Hauser speak to him in a very moving way. It is a conversation between a dead soul and a living one, which clearly indicates that Daumer is not referring to his own personality but to an impulse which comes to him through a discarnate soul, from the spiritual world.

For those who can accept that as true and take it seriously Daumer's work is in a quite different category to many other publications on this subject. The dedicatory poem, which gives the mood out of which all that has here been attempted to be expressed about Kaspar Hauser, runs as follows:

Life's pilgrimage will soon be done,
I feel my powers ebbing fast;
Yet once again, my poor child,
I see thy blood-drenched shadow rise.

Thy spirit lips they whisper soft:
'O thou, my friend, forever true,
My knight and my protector aye,
However hard the strife might be!

I was—that knowest thou full well—
Ne'er to gruesomeness disposed;
The one has struck me in the breast,
The others covered me with shame.

Thou strovest here, thou strovest there
The triumph of innocence assured
And in my dismal haven I
Slept once again in deepest peace.

But never rest the wiles of hell,
The rage of hell upon the earth;
After respite I am once more
Reviled and trodden underfoot.

O let me test thy love and courage
In the present battle too;
Take me under thy protection!
From above strength shall not fail.'

Thou speakest and I'm here at hand;
I and my sword serve as of old,
And sacred is the faithful bond,
Our duty now we shall perform.

The task of Feuerbach, the famous criminologist, was not this spiritual task with regard to Kaspar Hauser. During his whole life Feuerbach had been searching for the real motive for the crime committed against Kaspar Hauser. In spite of his deep understanding for the boy, he never arrived at a solution of the crime, because he could not understand its motive. This was bound to be something most significant—that was clearer to him than to anyone else. If it was a dynastic crime, why was Kaspar Hauser not killed immediately? This was the question which Feuerbach was ultimately unable to answer, because the reasons for it lie in the spiritual realm. One might well say that if Feuerbach had been aware of the anthroposophical study of man and the teachings about reincarnation, a person of his calibre would immediately have recognized the motive for the occult crime.

Pastor Fuhrmann's little essays are unfortunately and quite undeservedly very little known. His printed talks are real jewels of Christian opinion.

Even to this day Wassermann's novel is the easiest route to understanding Kaspar Hauser. One must only bear in mind that this novel is in the best sense of the word both fiction and truth and dates from the state of enlightenment which pertained at the beginning of the present century. Wassermann's novel is ultimately based on a 'vision', as he says himself,* that is to say on a supersensible impulse like the one which Daumer also experienced. Through that his novel has an enduring life-

---

* See notes section on p. 302 for this and all other asterisks in text.

force and contains a number of intuitive insights (for instance
the connection of Lord Stanhope to the horror lurking in the
background) which considerably deepen an understanding of
events.

Through Wassermann's novel Hermann Pies was also led to
his life's task. After reading this novel he felt it his duty to
discover the historical truth. Hermann Pies collected and
recorded the various facts in an admirable and painstaking
work which was the result of a lifetime of study. In almost 60
years of investigation he examined and published all the
relevant documents. The latter filled six volumes. In a concluding and summarizing seventh volume, which appeared in
1966 under the heading *Kaspar Hauser—Eine Dokumentation*,
he gathered the results of all his historical investigations
together. This work forms the indispensable prerequisite for
any work done in connection with Kaspar Hauser.[8]

It is both shattering and humiliating when it becomes plain
through the work of Hermann Pies that there are always
persons, untiring in the assertions of their commitment to
truth and science, who have demonstrably falsified and lied.
This phenomenon, which had already been noted by Daumer,
that in connection with Kaspar Hauser the simplest scientific
requirements have been abandoned without embarrassment,
also belongs among the factors to be noted in connection with
Kaspar Hauser. What the enemies of Kaspar Hauser succeeded in doing in this way can only be seen as a scientific
disgrace. Hermann Pies was able to demonstrate, for instance,
that the 'Authentic Records' by Julius Meyer, on which he laid
so much stress as being the historical and legally authenticated
truth, contained sense-distorting alterations, omissions and
even falsifications in abundance.

We who have been born later are indebted to Karl Heyer for
his book *Kaspar Hauser und das Schicksal Mittel-Europas im
19 Jahrhundert* ['Kaspar Hauser and the Destiny of Central
Europe in the Nineteenth Century'] in which he has faithfully
recorded and checked for their validity the statements of
Rudolf Steiner which do not appear in his lectures. The few
most important statements about Kaspar Hauser which are

integral to the present work, were given by Rudolf Steiner in conversation with members of the Anthroposophical Society. Furthermore Heyer has incorporated Kaspar Hauser into the consideration of modern history—a fact which is unavoidable; he is the first to treat Kaspar Hauser from the point of view of Anthroposophy in a wide context within the framework of his *Beiträge zur Geschichte des Abendlandes* ['Contributions towards the study of Western History'].

1. Kaspar Hauser's Path of Sacrifice

*The Child of Europe—Kaspar Hauser's biography
and history*

Whoever would recount the life and destiny of a human being will start, as a matter of course, with that person's birth, with a glance at mother and father and at the place and time of its occurrence. But if one is speaking about the foundling Kaspar Hauser, one is straightaway confronted by the remarkable fact that the place and time of his birth and his line of descent have long been debated and have been a matter of uncertainty. At the very beginning the impression arises that this child's birth was such an event that people came together who wanted to conceal it and make it ineffective.

An understanding of Kaspar Hauser's biography is made much more difficult because of the mystery of his birth. For that reason the first task for anyone wishing to understand Kaspar Hauser's life is to solve the riddle of his identity, because it is just with his birth that the factors are connected which give rise to 'the most remarkable of all remarkable criminal proceedings, the likes of which have probably never before occurred throughout millennia'.[9] Unending assiduity has been expended during the course of time in solving the riddle of his birth in a satisfactory way.

It is unreasonable in the light of modern scientific research not to acknowledge that Kaspar Hauser, born in Karlsruhe on Michaelmas Day, 29 September 1812, is the heir to the throne of the Zähringen dynasty, son of the then reigning Grand Duke Karl and his wife Stephanie de Beauharnais, the adopted daughter of Napoleon. There is no longer any reason today to doubt that the personality we know as Kaspar Hauser did incarnate on Michaelmas Day 1812. It is very understandable that the opponents of Kaspar Hauser even today are anxious to conceal or cover up this important fact by maintaining that it is not possible to ascertain who Kaspar

Hauser was and when he was born. But to that which can move our hearts belongs the fact that Michaelmas Day is the birthday of Kaspar Hauser and that this forms an essential component of his life.

The reasons will now be shortly stated which will necessarily lead to the conclusion that Kaspar Hauser was the heir to the throne of Baden. Feuerbach, in his famous memoir of 1832, which he sent to Kaspar Hauser's aunt, Queen Karoline of Bayern, was the first to uphold this statement, arising out of unknown sources and early bruited abroad among the people, as an established fact. He supported this view in the first place on the grounds that Kaspar Hauser could only be a legitimate child of high birth. There is no conceivable situation— Feuerbach studied that in detail—in which an illegitimate child, or one from a lower class, could be the cause of such an extensive crime stretching over more that two decades. There were bound to be circumstances connected with Kaspar Hauser's birth that appeared to necessitate such a dangerous criminal action, which at that time could have incurred the death penalty. By investigating the German families of the time in question, Feuerbach comes to the conclusion that it was only in the Zähringen dynasty where circumstances were present which could cause suspicion. It was conspicuous that Stephanie de Beauharnais had given birth to five children, of which two were sons, whose health had been expressly confirmed by the doctors, but who, nevertheless, both died suddenly as infants: the first of these on 16 October 1812; his brother, Prince Alexander, at one year old in 1817. Three other heirs to the throne perish under more or less peculiar circumstances, a fact to which Hermann Pies points, so that the unusual fact remains that, although five legitimate heirs to the throne existed, the regular Zähringen dynasty dies out in the male line. In this way Leopold, the son of the Grand Duchess von Hochberg, becomes the Grand Duke of Baden in 1830, that is during the lifetime of Kaspar Hauser. It would require a distinct degree of *naiveté* to believe in coincidence in this case. Apart from that, Feuerbach is able to point out that the dates of the letters which Kaspar Hauser carried with him when he first made his appearance fit with the dates belonging to his brother Alexander, probably also murdered. He is rightly of the opinion that here, after more than ten years, certain confusions have occurred between the two sons of Stephanie de Beauharnais. It is true that the thoughts which Feuerbach arrived at, even though they were the result of a very keen criminological reasoning can, to begin with, only carry a certain—albeit a very high—degree of certainty in this matter.

In 1875 the discussion regarding the princely heritage of Kaspar Hauser to the throne of Baden came to an end through the fact that the certificates of the birth, illness and death in 1812 of the heir to the throne were published. This circumstance led to an anomaly. The Hohenzollern Emperor, at that time William I, himself arranged for the publication of these documents. It is characteristic of the Emperor's lack of critical judgement and that of those around him that they never recognized the significance of these documents. From this it follows, namely, that in no sense was this a harmless or indisputably correct procedure; far rather it becomes evident that a proper identification of the dead hereditary Prince by the mother or the wet-nurse never took place. Furthermore it is noticeable that, with the illness and death of the Crown Prince, we are evidently dealing with a confused situation about which nobody was clear at the time. The autopsy was also not carried out with the necessary care. But above all it must be noted that the Prince born on 29 September was expressly stated to be in the best of health, which led to the fact that during the succeeding days the publication of further medical bulletins was relinquished, as the child's health demanded no further concern. The features which were observed on the dead child and which led to its death are difficult to reconcile with this diagnosis. There can be no question of an undoubted identification of the dead child. Quite apart from that, these documents do nothing to allay the suspicion that the Crown Prince was exchanged for a dying child.[10]

The question must now, of course, be asked: who was the

changeling and in what connection did he stand in relation to those who were intent on the criminal deed, especially to the Grand Duchess of Hochberg? The Kaspar Hauser investigator, Fritz Klee, actually succeeded in 1929 in establishing and clarifying this connection and discovering the identity of the substitute baby. Among the servants of the Grand Duchess of Hochberg was a family called Blochmann, to whom a boy with the name of Johann Ernst Jakob Blochmann was born on 26 September 1812. This child, like others born to the Blochmann family, was apparently not able to survive. The findings concerning the child which died on 16 October 1812 fit this picture very well. Klee set himself the task of finding out the dates of Johann Ernst Jakob Blochmann, who was born 26 September 1812. In so doing he came across truly astonishing facts. He first of all noticed that, contrary to all the other nine Blochmann children, whose death dates were entered next to the registration of their baptism, the death of a soldier, Kaspar Ernst Blochmann, was entered in the Protestant Death Register of 1833 as having died in Munich on 27 November 1833. One is immediately struck by the fact that here the Blochmann son has been given the wrong Christian name of Kaspar. This fact becomes still more remarkable when Klee discovered that in the Protestant Parish Registry of the City of Munich under the date 27 November 1833 the death of Ernst Blochmann was recorded. A corresponding entry is also made in the funeral register of the Graveyard Management Committee. The second Christian name Kaspar therefore only appears in the Karlsruhe death register. As the conjecture lay at hand that the entries were made on false information it became necessary for Klee to verify if a soldier called Blochmann had actually served in the Bavarian army at that time. Amazingly enough he was able to prove, with the help of the remaining list of soldiers, that at that time there was no soldier of the name of Blochmann serving with the Bavarian forces. From that Klee rightly concluded that he had the proof that those who were responsible for the crime were intent on giving the death of the changeling of 1812 legal status. Through that the abyss was revealed which ran through the whole of this affair and the cunning with which it was carried out: for we are here concerned with nothing less than an attempt to commit the perfect crime. If the Bloch-mann child of 1812 had really died in Munich in 1833 it could not then have been the changeling. The murder of Kaspar Hauser in December 1833 must have been planned in the autumn of 1833 and carefully prepared. Perfidiously enough it was necessary for the exchanged child to be made to die legally 17 days before the planned attack.

Criminal investigation and historical research therefore both lead to the clear conclusion that Kaspar Hauser, born on Michaelmas Day 1812, was the heir to the throne of Baden. Could one perhaps, if one were very sceptical, rule out one of the previously mentioned factors as being impermissible, an alternative possibility would be unthinkable under the given circumstances. Among the still active obfuscations is the fact that in the relevant biographical dictionaries and in many other books the facts connected with the heir to the throne of Baden are still subject to doubt.

In this connection we shall here take a cursory glance at the person of Prince Max of Baden. He is descended from the Hochberg line of the House of Zähring, that is the line which inherited the throne as a result of the elimination of Kaspar Hauser. On 9 November 1918, as the last Chancellor of the German Empire, he had the task of ordering the resignation of the Kaiser, Wilhelm II. A saying of Prince Max of Baden has been recorded to the effect that he intended, after his cor-onation (which never took place), to transfer the mortal remains of Kaspar Hauser to the royal grave of the House of Baden in Pforzheim.[11] From this remark of Prince Max of Baden we can infer that he—along with many others of the German nobility—was convinced that Kaspar Hauser was the legitimate heir to the throne.

If we now speak about the course of Kaspar Hauser's life it will only be a biographical sketch. Kaspar Hauser was carried off, after having been kidnapped, was apparently well looked after and even vaccinated. He grew up in isolation to begin with as a normal child. His captors were waiting for the time when he would be able to stand and had learned to walk. They first allowed the child to become stabilized in his incarnation. They even let him develop speech and thought up to a childish degree. What must have been decisive for those who committed the crime against Kaspar Hauser was, from the start, the age in which he would be able to form his first lasting memories. The great extent of the proceedings becomes apparent if one considers how, at the moment of awakening memory, the treatment changes radically. At a time which must have been between the ages of 2 and 3, Kaspar Hauser was imprisoned in a dungeon, in a cage in which he sat for the next 12 or 13 years. According to his own reports this cage was so constructed that he was forced to sit in dimness, that is in the dark. He never saw the sky, the sun, moon or stars. During the whole of this time he never saw another human being. His food, bread and water, were handed in to him, nursing procedures were carried out while he was in a state of stupor. He had only two wooden horses as toys. The cage was constructed in such a way that he was unable to stand up in it. The upright position, walking and also speaking and thinking were once more held back. Thus he existed in a dimmed state of consciousness, so that, for instance, it became impossible for him to know how long his imprisonment lasted.

Then—it must have been in the spring of 1828 when he was 15 years old—he was quite literally set on his feet. He was taught about 40 words of dialect, in addition to which he was taught by 'the man with whom he had always been', as he himself expressed it, to write 'Kaspar Hauser'. Then he was thrust out into the world. On a Whit Monday, on the afternoon of 26 May 1828, he appeared in Nuremberg. He could hardly walk, his feet and hips hurt him. The first people he met, two shoemakers, describe as eyewitnesses that he came swaying down the street carrying a letter in his hand. Their attempts to come into conversation with him were a failure. The letter directed him to the riding master von Wessenig. As the latter was not at home he is to wait for him in the stables. The beer and meat which was offered him he refused with disgust, but he accepted bread and water willingly and afterwards fell asleep.

The decisive moment in which the plan of his tormentors—to make him disappear in the world as a stable boy or groom—went astray was when the riding master, von Wessenig, arrived home that evening. Kaspar Hauser was wakened with difficulty. When he noticed the shining uniform of the riding master he became so fascinated by the sense impression that he fondles and feels it in a childish, childlike manner. The riding master, quite understandably, feels repelled by this behaviour of the young man, whom he cannot take to be a child. As he is unable to make anything out of what is said in the letter or by the lad, he abruptly lets him be taken to the police. The way to the police station was, as Feurbach so aptly says,[12] 'a martyrdom'. But the police are also at a loss to know what to do with him. Without meaning or context he repeats again and again the few words he has been taught. He puts his finger in a candle flame, burns himself and starts to cry. Finally, on a piece of paper presented to him, he writes his name by which he was henceforth to be known in the world, 'Kaspar Hauser'. Then, with pain and anguish, as he is unable to walk, he is carted off to gaol, where he is put in a cell with a butcher's apprentice who has the task of questioning him. He, however, sinks down on a sack of straw and falls into a deep sleep.

One must look upon it as a happy stroke of destiny that on the first day of his appearance in the world he is put under the care of the prison keeper of Nuremberg Castle, Hiltel. Hiltel is a simple man, a man of heart who possesses remarkable experience in the observation and judging of human beings. In contact with scoundrels of all types he was able to preserve the integrity and perspicuity of his powers of observation. The first thing that strikes Hiltel about the inconspicuous young man, who is quite unable to make himself understood, is his pure, innocent, childlike soul qualities. This has to do with a soul-impression, with the direct human experience of a reality connected with Kaspar Hauser. This incidence of direct human involvement takes place significantly enough with a man of the people whose heart is receptive for it. The impression of this event remained with Hiltel for the whole of his life. Self assured, definite and staunch, he remained a loyal witness for Kaspar Hauser. Nothing could disconcert him; even Stanhope later was unable to coax an unfavourable statement out of him. Daumer recorded a conversation with Hiltel by which the unusual impression that Kaspar Hauser made on him becomes just as plain as the inner independence of his attitude towards the affair. The memorable words are thus expressed: 'Hauser,' Hiltel assures us further, 'was a pure child to begin with, even less than a child. To fraudulently misrepresent such a phenomenon is beyond human capacity. His innocence is so patent that he would be forced to bear witness to it even if God Himself were to assert the opposite.' As he said this the man became quite red in the face with zeal.[13]

The human relationship of Hiltel to Kaspar Hauser shines through a remark in the court records of 1834. Hiltel states that Kaspar Hauser had given him so much pleasure by his good-naturedness and willingness to learn that he would never have wanted to part with him if he had not had eight children of his own.[14] Could the feeling of affinity be more modestly expressed?

Hiltel was not only sure of the fact that Kaspar Hauser was genuine, he was also the first witness to his unique childlike qualities and to the condition in which he was found when he first made his appearance. 'His whole behaviour was as it were the pure reflection of childlike innocence; there was nothing bad about him; whatever was on his mind he expressed—as far, that is, as his meagre speech allowed. Authentic evidence of his innocence and lack of knowledge was given on the occasion when my wife and I undressed him for the first time and washed his body; his behaviour then was that of a child, quite natural and unembarrassed.'[15] As lucky as the destiny is which brought Kaspar Hauser into contact with this person, so incomprehensible must it appear to an unbiased historical observer that in spite of this unmistakable, upright and in all respects serious witness, Kaspar Hauser could later be made out to be a fraud. Many books have been written about it which really are of no significance if a man such as Hiltel is to be believed.

On 28 May 1828 Kaspar Hauser was presented before the Nuremberg State Medical Officer, Dr Preu, who had to decide whether he was dealing with a sick person or a fraudster. Kaspar Hauser was thus confronted for the first time with a critical, scientifically trained observer. Dr Preu was an alert, impartial phenomenologist, the nature of whose profession had made him very sceptical. The observations he made about Kaspar Hauser led him to the immediate conclusion that in Kaspar Hauser he was dealing with a unique and exceptional case never previously observed. In his report Dr Preu summed up the result as follows: 'This person is neither mad nor stupid but has evidently been forcibly removed in the most brutal fashion from all intercourse with society and other human beings.'[16] Preu supports his medical evidence throughout on objective facts. One of the most important, the hollow of the knee, may be mentioned. Preu describes it in the following way: 'Both knees evince an unusual formation. The ends of the femur and tibia at the joint bend over steeply at the back and are sunk in deeply at the front together with the patella; thus when Hauser sits stretched out on the floor with his feet level with the hollow of the knee there is not room for a piece of paper to be inserted between, though with most people a whole fist would fit in.

'Along with this peculiarity goes another one to be noticed when Hauser is sitting in this position. His back is then perfectly upright, his hands stretched out freely in the air, whereas everyone else sitting with his hands stretched out in this position would have to bend forwards.'[17] This observation is especially important because it supports what Kaspar Hauser said later about his incarceration. Furthermore the length of time of his imprisonment in the above described cage, in which he was only able to sit, can be ascertained once more by this means. It is obvious that a malformation of this kind can only be brought about by years of sitting and that by a young child whose bones are still pliant. It is significant for the Kaspar

Hauser problem that, as far as I am aware, no opponent has come forward to question this phenomenon. In his body and on his bones he bears the material traces of his imprisonment, and yet, in spite of that, there were some who did not believe him.

Preu summed up all medical evidence once more in a later detailed report (3 December 1830). He arrives at the general conclusion that Kaspar Hauser was actually taken out of human society from his earliest childhood and reared in a secret place into which the daylight could not penetrate, and was kept in this condition until the time when, as if dropped from the clouds, he appeared among us. And with that we have a physical anatomical proof that Kaspar Hauser did not come to us as a swindler.*[18] The report by Dr Preu was confirmed and had further details added by the fuller report of Dr Osterhausen. Dr Osterhausen took over the care and medical examination of Kaspar Hauser in June 1828 as deputy for the ailing Dr Preu. Dr Osterhausen also comes to the clear conclusion: 'According to this Kaspar Hauser is not a swindler.'[19] Thus destiny has brought it about that Kaspar Hauser is described and recognized as a unique phenomenon by two scientifically trained observers independently of one another before any statements have been pronounced in this connection. This factor is usually overlooked when arguments take place about it.

First of all the being of Kaspar Hauser was perceived by a person with heart forces (Hiltel). After that his appearance was assessed and appreciated by the scientific methods of the time.

On the grounds of Preu's expert opinion (1 June 1828), the then Mayor of Nuremberg, Binder, as Chief of Police, takes over the interrogation of Kaspar Hauser himself, as the police—understandably—can get nothing further of any account out of him. In Binder Kaspar Hauser, to be sure, meets for the first time a highly placed representative of public life, but much more than as a mayor and representative of the police Binder occupies himself with the unique appearance of the person being interviewed by him. It is profound emotion which caused him to forget some of the police rules, and led him, 7 July 1828, to make the 'public announcement' of the 'strangest of all strange announcements,'[20] as was given with a certain amount of justification. For this public announcement—already on account of its unusual length—was fairly inappropriate in as far as it could advance the official police clarification of the case and in consequence earned Binder a not quite undeserved rebuke from his superior officers. The whole public announcement, however, is an eloquent witness to the deep sympathy which Binder felt towards Kaspar Hauser and which, also in his capacity as Mayor, he in no way wished to conceal. It was not his understanding but his heart which spoke out of direct experience, particularly in the following sentence:

His pure, open and innocent look, his wide and high forehead, the most exalted innocence of his nature, which knew and suspected no difference in the sexes and still today has only learnt to differentiate them by their clothing, his indescribable gentleness, his warmth and goodnaturedness which attracted all in his surroundings, and which, to start with, brought tears to his eyes and later, after gaining his freedom, expressed itself in tenderness even towards his oppressors, which was at first a deep yearning and home-sickness for his prison and his gaoler, then turned to a nostalgic memory and only now, through loving treatment, has become a gradually diminishing affection for the past, and the just as sincere touching loyalty towards all those who had constantly to deal with him and showed trust moreover towards all other folk, and his care for the tiniest insect, his aversion to anything which could cause the slightest pain to man or beast, his implicit obedience to and compliance with everything good, just as much as his freedom from any bad behaviour or vices, coupled at the same time with an inkling of what is wicked—and finally, his quite exceptional desire to learn, by which, with the help of an equally perceptive and reliable memory, he is enabled to enrich his vocabulary—which at first comprised only about

50 words—and acquired concepts and ideas about many
objects of which, with the exception of those he met with in
prison, he was entirely unfamiliar, and now also a conception of space and time, his particular preference for music
and drawing, which were previously unknown to him, his
inclination and skill in learning both of these arts and his
quite unusual love of order and cleanliness—in effect his
whole childlike self and his pure unsullied inner being—
these important aspects together give, in the same measure
in which they support and endorse his account of his illegal
imprisonment, the full conviction that nature has richly
endowed him with the most splendid gifts of spirit, disposition and heart.[21]

Binder is referring to the predestinatory character of the
meeting when as Burgomaster he declared: 'The community
which have received him into their heart, love him and regard
him as a pledge of love sent to them by Providence.'[21]

The announcement by Binder caused a great stir in
Germany and soon over a great part of Europe. Through the
detailed explanation of all the known circumstances the destiny of Kaspar Hauser was immediately made known to wide
circles. This historic service performed by Binder's impulsive
announcement took effect just because of its imprudence from
the point of view of the police. It called forth an echo from the
environment which accorded to a cry from the heart of this
man: 'The Child of Europe!' For his whole life from the time
of his first contact with him and initial shock, Binder remained
attached to Kaspar Hauser. And from the time of his first
deed, which was of such importance to Kaspar Hauser, the
thread of destiny continues until the obituary notice in the
Nuremberg newspaper of 19 December 1833 which com-
mences with the words: 'Kaspar Hauser, my beloved charge, is
no more.'[22]

Only a few days after his appearance in Nuremberg Daumer
visits Kaspar Hauser at the 'Luginsland'. What he experienced
on this first encounter he has not recorded. The 28-year-old
Daumer discovers his life's task in the 12 years younger

Kaspar Hauser. Without hesitation and with great energy he takes hold of his destined mission, the fulfilment of which is to immortalize him. He consequently visits Kaspar Hauser every day in order to give him instruction and was greatly astounded at the incomprehensible ability of his pupil's learning capacity. On 18 July 1828 Kaspar Hauser was handed over to Daumer for care and instruction at the instigation of the Mayor Binder. Daumer takes him into his own house, where he lives with his mother and sister. Kaspar Hauser had found a home for the first time, which was both a physical- and soul- and spiritual-home. Daumer describes this first period as follows:

I had known Kaspar Hauser for about three weeks before he came into my house (18 July 1828)—that is, since the end of June 1828—because I used to visit him in the Tower where he lived at that time. I found more than I expected, took a personal interest in the young man and visited him daily since then with the intention of doing something towards his development. The crowd of inquisitive folk which took up his time often allowed me hardly half an hour on my own with him, in spite of which he learned the rudiments of reading, counting, the pronouncing of number sequences, adding and subtracting; he progressed with his forming of letters in beautiful handwriting and learned off by heart a simple piece on the piano. I taught him to read by means of large letters, printed on single cards for children to put together; his exercises in handwriting were practised on his own according to patterns which I provided. But already by the third week I almost had to cease teaching him, because not long after the start of a lesson beads of perspiration gathered on Hauser's forehead and headaches set in. The twitching of his face which occurred with almost any kind of excitement became more marked; just at the time when he was given into my care he became so ill that he could hardly stay upright. Already by the second day of his stay in my house the obstruction from which he suffered was alleviated, but his digestive organs appeared to grow constantly weaker after that and his nervous system was in

great disorder. The spasmodic movements were of a terrifying kind; every loud word spoken or note of the piano
hurt his ear, a few words written or read by him, every white
or bright object he looked at, hurt his eyes; his hand trem-
bled like that of an old man when he grasped anything with
it; every kind of contemplation increased his affliction, from
which he only started to recover after a week. In this condition all intellectual and practical activities in which he had
previously been engaged—reading, writing, doing sums,
drawing, playing the piano—had to cease and I continued
part of my instruction only in the form of occasional conversation. I also kept him occupied with pasting, joinery and
gardening activities in so far as he was up to it, and with a
few games which allowed him to move about in the open air.
I also let him have a lukewarm bath occasionally (the latter
too proved beneficial). My attempt to do easy exercises with
him on the gymnasium playing field did not have the desired
effect, but riding lessons taken by the stable master von
Rumpler in my presence were a great success. His
convulsive movements, trembling and the results of over-
stimulation in general started to disappear.

Apart from rye bread and water, which had been his sole
diet previously, he now greatly enjoyed a soup made with
water thickened with flour, also plain chocolate, white
bread and milk dishes start to appeal to him and he received
great benefit from these for his still debilitated forces of
digestion by which rye bread could not easily be digested as
formerly. His appearance improved noticeably and he grew
extremely rapidly; in the last four weeks he gained about
two inches in height.

To describe his general physique I will say the following:
For as long as I have known him, and especially at the
present moment, he has a good appearance and a healthy
complexion, but his body is unbelievably frail, weak and
over-sensitive with regard to what he can do and what
influences him from without. A gentle touch of the hand has
the effect of a blow administered to him; when he walks for
a time against the wind he grows hoarse; he formerly

became dog-tired after a short walk, but latterly he has been able to walk for hours without getting exhausted. He used to stand and walk with his toes turned inwards and was always in danger of losing his balance; he was unable to make the smallest jump without falling over; now his step is hardly any different from that of other people. His hands and the soles of his feet had formerly been so soft, free of calluses and easily damaged that one could plainly see that he had been unaccustomed to walking and work.

When he was first entrusted to my care I found significant traces of blisters and sores on his feet acquired on account of his not being used to walking. When his senses were stirred, when he exerted himself, was alerted or sunk in thought his face, especially on the left side of his mouth and his left arm, would twitch convulsively. He got feverish spells if he ate meat and vegetable acid made him itch; sweet things were abhorrent to him, everything spiced and anything containing alcohol had terrifying effects on him. All his senses are very acute and refined. He can, for instance, smell things at a considerable distance which for normal senses seem quite odourless, he can taste a drop of meat broth if it should fall into his thin water-based soup and he can distinguish at a distance of about 100 paces the single berries of an elderberry cluster; in more than half that distance he can distinguish between an elderberry and a bilberry. His eyes, used to the dark, can see fairly well in a shade of darkness in which an ordinary eye can distinguish neither colour nor outline. He is still able to discern the difference between dark brown and dark red and between dark green and black in what for others is total darkness and he needs no light to walk around with confidence and find his way about the house at night time; yes, he can see better in the half-light than in broad daylight because the daylight dazzles him.

Strangest of all in his case are the phenomena which extend into the region of animal magnetism and clairvoyance. During the night in which his illness took a turn for the better he had a dream in which the transition to better

health presented itself in a friendly picture. When a person
approaches him unnoticed and unheard from behind he
becomes aware of it through a quite peculiar sensation
which the proximity of living beings arouses in him. If one
stretches out one's hand towards him he senses it as a
current flowing from it which he calls being 'breathed' on;
when a hand takes hold of him, almost invariably (except
in the case of some ageing people) he feels a cold shudder
come over him. The most violent reaction (for some
unknown reason) comes about when I am the one concerned. He feels it from about 125 paces away, when his
back is turned towards me and when I stretch out my hand
towards him. A similar sensibility is evinced by him in the
case of metals; as a result of the strength of attraction, he
feels and distinguishes between metals hidden under sheets
of paper of the existence of which he was unaware. These
phenomena grow less, however, the stronger and more
healthy he becomes.

As a description of his spiritual peculiarities in so far as
they have been revealed the following characteristics may
be of use: Kaspar Hauser possesses the greatest good-
naturedness and soft-heartedness, he mistrusts everyone,
however, to a greater or lesser degree, which is an understandable result of his experiences so far. His judgement is
keen and pertinent, his observation remarkably acute.
Authorities are of no account to him; he relies entirely
upon his own views, experience and insight. His understanding knows no bounds according to his standards and
demands absolute satisfaction; his moral code is rigorously
expressed; he is pedantic about outer tidiness and cleanliness. His persistence about things he has set himself to do
often borders upon obstinacy. His most prominent gifts
are those concerned with technology and art. With regard
to his capacity for expressing himself verbally he has progressed so far that one can converse with him without
much difficulty on any subject which lies within the comparatively wide range of his ideas and powers of comprehension.

According to his own admission the two greatest changes which took place in his way of thinking and view of
things were the following: the first was when I gave him a
box of letters and began to teach him to recognize them.
From that time on, he said, he had finished with playing;
the toy horses, which up till then had given him the greatest pleasure, were put on one side and from then on he was
only concerned with study. The second great change was
brought about in him by his perception of sprouting and
growth. He had previously thought that trees, leaves,
flowers and fruits had been manufactured by the hand of
man and, as I endeavoured to give him an idea about
growth and vegetable-life, he remained quite incredulous.
Therefore I let him plant seeds of various sorts in plant
pots and told him what would happen (August 1828). He
would believe all I told him, he said, if that was confirmed.
When the grains really sprouted he got into an indescribable state of excitement, of joy and wonder, and since that
time he looks upon nature with quite different eyes.[23]

Among those with whom Kaspar Hauser became acquainted in the first Nuremberg days was Anselm Ritter von
Feuerbach, the President of the Court of Appeal in Ansbach,
criminologist and instructor in criminal law. He took the part
of Kaspar Hauser with the whole strength of his fiery personality and became a witness to Kaspar Hauser's innocence
and a seeker who never ceased in his efforts to unravel the
mystery surrounding Kaspar Hauser's origin and destiny. In
1832 he basically solved the riddle of Kaspar Hauser's origin.
Further research by Feuerbach was made impossible by his
illness in 1832 and his sudden death on 29 May 1833. Daumer
was of the opinion that Feuerbach did not die a natural
death.[24]

Feuerbach's report about his first visit to Kaspar Hauser is
one of the classical records:

Kaspar Hauser had already been well over a month in
Nuremberg before I heard about him as one of the latest
topics of gossip. Official notice about the event had not yet

reached the Heads of State. I simply went along to
Nuremberg on 11 July (1828) as a private person out of
humanitarian and scientific interest to see this unique
phenomenon.

At that time Kaspar was still living in his lodgings in the
'Luginsland' Tower on the 'Vestner Tore' where anyone
who so desired was allowed to visit him. Truly Kaspar
enjoyed hardly any more peace from morning till evening
than the kangaroo and the tame hyena in the famous
menagerie of Mr van Aken. And so I went along to see him
too, accompanied by Colonel von D., two ladies and two
children and luckily we hit on a time when the scene of
interest was deserted. Kaspar's room was a small but clean
and bright apartment with windows which looked out into
the open, with a view which was both extensive and friendly.
We came upon him bare-footed, dressed in a pair of old
long leg coverings and for the rest only wearing a shirt.

Kaspar had decorated the walls as far as he could reach
with sheets of pictures which were presents from his many
visitors. He stuck them on to the walls afresh every morning
with his saliva, which was as sticky as glue [a note by
Feuerbach: the spittle was so gluey that when the pictures
were taken down, pieces of paper remained sticking to the
wall or pieces of the wall came away with the paper] and took
them down again as soon as it grew dusk to lay them in a pile
at his side. On the bench which was fixed to the wall all round
the room was his bed in one corner, which consisted of a sack
of straw with a pillow and a woollen blanket. The whole of
the rest of the bench was packed with a multitude of different
kinds of toys, with hundreds of lead soldiers, wooden dogs,
ponies and other Nuremberg goods. During the daytime he
seldom bothered with them any longer; and yet he went to
the not inconsiderable trouble of putting all these things and
bits and pieces together tidily in the evening and then, as
soon as he awoke, unpacking them and arranging them in
some sort or order. The charitable instincts of the good
citizens of Nuremberg had in addition endowed him with a
number of articles of clothing, which he kept under his pillow

and which he showed to us with childish pleasure and not a little pride. Among the toys on the bench various coins were also lying, to which, however, he paid not the slightest heed. I took a dirty Crown-Thaler coin and a quite new Two-Groschen piece in my hand and asked him to choose which he would rather have. He chose the small bright coin and called the other one nasty and pulled a face of disgust. When I tried to make him understand that the larger coin was nevertheless more valuable and that one could buy many more beautiful things with it than with the smaller one, he certainly listened attentively, but immediately fell into rigid contemplation and eventually let it become known to me that he did not know what I meant.

He showed not the slightest embarrassment or shyness when we entered his room, but rather a trusting acceptance and pleasure at seeing us. At first he turned his attention to the Colonel's bright uniform; he could not take his eyes off the helmet embellished all over with gold; next the ladies with their gay dresses drew his attention to themselves; at first he hardly vouchsafed a look at me in my modest black dress-coat. We each of us introduced ourselves to him separately and gave him our names and title. Kaspar went up close to each one as we were being introduced, stared at us closely and glanced with a quick penetrating look at each particular feature in turn; forehead, eyes, nose, mouth, chin, etc. And finally, as I clearly perceived, gathered the separate pieces of physiognomical information together into a comprehensive whole. He then repeated the name of the person to whom he had been introduced, and afterwards he knew the person concerned and, as later events showed, he then knew them for life.

He turned away from bright sunlight as far as he was able. He most carefully avoided the shafts of sunlight which shone in through his window. If, by any chance, a sunbeam such as this met his eye he blinked vigorously, frowned and showed obvious signs of pain; in addition to this his eyes were slightly inflamed and were altogether very sensitive towards light.

The left side of his later perfectly regular face was at that time noticeably different from the right. The former was clearly distorted and twisted; convulsive spasms often flitted across it like lightning. The whole left side of the body, but particularly the arm and hand, were obviously most affected. If he was shown something which aroused his curiosity or if someone uttered an unusual word with which he was unfamiliar, the convulsions started immediately and usually turned into a kind of numbness. He then stood there motionless, not a muscle of his face moved, his eyes stared straight ahead without blinking and as though bereft of life; he looked like a pillar which neither sees nor hears and which cannot be roused into life by any outer impressions. One could observe him in this state whenever he was sunk in thought or whenever he tried to find the right concept for a new word, or the right word for a new concept, or to relate a new experience to something with which he was already familiar, to make the former explicable by the latter.

What words he knew he pronounced decisively and clearly without hesitation or stuttering. There was no talk, as yet, of any coherent speech and his utterances were as scanty as was the range of his concepts. It was difficult, therefore, to make oneself understood by him. Hardly had one spoken a few sentences which he appeared to understand, than one introduced a word with which he was unfamiliar and the convulsions started again immediately as he tried to make sense of it. In all that he said the conjunctions, particles and auxiliary verbs were usually missing; his conjugation included very little else than the infinitive; and worst of all was the syntax, the parts of which were quite pitifully jumbled and mixed up. 'Kaspar very good' instead of I am very good, 'Kaspar tell Juli', instead of I will tell it to Julius (the son of the Prison Warder). This was his usual kind of speech. The word 'I' was seldom used; he nearly always referred to himself in the third person: 'Kaspar'; he also addressed others in the third person instead of in the second, for instance: 'You' was always Mr Colonel, Mrs General, etc. One might also not address him with 'Du', but with 'Kaspar' if he were to understand at once whom one meant.

The same word was often used in its various meanings which frequently caused a droll and laughable confusion of identity. Many words belonging to a particular species he used for the whole genus! Thus, for instance, the word 'mountain' was used to indicate every hillock or mound, for which reason he called a pot-bellied gentleman, whose name he had forgotten: 'the man with the big mountain'; a lady whose scarf hung down so low at the back that it trailed on the ground he called: 'the lady with the lovely tail'. One might think I did not omit to ply him with some questions which would give him occasion to relate something of his destiny. However, all I could elicit from him was such gibberish, mixed up and vague stuff that, not yet being familiar with his kind of talk, I could only guess at its meaning and much of it I could not understand at all.

It seemed of importance to me to test his taste for colours. He appeared in this respect to be like a small child or a so-called 'savage' human being. A red colour, indeed the most garish of reds, pleased him best; yellow was distasteful to him, except when it dazzled his eyes as shining gold, in which case his choice wavered between this kind of yellow and that kind of red; he was indifferent to white, but green was nearly as distasteful to him as black. This colour preference, especially his attraction to red, remained with him for a very long time, even after great progress had been made in his intellectual development, as the later observations of Professor Daumer indicate. If it had been left to him he would have clothed himself, and others to whom he felt well disposed, from head to food in scarlet or deep red. He took no pleasure in Nature on account of the basic colour with which it was adorned—green. To have been something beautiful in his eyes it would have to have been viewed 'through rose-coloured spectacles'. In the home of Professor Daumer, which he had exchanged for his abode in the 'Luginsland' soon after my visit to him, he was therefore not quite satisfied because the view there only looked out over the garden and what he thought of as the many 'ugly green trees and plants'. The home of a friend of his teacher,

situated in a narrow unprepossessing street, was much more
to his liking because opposite it and on all sides many lovely
red-painted houses were to be seen. When he was once shown
a tree covered with red apples he expressed the greatest
satisfaction with it; only, he thought, the tree would have
been much nicer if the leaves had also been red. When he,
who only drank water, once saw red wine being drunk he
said: 'If only I could drink something which looks so
beautiful'. He desired only one improvement to his favourite
animals, horses: that they could have been scarlet rather than
black, brown or white.

His curiosity and thirst for knowledge, as well as his iron
determination to persevere with things which he had set
himself to learn or to understand, surpassed all belief and
was deeply moving to watch. He did not bother any more
with his toys during the daytime, as has already been
mentioned; the daylight hours were taken up with writing,
drawing and other classroom subjects with which Professor
Daumer occupied him. He complained to us bitterly about
all the many people who visited him, leaving him no peace
and not allowing him to learn anything. It was touching to
hear his oft repeated lament that people in the world know
such a lot and that there is so much that he has not yet
learned. One of his favourite pastimes apart from writing
was drawing, a subject to which he brought just as much
talent as persistence. For many days he had set himself the
task of copying the lithographic portrait of the Mayor,
Binder. A whole big pack of quarto-sized sheets was filled
with these copies; they lay as they had gradually evolved in a
long series one on top of the other. I studied them one after
the other; the first attempts were just like the drawings of our
young children, who think that they have drawn a face when
they have scrawled a figure on a piece of paper which is
supposed to represent an oval with a couple of round
squiggles beside a few long and cross strokes. But in nearly
every succeeding attempt improvement was noticeable, so
that gradually these lines became more and more like a
human face and at last, though fairly rough and imperfect,

they resembled the original sufficiently to be recognizable. I expressed my praise for his latest attempts but he still did not appear to be satisfied and informed me that he would have to copy the picture many more times until he got it quite right; then he would make a present of it to the Burgomaster.

He felt himself quite happy with his life in the world; he longed to be back again with 'the man with whom he had always been'. At home (in his cubby hole), he said, he never had such pains in his head and people had not pestered him so much as they do now in the world. With that he was referring to the discomforts and pains which were caused by the many unaccustomed impressions, the various smells which offended his nostrils, etc., as well as the many visits of inquisitive people, their many questions and some of their thoughtless, not even human, experiments. About the man 'with whom he had always been' he had no complaints, except that he had not yet come to fetch him home and that there were so many things in the world which he had never shown him and about which he had never told him anything. He wanted to remain in Nuremberg until he had learned what the Burgomaster and Professor (Daumer) knew; then the Burgomaster was to take him home and he would show the man all that he had learned meanwhile. As I then asked him in response how he could wish to return to that wicked detestable man he flared up in gentle reproof with the words: 'Man not wicked. Man not do bad me.'

We were soon to get the most striking example of his remarkable memory, which was just as quick as it was tenacious. He was able to give the name and title of the donor of every small or large item in his room, of every large or small picture and by this means he encountered several people with the same surname. Then he distinguished them either by their Christian names or else by means of other qualities. About an hour after we had left him we met him in the street just as he was being taken to see the Burgomaster. We spoke to him and when we asked him to say our names, without any reflection or hesitation, he gave the full names of each of us, including our titles, which must have meant nothing to him. Dr Osterhausen, the medical doctor, had the following experience with him on a later occasion: When he was shown a bouquet of flowers and was told their names he was able to recognize the flowers and recall their names several days later. This memory faded later, however, and as it seems grew less in proportion to the rate at which Kaspar acquired more knowledge and his understanding was further engaged.

His obedience towards all those people who had obtained a fatherly authority over him, especially the Burgomaster, Professor Daumer and the Prison Warder Hiltel, was unreserved and unlimited. 'Herr Burgomaster, Herr Professor has said so,' was the final authority for his actions, which made all further discussion and consideration of the matter superfluous. When I asked him why he thought he ought to obey so instantaneously he answered: 'The man with whom I always was taught me that I had to do as I was told.'

But this acquiescence to the authority of others only applied in the case of doing or not doing things and had nothing to do with his knowledge, beliefs or convictions. In order for him to be certain about anything he had to have an inner conviction of its truth and this he gained either through sense observation or by reason of something which was for his powers of comprehension and for his almost empty head a convincing fact. In cases where one could not gain his understanding in either of these two ways he let the matter rest without contradiction until he had, as he used to express it, 'gained more wisdom'. Among other things I spoke to him about the prospective winter and said he would then often see the roofs of the houses and all the streets in the town completely white, as white as the walls of his little room. He thought that would be very nice, but showed that he was not going to believe it until he had seen it. When the first snow had fallen during the following winter he showed great pleasure in the fact that the streets, roofs and trees had been 'painted' so nicely and he quickly went into the courtyard to get some of the 'white paint'. But he soon came back upstairs to his teacher with his fingers spread out wide and crying and bawling out that the white paint had 'bitten' his hands.

The love of order and cleanliness, almost amounting to 'pedantry', was quite striking and inexplicable in this human being. Of the many hundreds of things he had in his small abode everything had its own special place, was put away properly, carefully taken apart and symmetrically arranged, etc. Uncleanliness, or what he imagined was uncleanliness, was an abomination to him, both on his person and on other people. He noticed almost every speck of dirt on our clothes, and when he saw one or two grains of snuff on my ruff he drew my attention to it with indignation, hastily admonishing me to brush the nasty thing off.[25]

This report was supplemented by a letter of Feuerbach of 20 September 1828 to Elise von der Recke:

But let us rather speak about the poor Nuremberg foundling, the good Kaspar Hauser, for whom I share the greatest concern, both officially and unofficially. Some things about this unheard of affair are a riddle and may perhaps always remain so in spite of the united efforts of all the magistrates and police authorities; at any rate, all the attempts to establish the site of the atrocity and to trace the perpetrator of the deed have so far been of no avail. But this, at any rate, is certain: the deed has been done and we see in Kaspar Hauser a 17- to 18-year-old prodigy such as the world has never before seen, a person who, since his earliest childhood, has been, as it were, buried and only since about six [should be four] months has seen the sun for the first time and has made the discovery that there are other folk on the earth besides himself and the monster who fed him with bread and water.

When he was seen for the first time in Nuremberg he could only speak a few words and had not the vaguest notion about the most commonplace phenomena of nature, as, for instance, when he tried to get hold of a candle flame, could not differentiate between what was close at hand or more distant, confused dead with living objects, or rather

knew the difference just as little as he knew the difference of
the sexes, etc. It was only with great difficulty that he could
feel about in front of him—and that was with his whole
hand; in the case of the separate fingers he was most
clumsy. Sunlight pained him; the scent of the most delicate
flowers, a rose for instance, was not only very repugnant to
him, but gave him great pain. When he first heard a regi-
mental band playing in the distance, he was beside himself
with delight, whereas it was painful for him close at hand.
He was only able to consume bread and water, every other
kind of drink, even milk, and the tiniest speck of meat
caused him not only nausea and loathing but also gave him
a temperature. He still eats neither meat, vegetables nor
fruit.

When I visited him in Nuremberg two months ago he had
not yet seen the moon or the stars, did not know what
winter was, could not grasp and did not believe that he had
once been smaller than he was at that time and had—as is
the case today—no sense for the beauty of a landscape and
for nature as a whole. Certain flowers gave him pleasure, the
rose, for instance, because he preferred the colour red above
all others. But next to black everything green was objec-
tionable to him and for that reason he looked forward very
much to winter when, as I had told him, he would then see
the view from his window no longer green but very often
quite white like the walls of his room for long periods at a
time. He had only learned quite recently what the growth of
plants signified, because he had been allowed to plant beans
and other seeds in pots and then had his attention drawn to
them; before that he had considered all plants to be the
artistic work of man and had been amazed how men could
have made so many flowers and have cut out so many leaves
on the trees and why they had done so.

Kaspar is, by the way, a person of excellent natural
talents, gifted with the quickest powers of comprehension
and an admirable memory. His thirst for knowledge, to
make up for all the things which the man 'with whom he had
been' had not told him, he always expressed in a very

moving way. He wants an explanation for whatever he sees and makes this dependent on concepts which are new to him, so he says sadly: 'Learn that too! Of that too the man with whom I always was, not said anything.' His progress was extraordinary, that which takes others months or years he learns in days. At present he is so far advanced that there are hardly any interesting psychological observations to be made about him. He already speaks in a perfectly understandable and coherent way, only sometimes he constructs his sentences like a child; his handwriting is firm, almost beautiful, and a few days ago my eldest daughter, who had visited him in Nuremberg and had given him a present on that occasion, received a very nice letter from him. Quite on his own account he started to draw and soon made admirable progress in that too. If he sees some art or skill being practised which rouses his interest, he wants to learn it straightaway, lets himself be shown how it is done, practises it for one or two days until he has gained a certain proficiency in it, but gives it up again as soon as he has learned it. It is altogether remarkable that the objects connected with learning do not interest him so much as the learning itself, which is his only passion. What is hardly explicable is his amazing love of cleanliness and order which he expressed immediately on his appearance in Nuremberg even though his body was covered with an accumulated crust of many years of dirt. When I visited him, all the countless things which had been given him by the people of Nuremberg, toys, articles of clothing, etc., stood most symmetrically arranged in his tiny room, every scrap of paper which lay on the floor was distasteful to him and was carefully picked up; he noticed every speck of dust or stain on his own or on the clothing of others. The people of Nuremberg have provided him with all necessary—and even unnecessary—articles of clothing, with stylish dress coats, waistcoats and so on, and now one expects to see him as a young lord when he appears in public.

From the point of view of morality Kaspar Hauser is a living refutation of the doctrine of original sin. Innocence

and goodness of heart was evident in all his doings and
speech, although he had not the slightest idea of right and
wrong, good and evil. He was not the slightest bit afraid of
other people and not even shy of them; people were all good
in his eyes and he regarded them all as beautiful. When,
among other things, I once expressed my indignation at the
villain who had kept him imprisoned for so long, he rebuked
me reproachfully with the words: 'He with whom he had
been' was not bad, but was his father—that is what he said
at the time I visited him about everyone into whose care he
had been entrusted—who had given him food and drink.
Only since about two months does it seem to have dawned
on him that he had been the victim of a crime and since that
time he has expressed the greatest fear at the mere thought
of falling into the hands of his gaoler once more. Of passions or bad inclinations there was no evidence, apart from
his newly awakened vanity.

    That the idea of God is not inborn in the human being but
comes to him from outside only, either by observing nature
or through being taught, is likewise demonstrated quite
clearly by Kaspar Hauser. I do not know indeed how it
stands with him at the moment, but not long ago there was
nothing to indicate that he had any idea of a God who was
the Creator of the Universe—dogmatism and the priest-
hood had, luckily enough, been kept at a distance from him
until now.

    The appearance of Kaspar Hauser is one of health;
meanwhile, as a result of the mighty impressions he had
received from the innumerable new things which constantly
stormed his senses from all sides, his nerves became
exceedingly sensitive, so that one could to some extent be
fearful for his life. Now, through the loving care and delicate and proper treatment he receives from his foster-father
and teacher, Professor Daumer, he is out of danger. For
some time the strangest physiological phenomena have
shown up in him; he can see at night—like a cockroach—as
easily as in the daytime and can distinguish objects at a
considerable distance just by their smell alone, etc. His

physiognomy has no special distinguishing feature but, especially when he speaks, the whole left side of his face twitches in an unpleasant manner; nevertheless the whole appearance of his face, through its expression of innocence and kind-heartedness, has a very undeniable charm. Whoever approaches him is immediately won over by him. Whoever, by the way, might imagine that Kaspar must have felt particularly happy in his situation at that time, which outwardly fulfilled all his requirements, would be badly mistaken. He certainly felt very pleased at times with many isolated things, when his senses were pleasantly affected or when his burning thirst for knowledge was gratified, but the basic tenor of his soul-attitude was one of silent melancholy which, especially now, frequently is expressed by pointed remarks.

There are some things which are unbelievable or enigmatic about his imprisonment and transportation to Nuremberg—certainly also some things which are not true. This account was elicited from him at a time when he had practically no concepts, no notions about nature or human affairs, least of all the appropriate words by which to express them; a time when he often said things in his muddled, murky gibberish which were not what he intended to say or which could give his questioner sufficient scope to interpret them in his own thoughts, opinions and hypotheses. But apart from that I have reason to believe that the barbarian in whose power Hauser had been, had given him a sermon of terrible threats on certain points, mainly intended to conceal the necessary clues towards an investigation of the location and the perpetrator of the crime. It must be noted that Kaspar rendered the utmost obedience to any person to whom he felt he owed esteem and gratitude. Only when his understanding is fully developed and equipped with the necessary moral concepts, when his notion of the villain with whom he had been united as though at the same time merged into one with him, has loosed its hold on his imagination and when, through long experience, he becomes convinced that he will always be

protected by a defence over which his former master has no
control—only then is it to be hoped that other and more
things will be elicited from him which may lead to the goal.

It would have been of the utmost importance for a
circumstantial diary to have been kept from the beginning
recording the many psychological and physiological
phenomena appearing in Kaspar Hauser. But that never
occurred to the Nuremberg materialists. It was I myself who
gave the first incentive for the fragments of those remarkable experiences to be collected together retrospectively.
Above all the people of Nuremberg treated our Kaspar as
an object of curiosity for months; his foster-father was a
prison warder; Kaspar was exhibited in social circles and in
public houses like some strange animal, was subjected to the
eager gaze of inquisitive people all day long and continually
made to submit to experiments, such for instance, as having
wine and similar things, of which it was known that his
nature was not able to stand them, introduced surreptitiously into his drinking water, so that he was in danger of
becoming spiritually and physically completely ruined
within a short time. The thought that one should put the
education of this unhappy person into the sole hands of an
educated man never occurred to the Burgomaster who
affected so much humanity in his precipitous and, by the
way, quite inappropriate public address. It was my journey
to Nuremberg which first brought a new turn to events by
drawing the attention of my worthy colleague, the District
President Herrn von Mieg, to what was needed and to the
whole nonsense which was being enacted around Kaspar
Hauser and begging him to visit Nuremberg and to see for
himself what was going on. Upon that Kaspar Hauser was
entrusted to Professor Daumer, who is a very good and
sensible man and who, with his family, lived completely for
the interest of his exceptional pupil. Soon after the arrival
into the peaceful quiet of this family Kaspar became
seriously ill, certainly only as a result of the foolish and
thoughtless treatment he had suffered in Nuremberg after
his release from his prison. As soon as something of

importance happens to Kaspar I shall not fail to write to you as far as it is communicable.[26]

Feuerbach's ability to recognize and describe the unusual is demonstrated, among many other things, by a not-to-be-forgotten sentence which he wrote concerning Kaspar Hauser's first days: 'In his soul, filled with childish goodness and gentleness which made it impossible for him to do harm to a worm or a fly, let alone to a human being, which in every respect showed itself so pure and untainted as the image of eternity mirrored in the soul of an angel, he brought with him from his gaol into the world of light, as has already been stated, no thought, no notion of God, not the shadow of a belief in any other more exalted invisible existence than that of the present.'[27]

The attitude of Feuerbach towards the personality of Kaspar Hauser and the deed perpetrated upon him is underlined by the following sentences: 'Also in the case of the history of the deed we have no further evidence at present than the account of the person against whom it was perpetrated. But the truth of the story is vouched for by the personality of him who tells it, the one on whose body, soul and spirit the deed itself is plainly inscribed in visible characters. Only a person who had gone through and suffered what Kaspar Hauser suffered can be like Kaspar. And whoever looks like Kaspar does must have lived under the conditions which Kaspar described to us. Thus the valuation we set on the credibility of someone who tells such an incredible story also rests for the most part on psychological evidence. But the results found in this way offer an attestation which is more convincing than any other authentication offered. Witnesses can lie. Records can be forged. But no person, other than a magician gifted with a certain amount of omnipotence and omniscience, could tell a lie of such a kind that from whatever angle it is illuminated it shows as the clearest and purest truth, as the personification of truth itself. He who doubts Kaspar's story needs doubt Kaspar's existence.'[28]

Then in Nuremberg, at the instigation of Burgomaster

Binder, Kaspar Hauser, while living in the care of Daumer, was placed under the guardianship of Baron Tucher. In the year 1834, that is to say after the death of Kaspar Hauser, Tucher expressed himself thus in a legal document sum- marised as follows:

I became acquainted with Kaspar Hauser during the first days of his stay in Nuremberg, that is in June 1828, but I only had the opportunity of observing him more closely in August of the same year. This took place from then onwards through almost daily visits and in constant exchanges with his foster-father of that time, Professor Daumer, until in December 1829, as a result of the assas- sination attempt, the investigation was put into the hands of the Royal District and City Court of Nuremberg which soon afterwards appointed me to be his guardian. Follow- ing this I took him into my house in May 1830, where he stayed until November 1831, that is to say, for as long as his stay in Nuremberg, and therewith my guardianship, lasted. Through that I have had the opportunity of closely obser- ving the development of this remarkable person from the time of his spiritual birth until the moment from which, from then onwards, the development of his character was unable to make any further important progress; that is, namely, until in moral and social aspect he resembled a young man of 18–20 years of age, although in his intellec- tual capacity he was like a boy of 13 or 14. This moral and intellectual development appeared to be the result of the peculiar circumstances of this marvellous, but in other respects quite normal, human being (that is one who is established in accordance with the nature of the human spirit) and there was nothing about his gradual, natural and in itself necessary development, no single instant which belied the nature of the thing.
This alone is sufficient to disprove all and every allegation that his appearance could be the result of deceit; yes, when all facts are considered and in connection with the most remarkable physiological effects, to be complete nonsense

even. I am referring namely to the fraud which thoughtless people, unacquainted with the facts of the case, have attempted to impute to him in manifold ways: Kaspar Hauser had falsely pretended by his behaviour, or had tried to awaken the erroneous opinion in people, that from his earliest years onwards he had been kept in solitary confinement and then brought to Nuremberg in a manner unknown to him. The possible purpose which Kaspar Hauser could have sensibly had through such deception the gentlemen fail to reveal.

Were one to consider such a deceit as this to be possible one would, even without considering a direct proof to the contrary which would be so easy to provide, invalidate the same owing to the fact that the carrying out of such deception would be something infinitely more enigmatic than the actual reality itself; yes, would even be an incomprehensible miracle, because it would not only presuppose such a fraudster to possess conspicuous intelligence and have undertaken profound investigation into the human spirit as is hardly possible for the most advanced philosopher, but simultaneously, armed with the exact study of the few similar cases preserved by history, to have a faculty of disguise which the most perfect actor would hardly be able to acquire—and in addition to that he would have to be able to exert a power over his whole body and over all its life functions to an extent of which no one since then has had any conception.

It is evident that a man of such unusual gifts and abilities would have never needed to assume a role such as that of Kaspar Hauser—a role which, in spite of the continual, most careful observation of many educated and experienced, nay, even brilliant people, and also, which says much more, many people hostile towards him, could be successfully played out simply for the purpose of being nourished on bread and water and being allowed to sleep on straw, after never-ending troublesome and strenuous learning, in order to progress far enough to become a copyist in an office and finally, living with his protectors and benefactors with all suspicion of deceit removed and confronted with a carefree future offered to him without effort on his part—to end his own life without any cause!

I think one would take such a person to be a madman rather than a swindler. But Kaspar Hauser was neither of these. In the first period of his spiritual life he was the innocent child with the purest unstained disposition, possessing all childish inclinations and instincts, who had no knowledge of the difference between good and evil and who knew of no other misfortune than that of bodily pain. His concepts were those of a child, but his soul-powers, which were quite differently formed to those of a child, seemed to have been formed in a manner analogous to that of the body; his mind, namely, was exactly that of a *tabula rasa*, one not yet influenced by outside impressions, which, with unending receptivity, absorbed into itself the whole world of concepts and, with an intensive reproductive force, which set all in amazement, all too easily created the impression of exceptional spiritual gifts.

The result, however, of the unintelligent treatment he had received during the first months, or perhaps on account of his changed life-style in which, for instance, he had been made to eat meat, soon showed in the over-stimulation of his nerves and of his whole soul-life which threatened his mind and body with great danger, but which at first caused stupidity and nervous irritability.

During this period it was noticeable how the seed of a regrettable moral corruption, which later showed up as deceitfulness and vanity, was implanted in him. His studies had practically to cease and all strenuous occupations had to be avoided. That led to him being left more to his own devices during the day, which could not at that time be avoided, but which had a very deleterious influence on his morality in the manner described. These defects in his moral education were certainly less the fault of the unhappy Kaspar than of a confluence of unfavourable circumstances.

The assassination attempt which took place in October 1829 brought about a great change in Hauser's mental capacities. The violent shock which it caused him loosened the fetters of his mind, his depressed mood disappeared almost entirely, he was able to study again properly and only now was it possible for him to start regular lessons, which he received under the guidance of experienced and gifted teachers about which, as from all that I, as his guardian, tried to give him, the deceased President von Feuerbach was informed, just as all that I undertook with my charge was submitted to that clever man for his opinion and approval . . .

As for the rest, however, Kaspar Hauser showed a high degree of natural good-heartedness and unselfish willingness to be of help to others. His feeling of being more or less dependent on others, however, encouraged him to ingratiate himself with people, especially with those whose favours he wished particularly to curry. In that he showed a remarkable skill at getting to know their weaknesses and turning them to his account, but in general he could adapt to all people. He fitted in with everyone to a high degree, perhaps merely out of cowardice, which was surely the result of his feeling of bodily weakness.

This cowardice, which was richly nourished by thoughts of the assassination attempt of October 1829, knew absolutely no bounds and nothing, not even the most serious admonitions, orders or threats, could persuade him to undertake anything which could in the least way put him in danger of his life; thus, for instance, no power could force him to bathe in the river for fear that he might drown; sailing in a boat on a pool to which I had forced him made him ill and I am convinced that this was more on account of the fear for his life than because he could not stand the rocking motion. With fear and trembling he twice drove across a pontoon bridge with me which would most certainly have caused him serious indisposition if his anxiety had lasted any longer.

Who could blame him for this fear of death, he who had hardly begun to live and who had once already had his precious existence threatened in such a horrible fashion! He expressed this countless times, always justifying it with the same reasons.

Otherwise, however, he showed a remarkable persistence and strong powers of endurance in everything he undertook. I already mentioned above that I could find no fault in him except for an all too great passion for learning. He pursued this in a manner which, as already stated, often awakened the greatest fears for his health. What, in the first period of his stay in Nuremberg, had been an unlimited and insatiable thirst for knowledge and wish to grasp and understand everything by reasoning, showed itself later as an untiring desire to learn, which, along with the most persistent and truly iron resolve, was unfortunately not rewarded with the success it deserved, for his powers of understanding, though not exactly limited, could none the less not be called brilliant.

That is how Hauser's character developed under my supervision. Regarding the fact that during the first period he showed not the slightest trace of mendacity, but rather an unusual love of truth and that his lying was nothing more than a habit acquired out of youthful lack of thought and, to begin with, the result of unhappy circumstances, that can be vouched for by Professor Daumer and also Professor Hermann in Munich who together and with me made observations about these extraordinary phenomena in 1828 and 1829.

Since November 1831, however, I have been out of touch with Hauser; I am unable to give any information about how his character has since developed.[29]

Hiltel, Preu, Binder, Daumer, Feuerbach and Tucher form the inner circle around Kaspar Hauser. They seem to have been chosen by destiny to be near to him and to serve him. Not one of them has been in any doubt about him during his life, not one of them has supported the later campaign of slander against him. Through an understanding partly based on feeling and partly on thinking, without any overall view of the background of the case, these men supported Kaspar Hauser by their conviction and knowledge of the truth.

The important phenomena which were observed in Kaspar Hauser, especially during the early period, have been established by the quoted evidence of the first witnesses. The childlike nature of the 15-year-old, which was evidence of his artificially retarded development, was expressed in innocence and purity.

A marked obedience and a childlike veneration for those in authority was his distinguishing characteristic. His memory verged on the miraculous. He could still recall word for word the names and complicated titles of a fairly large assembly of people weeks after he had been introduced to them—of course without understanding any of it. An immense ability for learning enabled him during his first weeks and months to learn and absorb within days what takes others years to accomplish. Especially in the beginning Kaspar Hauser was very eager and capable of learning, which does not in any way suggest that he was abnormal in the usual sense of the word.

The most striking thing about him was certainly the quality of his senses. Among the facts which again and again meet with disbelief, although substantiated by many witnesses and also expressly stated in a medical certificate by the doctors Preu and Osterhausen, is his capacity to see in the dark. After he had acquired his reading skills, he could decipher handwritten and printed matter in the total darkness of night. The strange thing about his ability of sense perception does not however rest only on his immense sensitivity, but also on the fact that he had preserved within himself his childlike purity of perception. Through Kaspar Hauser's disturbed development he was able to penetrate in memory back to the phase of early childhood to which memory normally does not extend. It is thanks to Feuerbach's attentiveness that this particular characteristic of Kaspar Hauser was noticed by him at all, and further, that when Kaspar had learned to express himself, Feuerbach was able to question him about it. He writes the following:

I was able to arrive at this remarkable experience, the whole significance of which only dawned on me some years later, through the following test to which I was led by a very obvious association of ideas between Kaspar Hauser, who only emerged from his dark gaol into the light of day when he was a youth, and the famous case of the blind man of Cheselden who lost his sight a few weeks after birth and only after a successful cataract operation in his youth was able to see again. I asked Kaspar Hauser to look out of the window, pointed to the expansive view into the beautiful landscape glowing in summer's finery and asked him if what he saw was beautiful? He obeyed me but drew back with obvious distaste as he cried out 'nasty! nasty!' Then he pointed to the white wall of his room and said: 'There not nasty!' I thought it clearly was not because of the impression that the light made on his sensitive eyes that he turned away. His countenance did not express pain in this instance, but rather disgust and horror. Added to that he was standing sideways from the window some distance away, so that he was able to see the view without being dazzled by any direct rays of the sun. When Kaspar Hauser shared my house for a few weeks in 1831, during which time I was continually able to observe him minutely and to amplify or correct my earlier observations, the above incident also was mentioned. I asked him if he remembered my visit to him in the Tower and then in particular if he remembered me asking him how he liked the view out of the window when he had turned away from the sight and had continually called out 'nasty! nasty!'—why had he done that? What had happened to him on that occasion? 'Yes, it's true,' he answered me, 'it was very nasty what I saw at that time. When I looked at the window it always seemed to me as if a shutter had been placed in front of my eyes upon which a decorator had splashed paint from his various brushes in a chaotic array of white, blue, green, yellow and red. I was unable to recognize and distinguish the single objects as I can now. That was therefore quite horrible to look at. And at the same time I was afraid because I thought that someone had closed the brightly chequered shutters so that I would not be able to look out into the open. It was only later, during my walks in the open air, that I realized that what I had been looking at at that time was fields, houses and hills and that which had appeared to me to be much larger than another object was really much smaller than it and that some large things were much smaller than I had observed them. Eventually I did not see the shutter any more.[30]

This is a unique testimony for the initial occurrence of pure perception in man. Rudolf Steiner describes it in his *Philosophy of Spiritual Activity* in the chapter entitled 'The World as Percept' as follows: 'Let us assume that a being with fully developed human intelligence originated out of nothing and confronted the world. All that is there perceived before its thought began to act would be the pure content of perception. The world so far would appear to this being as a mere chaotic aggregate of sense-data, colours, sounds, sensations of pressure, of warmth, of taste, of smell, and, lastly, feelings of pleasure and pain. This mass constitutes the world of pure unthinking perception. Over against it stands thought, ready to begin its activity as soon as it can find a point of attack. Experience shows that the opportunity is not long in coming. Thought is able to draw threads from one sense-datum to another. It brings definite concepts to bear on these data and thus establishes a relation between them.'[31]

Let it be said that Kaspar Hauser, who still had a certain amount of conscious perception of these things, was filled with aversion and horror until he succeeded in coming to a reasoned penetration of them. The concepts which gradually became attached to the things he saw profoundly altered his impression of them. The two sources of conscious human soul-life which are differentiated by Rudolf Steiner as perception and thinking in *The Philosophy of Spiritual Activity* still appear as separate soul activities in Kaspar Hauser, and it becomes clear how they are chaotically intermingled in ordinary consciousness.

Daumer realized too late that Kaspar's whole state of mind

was also connected with the fact that up till then he had never touched meat. He described later as his only, but greatest, educational blunder that he had introduced him to a meat diet. The calming and soothing influence he had exerted on wild or unruly animals, which was occasionally reported of him in the early period, grew less in the same degree that Kaspar Hauser accustomed himself to the usual form of nourishment. Above all it should be noted that with the awakening of his intelligence, the grasping of ideas, the alteration in his perceptive faculties, the change in his eating habits, a gradual lessening of his original abilities could be observed.

His development progressed so well under Daumer's supervision that in the summer of 1829 Kaspar's wish to write his autobiography became known to the public. This apparently drew the opponents into action. As appears from records or from police statements Kaspar was, however, not in a position to divulge any details which would have endangered the wrongdoers. Those in the background who were responsible for the crime had cast him out into the world to disappear or to perish. His whole progress in Nuremberg, the acceptance and sympathy which he found, could certainly not have been in the interest of those who had excluded him and had wished to destroy him. They had to admit that their plan to let him disappear had gone astray. News about his autobiography must have been alarming for them; their safety seemed threatened and they decided to risk the worst in order to avoid the danger which threatened them. Feuerbach writes: 'Whoever describes his life must have something to write about. It must have been a shock, therefore, to those who had every reason to remain in the darkness which they had woven around themselves and around the tracks which led to them when they heard the news of Kaspar's autobiography. The plan to drown poor Kaspar alive in the waves of the world, which was totally strange to him, had been frustrated. Now, as the secret villains may have thought, was the murder of Kaspar Hauser a kind of self-defence.'[32]

On 17 October 1829 in Daumer's house an assassination attempt was made on Kaspar Hauser by a man in a black mask. Feuerbach, in contrast to Pies,[33] supported the view that this assassination attempt was intentional and that only through a quick involuntary movement of Kaspar Hauser was his forehead struck with a horizontal blow from the murder weapon instead of his neck. Kaspar Hauser recovered from his injury fairly quickly, but a visible scar remained on his forehead. His attitude towards this event is described by Fuhrmann, of whom more later, as follows: 'His childlike mind felt only pain and fear about this event, not any bitterness or anger.'[34]

His so often described goodness of heart here shone forth, and a certain nervousness—who can fail to understand that?—took hold of him. He felt an uncontrollable fear, especially of knives and weapons. Did he have a premonition that his end was being prepared for him? From the psychological point of view it is therefore inconceivable that it could have been an attempt by him to end his own life as his opponents ever and again assert. First of all one places him in mortal fear of outward violence—and then one has the impudence to accuse him of having turned this violence against himself.

At the time of the assassination attempt Lord Stanhope, who later was to play such an incisive and disastrous role in Kaspar's life in Nuremberg, was travelling, as is said, on personal business, without paying any attention to Kaspar Hauser, who at that time was the best-known citizen of that town throughout Europe. One must regard it as symptomatic that Lord Stanhope appeared on the scene at this moment. Was not the publicly exhibited unrelatedness towards Kaspar Hauser intended to conceal the event just alluded to?

Some time after the assassination attempt Kaspar Hauser leaves the home of Daumer for various reasons, but continues to be educated and trained by him. After a short stay in the house of the merchant Biberbach he is taken into the care of his guardian Tucher. A short period of becoming accustomed to a bourgeois existence and a training for a future career follows. Then Lord Stanhope appears again in Nuremberg at the end of May 1831. He approaches the inexperienced youth as the serpent seducer who tries to dazzle him with promises and presents as well as confuse his mind by inciting him to vanity and mendacity. Lord Stanhope's behaviour is not only non-pedagogical, it is downright anti-pedagogical, so that it is hard not to recognize its evil intention. His Lordship must, however, have been an imposing actor and diplomat, for he succeeds to begin with in deceiving everyone and making them think that his intentions were unselfish and pure. Only Kaspar's guardian Tucher was undeceived and clearly saw the effect of Stanhope on the mind of Kaspar Hauser, recognizing his Lordship's perfidy and energetically opposing him—but unfortunately not succeeding against him. Tucher himself tells about this (in the court testimonial of 1834):

I can assure you by my pledged oath that during the one-and-a half years which Hauser spent in my house and before Lord Stanhope came to Nuremberg, there was not a single cause for me to rebuke, much less to scold, him and the only thing which I had to complain about was that I feared he might do himself bodily injury by studying too much. He gave sufficient proof of the fact that there was no natural wickedness in him and, with his lightmindedness, it required only a little supervision and consequential strictness to save him from the errors of mendacity and vanity and gradually bring him back to the proper path by accustoming him to what is good.

Unfortunately, however, the chosen path, which experience had shown to be the best, could not be followed for long. Lord Stanhope, who grew very fond of the boy, exerted a very adverse influence upon him, just in respect of the two defects already mentioned. This forced me, out of my duty as his guardian, to beg the latter to desist from all the insinuations unfavourable to Hauser's moral character or else to relieve me of the responsibility of my guardianship by taking over the care of my charge himself. Lord Stanhope chose the latter course, whereupon the guidance of my tutelage came to an end and I was wholly discharged of my duties by the Board of Guardians. That took place, as mentioned above, in November 1831.[35]

Lord Stanhope soon afterwards quickly changed from a paternal friend, benefactor and protector to a sceptical, aloof doubter and finally to Kaspar's worst enemy. That this opinion is justified is demonstrated by an experience which Daumer had with Lord Stanhope and which opened the eyes of the former, who was at first quite unsuspecting of his true motives. Daumer first spoke about the 'incomprehensible metamorphosis' of his Lordship from friend to enemy, incomprehensible because it was no such thing. This so decisive meeting with the person of Lord Stanhope is described by Daumer as follows:

Lord Stanhope honoured my unworthy self with many visits after Hauser's death while he displayed such an amazing activity for the purpose of calumniating the murder-victim. He sought me out, to my great astonishment, as I was still far from seeing him as an enemy in the Hauser affair, to mislead me into bearing witness against him. He would not listen to anything which I and my mother said in favour of the foundling from our personal and most valid perception and observation, for one would have thought he would have liked to have learned that his former pet had not been such a completely bad and unworthy person and he, the Count, had not been so disgracefully deceived. My mother, seeing what colours he bore on his shield, begged and entreated him with impassioned ardour not to spread infamy and discredit on the memory of an unhappy person who once trusted him in childish faith as his fatherly friend and benefactor and whom she knew for certain was no swindler or miscreant. 'It will not harm him any more,' he answered, became red in the face, broke short his visit and ran down the steps, never to be seen again in my house.
  I will not repeat what my mother thought and expressed (the Count was even obliged to hear a similar verdict from the mouth of a royal personage); appearances can deceive, she might have been mistaken. I will only describe what actually happened and what I can swear to on oath and what seems to me to be a part of this dark and ghastly story,

without accusing the Count of a crime or of complicity in it. I only go so far as to say that the Count's dealings were not performed solely in the interests of truth; that he must have had concealed motives and that therefore a true assessment of his character cannot hold him to be the sincere and credible guarantor which those on the side of the enemies, who see everything opposed to the unhappy victim as excellent, noble, above suspicion and authoritative, would accept and hold to be true.[36]

Lord Stanhope has drawn suspicion to himself in another way, namely, through the fact that he purposely and consciously wanted to remain without suspicion with regard to the murder. At the time this took place he was in Vienna, then travelled to Munich, where he posted a letter to Kaspar Hauser on 25 December 1833 and had it postmarked with that date. Does one have to believe that his Lordship had not heard of the assassination attempt on the 14 and the ensuing death of his foster-son and ward on the 17 December, even though this event was the talk of the day and was on everybody's lips? It only remains to be said of this: one can guess at the motive and one is horror struck.

This man is Kaspar's new guardian who takes him away from Daumer and his Nuremberg friends by bringing him to Ansbach. Only Feuerbach, who lived in Ansbach, remained in direct contact with him. One must not disregard the fact that it was Lord Stanhope who took his ward to the teacher Meyer in Ansbach, the one who later conferred with him in slandering and persecuting the dead Kaspar Hauser and whose son had previously played the infamous role already mentioned. Regarding the sort of lessons, as also the effect that teacher Meyer had on the mind of Kaspar Hauser, Feuerbach wrote as follows:

This poor neglected youth, who had only recently had his first sight of the world and had to catch up on things which our children learn at their mother's breast or on their nurse's lap, is suddenly called upon to martyr his brain with Latin grammar and exercises, with Cornelius Nepos and finally with Caesar's *De bello Gallico*. Pressed into Latin swotting his mind now suffers a second imprisonment. As formerly it was the prison walls, so now it is the dusty walls of the classroom which shut him off from nature and from life. Instead of useful things he is now given words and phrases, the meaning of which he is unable to fathom, and thus his childhood is once more extended in the most unnatural way. While he was wasting his time, and his in any case sparse energy, on dry scholastic frippery he was continually starved of the necessary knowledge of things which would have nourished and refreshed his mind and compensated his injured soul for its lost childhood and supplied him with a basis for some future profession. 'I have no idea,' he often used to say with annoyance and semi-despair, 'what I shall do with all these Latin things, as I am not going to be a parson, nor do I wish to become one.' When a pedant once retorted that the learning of Latin was essential for the German language, and in order to learn German properly one had to have a thorough knowledge of Latin, his common sense answer was: 'Did the Romans have to learn German in order to speak and write Latin properly?'[37]

Kaspar Hauser spent the last two years of his earthly life with his teacher Meyer, who certainly had no sense for such humorous turns of phrase. Is it not to be expected that Kaspar's nature grew outwardly hardened, that this treatment failed to arouse his faculties, that he was unable to have faith in and confide in a person like Meyer? He was treated in the most unsuitable and disagreeable manner in order then to have the results of this kind of treatment used against him and to be testified against by eye-witnesses and life-companions, as Meyer and his son did later. In inimitable fashion Jakob Wassermann has characterized Meyer in the person of the schoolmaster Quandt in his novel.

It is a happy stroke of fortune that Kaspar Hauser received his Confirmation classes from Rector Fuhrmann in Ansbach. For Kaspar to have met this person, who stands opposed to

Stanhope and Meyer as a Christian protagonist for God, is of
such significance, because through him he discovered living,
active Christianity. Fuhrmann, the evangelical parson of the
Gumbertus Church, appears from his later published sermons
relating to the Confirmation and funeral rites for Kaspar
Hauser to have been a man for whom the gospels were a
deeply felt truth and who was imbued beyond the bounds of
doubt and criticism with the basic facts of Christianity.

He was confirmed by Rector Fuhrmann in Ansbach on 20
May 1833, a few days before the death of Feuerbach. The fact
that it was not a mere formality or an outward event is shown
by the words spoken by Fuhrmann in his obituary address:
'He celebrated his Confirmation and his first Communion on
20 May this year with an emotion and exaltation of soul for
our Saviour which moved all who witnessed it and gave to me,
his religion teacher, the conviction that the gospel of Christ
which beatifies all believers had struck deep roots in his
heart.'[38]

The immediate effect which his person had on his surroundings was increased and elevated by the effect of the
Sacrament. That becomes plain through the following
impassioned and moving words of Fuhrmann. He says:

The 20th of May of last year was the festive occasion of
which hundreds still say it is a day of exaltation for them. It
was the day of Kaspar Hauser's Confirmation. The most
respected families of the district, in whose hearts feelings of
compassion were aroused for the pitiable young man,
surrounded him and his guardians and advisers who
accompanied him on his journey to the overcrowded Chapel
[a Chapel of the Swan-Knights][39]—our lovely Gumbertus
Church ... A prayer was sung in four parts by the choir:
'Prepare in me O Lord a heart that's pure and give to me a
new and steadfast spirit; cast me from Thy presence not
aside, nor take Thy Holy Ghost away from me.'

During the singing Hauser knelt on a prayer stool before
the altar. The moment, however, when he knelt, the emotion
with which he spoke the above words in the silence had an

unusual effect on the whole congregation. Every lip moved quietly in response; all hearts prayed with him and for him.[40]

Kaspar was 21 years old on 29 September 1833. Daumer became 33 in the same year. After his birthday Kaspar Hauser visited Nuremberg in the autumn. He met Binder and Daumer once more and resolved to return to live with Daumer if occasion permitted. He hoped in his *naïveté* that Lord Stanhope would allow him to leave his teacher Meyer in Ansbach and lead an independent life. One can only guess to what extent the secret criminals were alarmed by Kaspar Hauser's development. Did they guess that Kaspar's guiding spirit was nevertheless going to spread its wings in spite of the fact that they had done all in their power to mutilate them? It is in any case certain that his death had been decided upon by a secret council in the autumn of 1833. On 27 November 1833 the exchanged infant, Kaspar Ernst Blochmann, was made officially to die. On 14 December 1833 Kaspar was struck down by an unknown person, who lured him under pretext into the Royal Court Gardens while he was opening a purse which had been given him as a distraction. When on this Saturday afternoon towards four o'clock he staggered to Meyer's house, the latter did not believe his report. He got hold of the victim, who was later found to be mortally wounded in four places, and forced him to return to the palace gardens. It is amazing evidence of his death-defying life-forces that Kaspar Hauser was able to complete the greater part of the way back before he collapsed and had to be brought back to Meyer's house. Meyer continued to regard Kaspar's report as fiction. His verdict was that he inflicted the wound on himself to attract attention. When the doctors established that Kaspar's life was beyond saving, Meyer produced the slanderous argument that he was an inadvertent suicide and a thorough deceiver and liar. In that way the last three days of his life were, in a sense, overshadowed. 'Give up the Ghost in ignominy', as Wassermann lets him express it.[41]

His life draws to a close on Tuesday 17 December 1833 at

ten o'clock in the evening. As a painful reminder of an
unfulfilled mission sound his words: 'the monster was stronger'. But the monster was not strong enough to hinder Rector
Fuhrmann from being at his death-bed. At the moment of
death the light of Christianity blazed up brightly in him and
Furhmann is the world-historic witness of this event. Kaspar
Hauser thanks and forgives everyone, his teacher Meyer
included and even his murderer. Fuhrmann reports: 'The
departed uttered the word of forgiveness with his dying
lips'.[42] The central event of Christianity was planted by
Fuhrmann in Kaspar Hauser's consciousness. 'The more we
make the knowledge of Him (Christ) our concern, the deeper
we penetrate into it, so much the more intimately do we cling
to Him who is the Way, the Truth and the Life and without
Whom no one can approach the Father. The more willingly
we submit to His Providence, so much the more vivid is the
conviction that His Salvation and Blessing will be granted,
even amidst tears and sighs, and the more sincerely and con-
tentedly will we be able to pray: "O my Father, if it be possible, let this cup pass from me: nevertheless not as I will, but
as Thou wilt". Brothers and sisters gathered together with
deep feelings of pain among these grave mounds, where we
can also see that of the young man who engaged the sympathy and attention of practically the whole world, receive
now as a consolation and a lesson the prayer from Matthew
26:39, which was one of the last words he spoke. And a word
at the boundary of life, a word in the proximity of death, and
just through that in proximity of the Throne of Eternal Justice, does not easily emerge from a hypocritical heart, but
contains a person's whole soul and allows us an infallible
insight into his inner self.'[42]

Kaspar Hauser, whose whole life became one of self-
sacrifice as a result of criminal intentions, accepts his destiny,
accepts his death in the consciousness: 'Father, not as I will,
but as Thou wilt.'

Fuhrmann drew the attention of the dying Kaspar Hauser
to the fact that Christ had spoken these words as He was
preparing to sacrifice Himself in suffering and death. So

Kaspar Hauser crossed the threshold of death into the spiritual world with his soul filled with the Christ-impulse.

Daumer too speaks about the death of Kaspar Hauser. His report closes with an unforgettable expression which illuminates Kaspar Hauser's being like a flash of intuition: 'Truly this poor person had been afflicted with an atrocious amount of evil, even by those with whom he lived and into whose care he had been given; and yet he said out of his sheer goodness of heart: "no one ever did me any harm". He died with a lie—*but it was an angelic lie.*'[43]

'He was buried two days later: it was during the afternoon and the sky was a cloudless blue. The whole town was stirred. A famous contemporary, who called Kaspar the "Child of Europe", says that on that occasion moon and sun were both visible in the sky together, the former in the East, the latter in the West, and both heavenly bodies shone with the same pale light.'[44] Thus Wassermann assigns to Kaspar Hauser's death a special cosmic relationship. The Child of Europe, who was murdered shortly before Christmas, is carried to his grave on the occasion of an Easter constellation.*

It must be regarded as quite in keeping with Kaspar Hauser's view when Fuhrmann in his obituary address says about his murder: 'In a Christian sense we are sorry for the hand which brought an untimely end to his earthly life; in a reconciliatory sense we pray for the unhappy person who wantonly destroyed what might have led to a happy turn in his destiny and we hold fast to the belief that those who are able to kill the body are unable to extend their dark powers to the soul as well.'[45]

Kaspar Hauser made his appearance among men as an innocent, pure soul and he departed from the earth as the victim of criminal manipulations by deeply uniting himself in death with the central event of earthly evolution, with the Christ impulse as it was expressed in the Mystery of Golgotha.

An offence against the human soul out of occult motives (according to Feuerbach)

If one follows the story of Kaspar Hauser as it here stands and is portrayed, one can only regard it as a riddle of our time. Apart from verifying the facts and the suggestion of a successfully committed dynastic crime, science has no explanation to offer, for with the means at its disposal the whole mystery can neither be solved not understood. Even Daumer and Feuerbach are well aware of the fact that the whole affair ultimately remains an enigma.

What deep-seated motives can lead to a child, later a young man, being treated in such a way as that? It was a very dangerous procedure which, from the start, necessitated a long-drawn-out course of action—in this case more than two decades. A whole series of people must have been engaged in preparing these events long in advance. Considerable means were demanded and have been employed. In connection therewith we have to regard the action against Kaspar Hauser as taking part in at least two stages.

The dynastic crime, in which the Empress of Hochberg must have played the instigative and decisive part, is so much in the foreground that it appears to hide a much more important event in the background. A hint in this direction is given by the fact that the dynastic crime fails to explain the kidnapping and in particular the special way in which the imprisonment was carried out. All investigation along these lines remains ultimately unsatisfactory. Even Feuerbach only reached the conclusion that a benefactor of Kaspar Hauser wished to protect him by this means. But it is not obvious how such protection can be reconciled with such an enormous amount of cruelty towards a child. Protection could in any case have been given in a different way. From the inexplicability of the imprisonment its connection with the dynastic crime has been set in doubt or even denied outright.

Kaspar Hauser's imprisonment confronts everyone who gives it consideration with an almost insoluble riddle, but, nevertheless, the solving of this riddle is of the very greatest importance. One starts to overcome the difficulty when one realizes that the problem is not to be solved by knowledge based on the senses alone, for the simple reason that it is an occult event. 'Where outer senses' knowledge ends, there and there only is the gateway that leads to the realities of life' is how Rudolf Steiner expresses it in one of his *Verses and Meditations*. Whoever looks for an explanation of Kaspar Hauser's treatment is led of necessity to the threshold of the spiritual world and only the knowledge of man as Rudolf Steiner developed it through his passing of the threshold into the spiritual world is an appropriate means of progressing further. The fact that Kaspar Hauser can only be understood in essence by Anthroposophy, means that he stands in a very special relationship to it. When one looks at Kaspar Hauser with anthroposophical insight an almost frightening light is thrown on the treatment meted out to him.

To begin with one can say that the child was carefully reared, that he was allowed to develop until the moment when the ego had become consolidated in the physical body in walking, talking and thinking. Everything depended upon the fact that a certain amount of power was to be gained by the physical body over the spiritual and soul nature with which the ego wished to be united during its incarnation. The perpetrators therefore were only interested in the living Kaspar Hauser, whereas the dynastic crime always favoured the murder, as happened to the brother of the Crown Prince Alexander in 1817. The crime against Kaspar Hauser, therefore, comes into the second category, resting only on his personality. The latter is to be kept away from its earthly task, from its historic mission. For that reason it was necessary for him to remain alive. Rudolf Steiner indicated that if Kaspar Hauser had been killed he would soon have incarnated again. This corresponds with a certain law of the study of man. A small child carrying with it into incarnation a rich web of destiny sufficient for the whole of its future life, can very quickly reincarnate—better said, look for another body—if, for any reason, it dies young. The perpetrators knew this law and treated the young child accordingly.

Then follows the life in what he himself described as the dungeon. He was transferred there as soon as the permanent memory started to develop. This would certainly have been dangerous for the conspirators. It was predicted by them in advance. The development of the capacity for memory indicates that the ego is taking hold of the physical body more strongly. Through that a further consolidation of the incarnation takes place so that there is not so much fear of the child dying. It was placed in a condition between life and death, between waking and sleeping. It was made impossible for it to develop on the earth as a human being, but at the same time it was prevented from returning to the spiritual world by means of death. As follows from his own account Kaspar sank into a kind of dreamy state. His bodily development is very much retarded, his mind and soul remain for the most part static. It is not only a physical but also a kind of inner spiritual imprisonment. It revolves about the fact that the individuality is held in a suspended condition whereby it is eliminated.

Kaspar Hauser sitting in the dungeon can be seen as the archetypal picture of modern man. Man is hindered from developing his ego and his destiny—he is rammed down below the level of his possible achievement. Kaspar Hauser is then prevented from standing upright, from asserting his individuality on earth. He is not allowed to roam about and thereby meet his destiny. He is unable to speak and think and above all he cannot meet any other people. All of that forms a counter-image to what Kaspar Hauser really wanted. But it has fallen to his lot in an archetypal and horrible way to experience the destiny of modern humanity in advance. Innumerable people today can be experienced as sitting in invisible cages. They are thrust into them in childhood, through medicaments which fetter them rather than heal them, through pedagogical measures which cause young people to freeze in their intellectuality, through nutrition which is looked upon as a purely chemico-biological process and through much else as well.

After having sat for more than twelve years in his dungeon, Kaspar Hauser is thrust out into the world by those who wished him mischief, so that he might perish there. The plan to make him disappear into a cavalry regiment apparently went astray. His development takes a different turn to that which those in the background expected and wished for. That is supported by the attempted assassination and the murder itself, which were in any case dangerous final expedients. The opponents have been misled about Kaspar Hauser's possibilities of development as well, above all, as about the people to whom he came, to whom he belonged and by whom he was understood.

Lord Stanhope was sent to corrupt him when his development diverged too far from that which the corrupters could allow. Lord Stanhope does all he can to hamper his mental development—a great updating process—by inciting his vanity and trying to mislead him into telling lies. Then he prepares a second imprisonment for him through the materialistic attitude of his teacher Meyer. He also succeeds in separating him, at least physically, from people like Binder, Daumer and Tucher. Through Lord Stanhope our attention is clearly drawn to the second stage of the felony committed against Kaspar Hauser and to the people behind it, and this track leads inexorably towards the West.

Lastly, the assassination of Kaspar Hauser, which takes place a bare three months after his 21st birthday, goes back to considerations of human development. His personality starts to assert itself. He united himself deeply with Christianity during the celebration of his Confirmation. He underwent certain supersensible experiences, as Wassermann describes them in his novel. The opponents' schemes had in a sense miscarried. His death was planned in order to prevent any further risk.

From this it clearly emerges how certain groups in history have concretely contributed towards helping the forces of opposition. Behind the crime carried out on Kaspar Hauser there is obviously a deep-rooted occult knowledge, which was not publicly recognized at the time. This recognition has to do with what happened before Kaspar Hauser's birth, it concerns the when, where and how of his appearance in public. The approach and entry of this individuality into earthly life and its terrestrial mission must have been under observation. The Empress of Hochberg with her ambitious plans and dynastic intentions must have served purposes of which she was probably quite unaware. The instigators of the crime against Kaspar Hauser possessed significant spiritual insight. Their rank, not their morality, is equal to that of the Three Holy Kings. They saw Kaspar Hauser's star rising. But they do not use their secret knowledge for the salvation of humanity or for the development of a personality, but for the establishment of power and rulership. A dark kingdom becomes visible whose icy wisdom turns deliberately against the Christ impulse. In this sense the instigators serve extensive plans in the history of mankind. Their method of working is determined by the fact that they employ people to serve their schemes without those concerned being aware of, or allowed to understand, what is happening. It is of fundamental, nay paramount, importance to know that there are people possessing significant occult knowledge of things such as reincarnation and karma and the nature of man, who use it to the detriment of humanity and place it in a devastating form into the evolutionary history of mankind. If the activity of these dark Kings who are only intent on gaining power over Kaspar Hauser's destiny is recognized, a part of their power will then be destroyed.

In many souls something rebels at acknowledging such a dark, intentionally wicked trend in history. Kaspar Hauser's destiny has not been lived in vain if through serious recognition it throws light on the evil background which would itself rather remain in the dark.* In this way those people who wished to destroy Kaspar Hauser can be recognized and unmasked by a science which takes the spiritual world and its beings as a serious reality. It behoves those people who have come to an understanding of the spiritual world through Anthroposophy to attribute this meaning to Kaspar Hauser's sacrifice. After Kaspar Hauser's sacrificial death at the hands of these unholy ice-cold Kings, the latter did all they could in a hidden way to nullify what came from him, so as to bury the thought of him and to paint over his true image. To the best of my knowledge no one in recent history except Rudolf Steiner has been so slandered and misrepresented as Kaspar Hauser. That will only seem logical to those who understand the occult motives of the instigators and can know through that that they had to, and wanted to, remain incognito. The simplest means to this end was to make Kaspar Hauser out to be a liar, deceiver, a beggar and a suicide.

'He will be as mighty in death as he was powerless in life'
(Jakob Wassermann)

If one reviews the biography and destiny of Kaspar Hauser with a glance which is directed at first to the outer events, one has the picture of something incomplete, inferior, defeated— even scoffed at and derided. This impression is strengthened still further by what was rained down upon him after his death. Only a small circle of friends took up his true inner nature into themselves, protected it and bore it into the future. The destiny which Kaspar Hauser suffered in his life is a path of ultimate testing, which can be compared with the Stations of the Cross of Christ. By withstanding these trials humbly and uprightly till the time of his death he is a bearer of the Christian destiny of the nineteenth century. For the spiritual world the opponents have thereby been robbed of their triumph. The same thing happens for mankind's history when human beings recognize this fact and grasp it in the spirit.

Kaspar Hauser's whole life on earth was, as Feuerbach so aptly said, a martyrdom, a path of torture and self-sacrifice. This sacrifice is first of all imposed on him from outside. His mission was annulled, his life's plan destroyed. An indication by Rudolf Steiner, given to Friedrich Rittelmeyer about the First World War, but which applies equally well to many another historical observation, can be of help to us here too: 'It should not have happened like this but what has happened was necessary.'[46] Kaspar Hauser acted in the sense of this saying which is so difficult to understand when, at the point of death, he uttered the Christ-words: 'Father, not as I will, but as Thou wilt'. He lived in the acceptance of his destiny. He took up his Cross, he transformed his way of suffering into a free deed of sacrifice. His self-sacrifice acquires the significance of a Christianization of the individuality. Looked at in this way Rudolf Steiner's saying becomes understandable: 'Next to Christian Rosenkreutz, Kaspar Hauser had the greatest feeling for the suffering of Christ.'[47] When a person accepts a destiny imposed upon him—a destiny which does not result from the karmic debt of the individual concerned— as Kaspar Hauser accepted and transformed his destiny in a Christian sense, it brings about a situation which the powers opposing human evolution and the human beings that serve them are not able to understand or foresee. Their plans are frustrated, the limits of their insight are made visible and their power is curtailed.

By changing his self-sacrifice into a free deed of sacrifice Kaspar Hauser becomes a companion of Christ. The sacrificial death finds fulfilment in resurrection. Humanity will take part in this by spiritually recognizing who he is. One can guess how his future activity will give expression to the resurrection forces, which have been strengthened by his sacrifice, and how he whom the evil forces wished to corrupt in the most horrible fashion is working for the redemption of the evil forces. Through his sacrifice Kaspar Hauser has become one of the great Christian figures of humanity.

At the present time the picture of one who has been defeated can change into that of the Comforter, the Comforter who has experienced in His own being the destructive effects on humanity of indolence of heart and has therefore become the inspirer of heart's courage. If one were to ask oneself what was the attitude of Kaspar Hauser towards his own destiny, one could find the answer expressed in the saying of Novalis: 'All that happens is what I will'. The highest spiritual activity links up with what—as mentioned above (p.63)—appears, in a historical sense, to be a forced necessity. Through that the ego unites with the stream of world events and frees itself—paradoxically enough—by that means from compulsion.

For the observer who wishes to participate in this event

himself, his task will be to overcome the aspect of the defeated sacrifice. One can feel that this task, which demands courage, is a Michaelic task, which we owe to Kaspar Hauser.

Still another motive is shown by the inner connection which he, who was born on Michaelmas Day, has to the Being we celebrate on that day. By the destiny he suffered Kaspar Hauser leaves other people completely free. What he accomplished outwardly on earth is quite insignificant. What has been handed down about him in a historical sense does not in the least reveal the possibilities of his individuality. So there is no kind of compulsion exerted by him, he leaves everything to a person's own judgement. His essential being is only accessible to an understanding which can raise itself to the supersensible world.

There is still the question as to how the opponents could acquire power over him. The way that an important personality affects a larger group of people does not depend upon him alone, but also on what is offered him by his surroundings. Especially in the case of a spiritual mission, which relies on the free recognition and selfless actions of many people, is this of decisive importance. Now we can easily see that the spiritual guidance of history had been thwarted and hindered even before Kaspar Hauser appeared. Above all Count St Germain had done all he could to give Louis XVI spiritual incentives to bring about the necessary social changes in a healthy way. Count St Germain's efforts, however, tragically failed to produce an effective historical result. The French Revolution with its ideals of Liberty, Equality and Fraternity only allowed these deeper forces of the future to appear in a chaotic way. Without being understood they did not have the strength to intervene in the social structure in a formative way. Consequently the activity of Napoleon ultimately replaced this impulse.

It is also important to realize that the spirit which proceeded from Goethe and Schiller was also not taken up as it should have been. It is particularly conspicuous that Schiller succumbed in 1805 during a spiritual battle as he was about to write the destiny of Demetrius. This destiny, which Schiller

wished to portray seven years before the birth of Kaspar
Hauser and because of which he died, shows a certain similarity to the destiny of Kaspar Hauser. Demetrius is
manipulated from childhood on by an occult clique which
wishes to use him for its own purposes. He was to have been
isolated from his destiny and above all from his own ego.

But in the individuality of Demetrius there are latent forces—similar to those of Kaspar Hauser—which cross their
plans. The attack on his ego does not succeed as it was
intended. Demetrius, however, as a 'deceived deceiver' is
unable, through his individuality, to rectify what had been
perpetrated upon him. That brought about his tragic downfall
which destroyed his temporal being, but caused his spiritual
being to shine even more brightly.[48]

The impulses of the spiritual world which stirred in Goethe
and Schiller and in many others were unable to work down
strongly enough into the physical world. The bridge from the
spiritual to the physical world as it is pictured in Goethe's
Fairy-tale has to be built every time afresh for modern mankind if it is not to be dragged down into physical decay. A
human being had to build that bridge. It was built by Kaspar
Hauser's path of sacrifice through which he surrendered his
personality. That is the significance which he had for his own
time and which continued to work on into the nineteenth and
twentieth centuries. Rudolf Steiner expressed the mission of
Kaspar Hauser with the following words: 'If Kaspar Hauser
had not lived and died in the way he did the contact between
the earth and the spiritual world would have been completely
severed.'[49] This statement shows how, instead of a personal
task, a cosmic mission for the whole of mankind has been
fulfilled. He lived and suffered and died for others—for
mankind.

By his sacrifice he joins himself to and is penetrated by the
Christ and is enabled, through those who wish to know him, to
work into the present and the future. 'He will be as mighty in
death as he was powerless in life.'

In the three sections of the first chapter an attempt has been
made to draw three great and moving pictures. The many-

layered and differentiated whole becomes visible when we do not let the single pictures remain isolated and static, but interweave them with one another. A summing up can be found, strangely enough, in the thrice-urging motto on his gravestone. There stand the words:

Hic jacet Casparus Hauser
Aenigma sui temporis
ignota nativitas
occulta mors.

(Here lies Kaspar Hauser, a riddle for his age, his origin unknown, a mystery his death.)

'His origin unknown': His birth as the heir apparent to the throne of Baden on Michaelmas Day 1812 was revealed and his life as 'Child of Europe' was described in the way it can now be sketched according to the facts which have been discovered.

'A riddle for his age': For science his abduction and imprisonment remain a mystery. Only through Anthroposophy is it possible to recognize and understand the occult motives which led to the crime against a human soul. A dark background to history is revealed and must be borne courageously.

'His death a mystery': Something of this mystery can be revealed if his death can be understood as the final chapter of a path of sacrifice which raises him to be a companion of Christ. His death gains cosmic importance for mankind and for the earth.

A saying of Rudolf Steiner which he gave for the leading geniuses of mankind, and in which he expresses the duty which human beings owe to these geniuses, is here appended:

Es leuchten gleich Sternen	There gleam like stars
Am Himmel des ewigen Seins	In the heaven of eternal being
Die gottgesandten Geister.	The God-sent Spirits.
Gelingen mög'es allen	May all human souls
Menschenseelen,	In earthly evolution
Im Reich des Erdenwerdens	Glimpse their flame of light.
Zu schauen ihrer Flammen Licht	

2. Kaspar Hauser's Karmic Surroundings

Figures around Kaspar Hauser

The people with whom Kaspar Hauser came into contact after being released into Nuremberg seem to have been predestined to meet him. Let us just recall in the sequence of their appearance the figures whom he met without any effort on his part. First of all there is the prison keeper, Hiltel, whose heart-forces made him clairvoyant for the purity, innocence and integrity of Kaspar Hauser. There followed the medical doctor, Dr Preu, who by close observation of the phenomena immediately formed the idea of an intentional retardation by means of imprisonment. Nuremberg's Mayor Binder greeted Kaspar Hauser as a 'token of love' in which 'Providence' had allowed the community to share. Through Binder's proclamation Kaspar Hauser quickly becomes a concern of Germany—nay of the whole of Europe. The foundling becomes 'the Child of Europe'. The appearance of this outstanding child attracts the attention of the schoolmaster Daumer, who becomes his foster-father in the sense of a true self-selected kinship. He gives a comprehensive description of Kaspar Hauser with loving artistry, he supported him in life, defended his integrity after his death and is allowed, when he is very old, to let the deceased speak through him (see the obituary poem in his Kaspar Hauser book of 1873—p.5). 'The not highly enough to be esteemed Professor Daumer' (Rudolf Steiner) has the historic merit of having taken up and preserved in a unique way the figure of Kaspar Hauser. Without Daumer's life's work we should have had a far less significant, smaller and fainter picture of Kaspar Hauser.

Next to him stands President Feuerbach as criminologist, lawyer and psychologist, a fiery-headed person who never had any peace during his lifetime for wanting to solve the mystery of the unique crime. 'For years he (Kaspar Hauser) has been the primary and most important object of my observation, investigation and concern, my chief preoccupation as a human being, scholar and State Official,' he writes in 1830.[50] He succeeded in solving the riddle of his identity (*Memoirs* of 1832), he starts to see through the evil machinations of the dubious Lord Stanhope and—as a result of his dangerously growing insight—he had to die. The first official guardian of Kaspar Hauser was the Frankish nobleman, Baron Tucher, appointed at the instigation of Binder. In him Kaspar Hauser finds an unusual amount of uprightness, honesty and nobility.

To these six figures with whom Kaspar Hauser became acquainted in Nuremberg must be added a seventh, Pastor Fuhrmann from Ansbach, where Feuerbach lived, a representative of living Christianity in the garb of the Protestant religion. Pastor Fuhrmann is the appointed witness of the Christianity of Kaspar Hauser. He acts in the sense of Kaspar Hauser's essential being, which was truly affected by the Christ impulse, when at the grave of the assassination victim he prays for the murderer.

These seven figures are gathered about him in an intimate circle. Each one of them feels that in Kaspar Hauser they have encountered the greatest karmic event of their life. These people who, of course, represent a much wider circle, form a delicately composed whole which is inwardly connected to him.

Within this circle of people Kaspar Hauser was able to live in such a way that his individuality and the mission attached to it began to awaken. No other circle of people but the one in Nuremberg and Ansbach could have achieved the same. What relationship would these people have had to him if he had been centred in the Court in Karlsruhe? If the karmic community here portrayed represents a spiritual reality, then the connections in life would have had to develop under different conditions.

A still greater riddle is presented to us if we consider how, strangely enough, Kaspar Hauser was released into the world just in Nuremberg. It is the place where people who are predestined and able to understand him are waiting in readiness. If one does not want to accept the fact that the opponents had

given up their plans—and there is no evidence for this—one is
again faced with the fact that they could not have foreseen the
results of setting him free. For it could not have been the
intention of the opponents to let Kaspar Hauser come to just
those people who—each in his own way—could recognize
something about him which was exceptional and unique and
at least guess at his historical greatness, but above all could
treasure and love him. It is unthinkable that the opponents
could have intentionally put themselves in this position. (The
third chapter will deal with those powers which led to Kaspar
Hauser's release from captivity.)

This view is confirmed by the fact that the opponents
naturally—in their way—soon noticed that they had made a
fatal mistake. This mistake of theirs was to be compensated
for by the arrival of Lord Stanhope. It would be karmically
wrong to number Lord Stanhope among those who belonged
to a group connected to Kaspar Hauser through destiny. Lord
Stanhope was consciously *sent* to Kaspar Hauser with certain
definite antagonistic, ultimately murderous intentions. What
the connection of this person could or should have been to him
is not relevant in this case. The only decisive thing is the task
that was given him. This contract had as its aim to corrupt
Kaspar Hauser morally and, if this did not succeed, to
eliminate him by force.

The connection between Kaspar Hauser and Lord
Stanhope does not arise—as the others described it—out of a
human karmic encounter. Through Lord Stanhope's manipulation Kaspar Hauser is parted from his Nuremberg friends
in 1831 and brought from them to the wretched teacher Meyer
who makes Kaspar Hauser's life more and more miserable.
Meyer stands in contact with the police sergeant Hickel who
apparently pursued Kaspar Hauser's life with mistrust and
enmity at the behest of Lord Stanhope.

So it happened that those who were the opponents of
Kaspar Hauser and who gave evidence against him after his
death had been chosen for this role by Lord Stanhope. Lord
Stanhope brought about these connections intentionally. The
enmity against Kaspar Hauser did not arise out of unpreju-

diced personal experience, out of an impartial encounter, but was the result of an intended course of action. It deserves to be recorded that no enemies have been made by Kaspar Hauser in his dealings with others. From direct contact with this affable and good-natured human being no one has had anything to complain about.

This is underlined by the fact that Merker, the police superintendent for Berlin, who was the first to write in defamation of Kaspar Hauser during his lifetime, never took the trouble to interview him in person.[51] From an unbiased human experience of Kaspar Hauser there arose in everyone who wished to accept it at least an inkling of the source out of which his goodness flowed.

About the name 'Kaspar Hauser'

The name Kaspar Hauser was written on a sheet of paper in the Nuremberg Police Station by the individual who bore that name in life. This was on the evening of Whit Monday 1828, the day when the person concerned was released into the world.

One only knows as much as he himself has told us about the giving of the name. According to that, 'the man with whom he had always been' had taught him to write this name a few days before his release; apart from this he only knew a few letters.[52]

Was the reason for this name-giving only to comply with the outer necessity of not sending anyone out into the world without giving them a name? Did one wish to avoid the situation that without a name this youngster would have been more conspicuous than ever? Is the giving of the name accidental and unimportant or not? All these questions can lead to an investigation of what lies in the name 'Kaspar Hauser'. 'Since the world began there was never a king with the name Kaspar' wrote Adolf Bartning.[53] Bartning—entrapped by modern culture—overlooked the fact that Kaspar was the name of one of the 'Three Holy Kings'. If one works from the basis that Kaspar is the name of the Black King, the Negro King, an inner connection can then certainly be found.[54]

The Negro King represents the will element in the trinity of
the Kings. It is the future part of mankind. Man's will, in all its
movement and activity, is always directed towards the future.
It is that which goes beyond the reality of the moment. It is
that which appears during life, but can only be experienced in
its growing significance in the life after death. It is a reality
which, in growing, will only be revealed in a future human
life.[55] In this sense Kaspar is a figure belonging to the future,
around whom is the promise and anticipation of what is still to
come. Kaspar is the king who greets the coming of Christ,
Epiphany, with vigorous youthful enthusiasm. The Christ-
Star has led him out of the farthest distance into the presence
of the Logos become man, which will be the goal of his
endeavours ever afterwards.

Kaspar offers myrrh to Christ. Whereas the properties of
gold are openly revealed, those of incense on being burned,
myrrh has to be experienced directly. Its essence remains
hidden, its essential part is held back. It cannot be revealed
openly, but behind its inconspicuous exterior strength and
potency lie hidden. One can imagine the Negro King who
offers myrrh as a person wrapped in what is hidden or occult.
This king has a black skin not only on account of his race. One
can experience through the black colour something that stays
in the background, whereas the white colour comes to the fore.
Black is the colour of the hidden spirit, it conceals what is
contained within it—just as the black carbon conceals the
shining diamond, which is of like nature. Understood in this
way, what is black can be experienced as that which lingers in
the spiritual world, whereas that which is white is the spirit
revealed in the world of appearance and is the expression of
what is incarnate.* If one is able to grasp the significance and
secret of the Black King Kaspar in this way, then one's insight
will likewise be opened for the inner character of Kaspar
Hauser as it is expressed by his Christian name. This will be
especially elucidated in the final chapter of this book.

The question must remain unanswered as to whether the
name-giving followed the intentions of his mother Stephanie
de Beauharnais to call her firstborn Gaspard, about which no

accord could be reached with the father, the Grand-Duke Karl, by the time of the supposed death of the child on 16 October 1812, so that the name-giving and baptism had not taken place at that time.

If one turns one's attention to the surname 'Hauser' the word Haus [house] catches one's attention and can first of all be interpreted as describing what the destiny of this person had been—sitting in a house for nearly all his life. Imprisoned in a house, isolated from nature, it remained unknown to his senses and estranged from his experience. It will be explained in the fifth chapter of this book how by continually confining Kaspar Hauser in a house it was intended to preserve in him an ancient Atlantean kind of consciousness. In this sense the word 'Hauser' does not refer to the place of his suffering, but to the state of his consciousness which it was intended to induce in him.

A further possibility of linking Hauser's name to the individuality is to interpret the word 'house' as being a 'tabernacle' in the sense of the Gospel of St Luke: 'Let us make three tabernacles...'[56] The building of a tabernacle in the Gospel denotes the creating of a 'fixed abode' in the spiritual world to which all one's endeavours and work can be related. Through the building of the tabernacle a person becomes a citizen—or rather a 'Hauser' [house-dweller]—in his heavenly home. He has then acquired an inner rank which gives him sovereignty to linger in the supersensible world.

Can one be in any doubt that this rank fits the person who bore the name of Kaspar Hauser? He has built his tabernacle in the immediate neighbourhood of the Christ-Being. Only by this means was Kaspar Hauser able to endure such unique suffering as a prisoner in an earthly house. To summarize what a reflection on the name 'Kaspar Hauser' has to offer us we can say that the surname expressed more the facts of his life—rank, experiences and suffering—the Christian name more the elements which lead into the future.

Who was it who gave Kaspar Hauser these names which, when they are understood in this way, make his individuality so apparent? Are the opponents showing the limitations of their knowledge and power in this, as they did anyway in releasing Kaspar Hauser? The higher power which set him free and led him to the people who were waiting to receive him also furnished him with the name which was appropriate to him. This happened independently of that which the man who taught him to write thought about it at the time. With that we have touched upon the mystery that those who kept him in captivity were unable to conceal him for ever from the world— by setting him free they had ultimately, but unwittingly, even served his individuality.

Kaspar Hauser and the German Folk-spirit

The greatness of Kaspar Hauser's sacrifice can only be gauged by the importance of his mission. His task in connection with the German Folk-spirit was to bring this Folk-spirit into the closest possible contact with the Folk-body, the mass of the physically incarnated German population. Beginning with the forties of the nineteenth century, Kaspar Hauser, as the heir to the throne of Baden working from his centre in Karlsruhe, was to have converted what existed as the spirit of Central Europe during the time of Goethe into social activities and forms. The spirit, as formative life from the supersensible world, was to have penetrated all human and material relationships.

The current of history in Central Europe was in need of a real spiritual unfolding, because the spirit that does not enter reality withdraws and dematerializes. Because Kaspar Hauser, as the mediator for the German Folk-spirit, was obstructed in his mission, an incalculable calamity, a process of disease, ensued: the German people became estranged more and more during the course of the nineteenth century from the connection to their spiritual self. Rudolf Steiner, in a conversation with Count Polzer-Hoditz in November 1916, described in the following words what might have been achieved through Kaspar Hauser: 'South Germany should have become the new Grail Castle, the new champion of the spirit, the cradle of future achievements. The arena for the spirit had been well prepared by such personalities as Goethe, Schiller, Herder, Hölderlin, etc. Kaspar Hauser was to have gathered around him all that flourished in the arena thus prepared. But that was not wanted by those circles (western Lodges and Jesuits). They could not allow a centre to awaken if they were not to relinquish their control and power-aims. Goethe's kind of spirituality frightened them.'*

The fact that Kaspar Hauser had been hindered in his work meant that not only for him personally, but above all for the whole of his social surroundings, something calamitous had happened. Innumerable people, even the destinies of nations, depended on the fact that this individual's single destiny could be fulfilled according to the spirit's wishes. The destiny that Kaspar Hauser suffered is the greatest imaginable catastrophe that has occurred up till now in the development of the German nation. The perpetration of this fateful event has resulted a century later in the exact opposite having come about in historical reality to that which had been intended through Kaspar Hauser. As the effects of selfhood had not been successfully established in the German Folk-body, the powers directed against the ego asserted themselves of necessity in a disastrous fashion.

The true German Folk-spirit can only work into the Folk-body by way of the ego. The ego, however, is without doubt the most endangered and unstable member of man's constitution. If it is able to realize and take firm hold of itself as a supersensible being in the spiritual world, then it can control and regulate the whole of man's being through its spiritual activity. If this does not happen, if the ego is unable to retain its spiritual involvement, then it will not result in a mere suspension of activity, but will produce an emptiness, a force of suction, which will attract the most evil forces, in contra-distinction to the best possible ones. Because the German Folk-nature is based on the nature of the ego, it all depends upon the fact that the ego is implanted into the spirit, through which a real spiritual fulfilment is obtained—otherwise the most terrible abyss will open up before it.

The opponents of Kaspar Hauser, about whom a more

detailed account will be given later, knew from their under-standing of Folk characteristics what far-reaching results could be achieved by preventing—through Kaspar Hauser—the possible connection between the Folk-spirit and the Folk-body. Knowing this Rudolf Steiner tried with utmost spiritual endeavour to check this fatal trend in the German nation. In continuation of Goethe's work he extended the Central European spirit to rouse it and induce it to act. A visible success on a historical scale was not achieved to begin with.

In the introduction to his concluding volume of *Kaspar Hauser* (1873) Daumer recounts an argument he had with Meyer about the relationship of the German people to Kaspar Hauser. The thought lived intuitively in Daumer that Kaspar Hauser was deeply connected with the destiny of the German people. This is what he writes: 'Dr Meyer's book closes with the following remark: "Schlosser in his history of the eight-eenth and nineteenth centuries refers to the story of Kaspar Hauser as a fable which is believed by the German people." Meyer underlines the word 'fable', but not, of course, the words which we underline; it is these latter, however, which are important to us. The belief in this story is inherent in the German nation; the nation does not need to be ashamed of that, it is a part of its feeling for truth and justice and it will not let anyone deprive it of that. Whoever would try to take this away from it is not standing on the true ground of the German nation;* but we, the defenders of Kaspar Hauser, are such and we hope to win popular support for that. We are not just here on behalf of the unhappy Kaspar Hauser, nor for ourselves who have been victimized and abused on his account. We are here to stand up for our nation and for our national character. Should a book such as Meyer's meet with convincing success, should the people let themselves be converted to the heartless and spiritless criticism which would make this story into a fable and act with so much harshness, lying, falsification and malice, it would no longer be a truly German people and we on our part would not feel very proud of being German.'[6]

In order to see the full significance of Daumer's comments, one ought to know how highly he values faith. 'What I understand by faith—to state it positively at last—is the acknowledgement of what is unusual, even if it contradicts what is generally accepted; the devotion to the facts which have been presented and can only be denied by violence; the deep and inner relationship in which things stand to one another; the acknowledgement of things which are not immediately obvious, not to be understood materially and mechanically and yet are true and real, but which the common materialistic understanding feels so antagonistic towards that it seeks to get rid of them at all costs and by any conceivable means. On this faith rests not only all religion, but also all *culture* in the full human sense of the word; it is not just at the command of an outward regulation and authority, but a demand of *reason*, of genuine, impartial *search for truth* and *science*; and if this does not succeed, then the path which mankind treads—in spite of all the outward benefits of technology, industry and its materialistic-rational direction and activity—will lead to barbarism and the destruction of the whole of man's being, to the loss of man's higher dignity, to the suffocation of all the more delicate and noble feelings of the human heart and of all the deeper insight of the human spirit, to an unbearable impoverishment of man's disposition and life and therefore to a general decay and dissolution, which may not be outwardly visible, but nonetheless is inwardly so.'[57]

The faith of the German nation in Kaspar Hauser and his destiny was what Daumer saw could provide the possibility of preserving its connection with the spirit. Daumer clearly saw the danger that, without this faith, it would lose the ground from under its feet and plunge into the abyss. He was quite aware of what the spiritual needs of the life of the German nation were; he sensed that through Kaspar Hauser the connection with the German Folk-spirit could be maintained. Daumer discovered that the German nation would have to relinquish its true mission if it were really to lose Kaspar Hauser for ever.

The signs of doing so confront the German people in the nineteenth and twentieth centuries. Among those at the turn of the nineteenth to the twentieth century who clearly saw this task and also the danger involved was Schiller, who wrote in the draft of his poem *Deutsche Grösse* [German Greatness]:

> This is not a German's greatness
> That he conquers with the sword—
> But to penetrate the spirit,
> Overcome his prejudice,
> 'Gainst illusion to do battle,
> That's a worthy cause for strife.
>
> He hath won a higher victory
> Who hath fought with lightning's truth,
> Who hath set the spirit free!
> Freedom for 'good sense' to battle
> Means to argue for mankind,
> For ever that holds good.

Schiller notes in this connection that it lies within the German character 'to serve above all the spirit'. He, the German, has been chosen by the world spirit 'to work upon the everlasting edifice of human culture'.[58]

As those spirit-given tasks could not be fulfilled in the appropriate way the loss of the spirit manifested in three ways: in arrogant nationalism; in humanity-scorning militarism; in the aimless development of economic power. In contrast to that the greatness of the Folk-mission demands the deepest humility and a truly cosmopolitan sense; the propagation of the spirit creates peace and non-violence, the humanizing aim restricts the economic process. Kaspar Hauser would have enabled the Folk-spirit to revive these intentions; the opposite events have estranged the people to the greatest imaginable extent from their Folk-spirit and have dimmed the image of Kaspar Hauser.

But it is now time for a transformation to take place in the greatest misfortune that could have happened. For that it is necessary for us to consciously experience Kaspar Hauser as the mediator of the German Folk-spirit. As nothing of all that could have become reality has actually taken place, it only remains for us to consider in our heart that the 'Child of Europe' is the representative of the spirit. The already mentioned childlikeness of the Christ-awakened human being is a necessary part of his activity. He does not assert his personality over his surroundings, but rather receives it from there, as the heart receives its life from the forces of the periphery and regulates and rhythmizes this within itself and thereby gives it a new impulse. The German spirit in Kaspar Hauser is thus from the start not a national spirit but a European, cosmopolitan one.

Through the destiny suffered by Kaspar Hauser the path which leads to the German Folk-spirit has been greatly changed. Just as the activities of other Folk-spirits manifest in important observable events, so would the German spirit have been revealed in the ordering of social life in accordance with the precepts of the spirit. Through the blows of fate which were dealt to Kaspar Hauser it was concealed from humanity in general that he appeared on earth as the bearer of the German Folk-spirit and was foreordained to work towards that end. Contrariwise, deception and mendacity surrounded him on all sides and it requires the serious and honest endeavour of independent spiritual knowledge to perceive and recognize his true image. Thus through the self-sacrifice of Kaspar Hauser the pathway leading to the German Folk-spirit has become something which can only be compared to Faust's visit to the Mothers.[59] The 'loftier mystery' is that the pathway here referred to [in *Faust*] is really 'no way, a way to the unreachable, ne'er to be trodden' [*Faust*, Part II, Act I, Scene V. Bayard Taylor's translation, p.329], which has to be trodden if the spirit is to be attained. It stands within the freedom of every person to tread this path, which is 'no path', and along this path freedom will be attained, just as Faust gained freedom from Mephistopheles by his visit to the Mothers. It belongs to the destiny of the German peoples that Kaspar Hauser was sent to them and it is deeply connected with his destiny that Kaspar had to offer himself as sacrifice. However, there is no outward proof of such an inner event.

Through his self-sacrifice Kaspar Hauser has brought about

an element of freedom. He does not force anything because he did not act as a historical person of authority. In this sense he can only be discovered in the spirit, as can Christ, too. Thus he shows once more that he is a companion of Christ.

One now has to ask oneself in what way the opposing forces which have proved so disastrous in German history can be overcome. It demands spiritual effort which can really penetrate into the powers of the spiritual world in such a way that the evil powers become paralysed. This is meant in the sense indicated by Rudolf Steiner when he says that it is the task of the progressive spirits to carry evolution forward by transforming bad fortune into good. Without this effort to comprehend it, however, the German nation will never arrive at a true understanding of the facts or of itself. The spirits will be divided over the figure of Kaspar Hauser and the German destiny will be decided through that.

The greatest mistakes have been made by the Germans in their stupid show of strength during the reign of Emperor William II and in the destructive use of power during the Hitler regime. The path leading to Kaspar Hauser as the servant of the German Folk-spirit can only be trodden if the way of perfect powerlessness, of implicit harmlessness, is taken. The strength of the spirit can only develop beyond the region of force and violence.

The blossoming of the German spirit will come about in the future when Kaspar Hauser, as a spiritual being working from the supersensible world, giving inspiration and kindling impulses, will be experienced and grasped by the members of the nation. This will create the cohesion of the nation, not however a physical union, such as a state or a kingdom. The power which can bring about the necessary fulfilment of the German Folk-spirit's destiny lives as expectation, as a longing for the future in Kaspar Hauser's spirit-being. In the opinion of people of the present day this may seem nonsensical or presumptuous, but the breath of the spirit of history stretches throughout centuries.* Such a powerful destiny as this cannot find compensation and healing from one day to the next. It rests with discerning human beings to ensure that what has fallen into the abyss of the demonic forces may be revivified on the basis of the spirit. Here we are reminded about the verse which Rudolf Steiner spoke in Berlin on 15 January 1915:[60]

Der deutsche Geist hat nicht vollendet,
Was er im Weltenwerden schaffen soll.
Er lebt in Zukunftssorgen hoffnungsvoll—
Er hofft auf Zunkunftstaten lebensvoll—
In seines Wesens Tiefen fühlt er mächtig
Verborgenes, das noch reifend wirken muss—
Wie darf in Feindes Macht verständnislos
Der Wunsch nach seinem Ende sich beleben,
So lang das Leben sich ihm offenbart,
Das ihn in Wesenswurzeln schaffend hält?

The German Spirit hath not yet fulfilled
Its task in evolution of the world.
It lives with future cares in hopefulness,
It hopes for future deeds with liveliness—
It senses mightily within its soul
The hidden things that must to ripeness grow—
How dare the hostile powers in ignorance
Harbour the thoughts which gloat upon its end,
As long as life reveals itself therein,
Keeping it active in creativeness?

Kaspar Hauser—a Parsifal figure of the nineteenth century

Revealed in the countenance of every century are features connected with historical growth and the gradual unfolding of Christianity. What is meant by Christianity in this case is best expressed in the picture of the Holy Grail.[61] In the image of the Grail the fruit of Christianity lies hidden. Whoever, as a Christian, comes into contact with the Grail expresses not only faith and conviction, but also knows himself to be in living contact with an invigorating source of life. In the Parsifal saga of the Middle Ages (of Wolfram von Eschenbach) a significant

change is portrayed in connection with the Grail. On the first
occasion Parsifal finds his way into the Grail Castle by the
path of destiny. He behaves according to how he has been
taught. He is silent in face of the sight and experience of what
should have provoked pity and deeply moved him. His destiny
and upbringing, however, have not provided him with what
was most essential: to find the courage and strength to ask the
question in face of the spiritual events which he encounters.
After many journeys, during which he was able to defeat the
evil kingdom of Klingsor, Parsifal has to acquire an alert and
independent consciousness out of which the redeeming question is asked. When Parsifal has matured in this sense he is
called to the Grail for the second time. He shares in the grace
which enables him to heal the suffering Amfortas: not because
he has sought grace, but because he has discovered the way to
himself—that means, in the highest sense of the word, to the
Grail. Parsifal thus becomes the Grail King and gains the
possibility of enabling the Grail to work in diverse ways into
life.

During the course of the Parsifal saga the intimated change
in the relationship of mankind towards the Grail is expressed:
to begin with the events are described in the sense of the fourth
post-Atlantean cultural epoch (intellectual and sentient soul).
The appointed person receives into himself what is spiritually
due to him by destiny, and in absorbing the supersensible into
himself all necessary steps have been taken. But now, amazingly, something quite new is required—his own question.
This is the task of the consciousness soul in which the setting
free of consciousness and the development of the personality is
of foremost importance. One's own reasoned understanding
of the spiritual world is what matters. Parsifal pursues this
path to the end, till he grasps the Christian essence of the
spirit, i.e. the Grail. In the Parsifal saga is recounted the story
of an individual who has already trodden this future path in an
archetypal and exemplary fashion. Even before the beginning
of the modern age this poem, which nevertheless is based on
spiritually real events, spoke about the Parsifal way of the
future.

The Kingdom of the Grail has not previously been manifested in a historically effective way.* By the nineteenth century the development should have progressed so far that for the first time in history the story of the Grail Kingdom could have played an immediate role in life. The individuality living in Kaspar Hauser was that which was capable and destined to be the Grail King. In this context is the remark made by Rudolf Steiner that 'South Germany should have become the new Grail-Castle of the new Knights of the Grail' in which Kaspar Hauser would have been the Grail King, which would have accorded both with his inner and outer status. As an initiate in the Rosicrucian sense, Kaspar Hauser would, as already indicated, have implanted spiritual impulses into society to prevent the nineteenth century from sinking so deeply into materialism and to prepare for the epoch of light. Of course it was not intended for the monarchy to be preserved indefinitely, but what was new and based on the individuality was to have been joined to the old in a reasonable fashion.*

The Grail-Kingdom of Kaspar Hauser would have been attached to the knowledge of reincarnation and karma. Out of this source the social organization should have flowed. Rudolf Steiner has often indicated that a solution to the social question commensurate with human dignity is not possible if this knowledge is lacking. The decisive motive of the opponents of Kaspar's Hauser's Grail-Kingdom, which was the aim of the leaders of humanity, is to be seen in the hindering of his mission and Kaspar Hauser's elimination. It succeeded in separating the Grail King from his historical task. The nineteenth century is most deeply characterized by the fact that the foreordained Parsifal was not able to carry out his mission.

As a result of the destiny which Kaspar Hauser suffered a new image of Parsifal is presented. Kaspar Hauser comes into the world not only without knowledge of his parents, but after having been deprived of them. He is a foundling, whose parentage remains hidden from him. He is the Parsifal who has emerged from the actual darkness of imprisonment, over against which stands the withdrawn and secluded life of the

other Parsifal in the isolation of the forest. His destiny with
regard to his mother and father (his father died in 1818 when
he was six years old) was not the result of forces which resided
in him, but was inflicted upon him. A hostile force presses
upon him from outside and prevents him from following his
predestined way. He accepts the path of sacrifice. The Parsifal-
destiny of this child is in this sense highly pitiable. The child is
prevented from reaching the stage of questioning. The situation has been reversed. This particular Parsifal-destiny poses a
great question to mankind which might help them to awake.
The Parsifal image of the nineteenth century reveals a child
vicariously suffering in imitation of Christ, whose life is
eventually violently destroyed.

   The spiritually intended, but not realized, image of Kaspar
Hauser as Parsifal is revived in Wagner's *Parsifal.* Wagner,
born hardly a year after Kaspar Hauser, belongs as an artist to
his spiritual environment. What an enhancement of his artistic
faculties would have been made possible if Wagner could have
met and experienced Kaspar Hauser! In his *Parsifal*—without
having a conscious knowledge of the fact—he portrayed in the
guise of a stage-festival the inner way traced out for Kaspar
Hauser as the nascent Grail-King.

   Parsifal, the artless fool—an indication of his childlike
nature—is victorious over Klingsor. The spear, which is
intended to kill him, cannot do so because he takes hold of his
destiny and fulfils it. The sign of the Cross, made with the
spear, causes Klingsor's might to collapse. Amfortas is healed
and redeemed from his unbearable suffering by the re-won
spear. The might of the spear is the knowledge-deed of the
spirit which has been conquered by a human ego. The re-
winning of the spear is in this sense the task of the Michael
Age, the first epoch of the Age of Light.

Faust and Kaspar Hauser

Faust is rightly looked upon as the representative of the
striving human being of the fifth post-Atlantean cultural
epoch. Faust joins himself to Mephistopheles in his inner-

most being—in his blood, in which the ego lives. The greatest imaginable danger to the existence of the ego is presented by this alliance. It comes to the limit of its individual existence, it plunges into the abyss as is tragically exemplified by the entanglements of Faust's destiny. In this sense Rudolf Steiner once indicated that in Faust Goethe portrays a human figure 'who has wholly lost his humanity'.[62] In life and in his dealings Faust often succumbs to Mephistopheles. He is only able to break free from him to begin with by his discernment (visit to the Mothers, meeting with Helen, classical Walpurgis Night). When he tries to intervene actively, he is unable to withdraw from his involvement with the evil forces, he cannot recognize them and is unable to control them, so in the end Philemon and Baucis are killed and he dies under the illusion that he 'stands on free soil among a people free' whereas actually he is dependent on Mephistopheles and the Lemures. Goethe did not lead Faust to the point where he could actually overcome Mephistopheles in life, where his ego would find the strength to free itself from the abyss which threatened it. 'Goethe felt it was necessary for Faust to find redemption here on earth. Goethe should have framed his question as follows: How does Faust find confirmation of the Pauline words: "Not I but Christ in me"? Goethe should have arrived at the point where Faust does not merely say "stand on free soil among a people free", but: on free soil with Christ in my soul leading human beings in earthly life towards the spirit—Goethe should have let Faust say something to that effect. Goethe, of course, is honest; he does not say it because he has not yet fully comprehended it.'[63] It is only after his death that Faust attains that which he had striven for in life: to gradually free his ego from the powers of the Evil One. 'Goethe, on the other hand, was not able to arrive at a real comprehension of the spiritual world; that is why he turned back.'[64]

It was not possible for Goethe to recognize the living person as a spiritual being on the earth. Goethe could not connect the *incarnated* ego with the Christ impulse in such a way that a human being appeared who could reveal his con-

nection with the spiritual world by his recognition and
actions.

Thus we see that the Faust figure needs to be extended and
developed further, which we gather from the above indications
by Rudolf Steiner. The Faust which Rudolf Steiner depicted in
the cupola paintings of the First Goetheanum—the picture of
archetypal man in the fifth post-Atlantean cultural epoch—
was designed to illustrate the development here mentioned.
The detail we reproduce shows the contemplative Faust,
whose powers of concentration have conjured up before him
the ego through which the forces of evil have lost their hold
over him. In its place the child, as fruit of the conquest of evil,
is attracted by the ego as it flies towards Faust. Faust's way is
that of the renewal of mankind by grasping hold of the ego in
which Christ is living. This renewal of mankind becomes
reality through the child when the restored human nature
appears as a result of the Easter event. Only in this condition is
the endeavour of Faust fulfilled. If one observes the trinity of
Faust-ego-child, one will be able, after all that has been said,
to find the child-nature within Kaspar Hauser. One can
experience Kaspar Hauser as a picture of childlikeness about
which it is said: 'Unless ye become as little children ye can in
nowise enter the Kingdom of Heaven'.[65]

Faust is able to share in the child within him through his
striving after the EGO. He will thereby be able to take up
during his life what Goethe's Faust only achieved after death.
In this sense must he who strives like Faust take into himself
the Kaspar Hauser element as the higher, not-yet-realized
spiritual nature. Faust must grow towards the Kaspar Hauser
element so that man may be completely renewed. Kaspar
Hauser in his child's nature is the future which Faust needs in
order to attain his goal of defeating Mephistopheles.

The Faust picture by Rudolf Steiner in the Goetheanum
cupola thus contains an image of the future development of
the consciousness soul. Faust attains in this picture the stage
of consciousness into which real spiritual knowledge enters.
Lucifer and Ahriman have no part in spiritual-scientific
knowledge—as Rudolf Steiner often emphasized. In their

place the child appears, promising that all real spiritual knowledge carries within it the power to grow in a way which will create reality.

A picture of this child has been presented to mankind by the powers of destiny in the person of Kaspar Hauser as he appeared soon after his release.

Still another connection between Faust and Kaspar Hauser presents itself if one approaches it from the aspect of 'active' and 'passive'. Faust takes an active role in his dealings with the devil. That which, as his higher nature, he is bound to forfeit thereby remains in the background. This higher nature is condemned to inactivity. Passivity or suffering is imposed upon it, through which, however, it is preserved. To express it figuratively we could say: For as long as Faust is entangled in the meshes of the evil power, the child Kaspar Hauser, condemned to idleness, must sit in his dungeon. In this relationship of activity to passivity and suffering man can also take part if he can find the way to free himself from the clutches of Lucifer and Ahriman. The imprisonment of the child Kaspar Hauser is an expression of the situation where man forfeits his own spiritual nature during his struggle. If this can be won back through true spirituality then the child Kaspar Hauser will be released from his imprisonment. Behind many present-day human beings the picture of an imprisoned child—a Kaspar Hauser—can be discovered. The condition which prevails in man's higher nature is altogether dependent upon his state of consciousness and his activity in life.

Rudolf Steiner, Faust-Motif. Detail from the painting on the ceiling of the
small cupola of the first Goetheanum in Dornach, Switzerland.

Rudolf Steiner, Child. Detail from the painting on the ceiling of the small cupola of the first Goetheanum.

Rudolf Steiner. Section of the painting on the ceiling of the small cupola of the first Goetheanum.

3. Kaspar Hauser in the Karmic Proceedings of the Nineteenth and Twentieth Centuries

The Gods geometrize
Novalis

People enquire about the
Riddles of existence
And forget thereby
To observe how life
In its rhythmic sequence
Is the true answer
To this question.
Rudolf Steiner

The 33-year rhythm of history

If it is true that one of the most important human individualities lived in Kaspar Hauser and that he had a particular task to fulfil for the healing of mankind, then it must be possible to discover how in the further progress of history events take place which can be traced back to the fulfilment—or respectively non-fulfilment—of this individual's task.

A rhythm which encompasses human events in their metamorphosis and effect in time has not yet been discovered by historical science. If, however, a way is nevertheless sought to gain an understanding of the historical connections, a decided help would be to apply the 33-year law of history discovered and demonstrated by Rudolf Steiner. Rudolf Steiner first spoke about this result of his spiritual research in Basle on 23 December 1917. The lecture bears the relevant title 'Et incarnatus est—the time cycle in historical events' and contains suggestions to which up till now far too little attention has been paid considering their far-reaching importance.

These expositions of Rudolf Steiner can become a turning-point for all contemplation of history in the light of Christianity if they are taken up. Two sentences of fundamental significance are here noted: 'Connections in intervals of 33 years bring understanding for the continuing current of historical progress'.[66] By this a progressively unfolding element of historic development is pointed out. The special feature of this process is described by Rudolf Steiner as follows: 'That which happens in approximately this length of time—one can, of course, only speak of such things in approximate terms—points to a moment of birth 33 years previously and is itself the birth-point for what will happen in the course of the next 33 years.'[66] *

The deeds of men set in their historical current call forth a rhythmical effect which grows greater and then finally ebbs. The world-historical 33-year impulse-rhythm for those who increasingly take note of it can become a fully justified spiritual proof of Christ's incarnation and, since the Easter Event, of Christ's power in connection with human evolution. In this respect the previous views of history may be regarded as a 'fable convenue' which, quite frankly, appears to serve the purpose of covering up this reality.

It is one of the most difficult features in the understanding of the 33-year rhythm to realize that '*everything* in history rises up from the grave in a changed form after 33 years'.[66] This change makes it difficult to see the connection in isolated cases, because detailed, hidden and secret relationships appear which are to some extent so unusual that they may strike one as being unbelievable. Rudolf Steiner explicitly emphasizes that *all* things are reborn after 33 years. With that an important 'open secret' has been indicated to which a solution has to be found. One is reminded here of the words of Ariel (*Faust*, Part II, Act I): 'Be he holy, be he vicious,' and an impression of the cosmically extensive dimension of the Christ impulse can be obtained, which enfolds and includes all things and from which nothing escapes.

A serious but necessary question which has to be asked concerns the 'might of the most holy and redemptive factor received by mankind from the Mystery of Golgotha'.[66] From the superlative way in which Rudolf Steiner expresses himself, one gets an inkling of the fact that a deeper level of the secret is being touched upon.

The first step towards a comprehension of it is made when one takes one's start from the fact that after 33 years all things are revealed by this force according to their true and original impulses and that the hidden, unuttered, but effective powers are so placed before man's understanding that they can be grasped in their reality. The transformation which comes about through the power of Christ makes it possible for every illusion to be recognized for what it is. This force works in such a way that man is set at liberty by being able to know. The first release of which man partakes today through knowledge of the 33-year rhythm is the release of knowledge in the sense of Christ's words: 'And ye shall know the truth, and the truth shall make you free'.[67]

Another point of view from which to understand the 33-year rhythm of history is provided by the Ego-nature of Christ. The 'I am the I am' brings about the consequences which lead to compensation. If these compensatory consequences are felt by us human beings to be exceptionally hard we must raise ourselves above the restricting aspect of the punishment and soar up to the emancipating feeling of healing and deliverance. In this sense of putting things right and straightening up one can also see what Schiller meant when he said: 'World history is World-judgement'.[68]

If one investigates the historical significance of Kaspar Hauser's destiny, his birth and death stand out as the decisive factors in this respect. From these we shall follow up the 33-year rhythm beginning with his birth in 1812. The dates which follow are:

1845, 1878, 1911, 1944, 1977, 2010.

The sequence of dates reckoned from his death are as follows:

1866, 1899, 1932, 1965, 1998.

Even a hasty glance at these dates can immediately show that decisive turning-points, high- and low-points of history of the nineteenth and twentieth centuries, are contained in them. We shall next investigate these dates individually to find out if and in what way they might have a bearing on Kaspar Hauser's life.

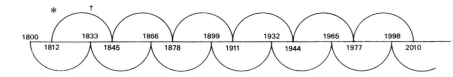

The birth and death sequences of Kaspar Hauser in the 33-year rhythm

The birth sequence—1845

If, to begin with, one takes account of the fact that in 1845 Kaspar Hauser would have been 33 years old, one should also bear in mind that in 1841 Michael's fight against Ahriman began in the spiritual world and that this battle ended in 1879 with the casting out of the ahrimanic spirits on to the earth.[69] Through that the spirits of evil unfold their activity on the physical plane ever more strongly from 1841 onwards. They penetrate the sphere directly adjacent to the sense-world with such strong forces that in the interest of Ahriman they act in a highly seductive manner upon the incarnated human beings. The result of this is the disastrous eruption of materialism in the nineteenth century which affected chiefly two spheres of life. On the one hand the impulse of natural science springing from the consciousness soul, which has the ultimate objective of seeking the spirit in nature, becomes more and more restricted and distorted by materialism from this time on. At the present day mankind is still living to a large extent with the results of this seduction in the realm of science.

On the other hand the ahrimanic spirits started at that time to tempt in the most dreadful manner those human beings who were inclined towards them. In this way people became inspired with thoughts about their life and work which, under the illusory image of more humane conditions, engendered in them hate and destruction of world-wide proportions.

The works and thoughts of Karl Marx must be looked at from this point of view, especially his ideas about human work-capacity. He certainly wanted to eliminate the 'goods' aspect of work. Because, however, he would not acknowledge the paramount spiritual motivation of work, it led to a flagging of interest and an undermining of the will to work.

A world-historic date in this development is the publication of the Communist Manifesto in 1847. Again it is made plain that the impulses and thoughts then evolved have intervened to make their mark even on present-day reality. Not only does a large part of humanity live in the thoughts which derive directly from this spirit, but also the remainder of humanity is firmly harnessed to a one-sided materialistic process of production. In present-day output the role of the working human being is visualized and practised completely in the sense of the ahrimanic seduction, namely in such a way that work is not looked upon as the direct karmic expression of man's spiritual nature but as something akin to the concept 'goods' and becomes saleable.[70] From all of this we may infer that the decisive turning point of evolution up till our own day and far beyond it came in the early forties of the nineteenth century. Mankind became deeply connected with the ahrimanic powers.

In its wisdom the spiritual guidance of mankind had placed the individual, Kaspar Hauser, onto the physical plane to act as a counter-force to the spirits of darkness in the hour of their expulsion onto the earth. It was a precaution to ensure that the ahrimanic powers, working out of historical necessity, would not be able to drag man down too deeply into earthly affairs. Kaspar Hauser was the one who was predestined, had been made ready and was able, to create an opposite reaction to the ahrimanic activity on the physical plane. He could therefore prepare for the coming Age of Michael. One can observe with dismay how well Kaspar Hauser's opponents recognized the decisive role to which he had been appointed and how far-reaching were their aims.

Only think what a spiritual personality such as Kaspar Hauser could have achieved from his centre of activity in the

Court of Baden in Karlsruhe, for instance by setting the people of his country spiritual tasks in the social life of the district.

An essential motive for the deeds of those who got Kaspar Hauser into their clutches can be seen in the fact that they wished to sever from the foreordained goal of mankind not only Kaspar Hauser himself, but the greatest imaginable number of people—a goal which they also achieved. It was their aim to strengthen the effect of Ahriman on man in general for their own purposes. It was the conscious goal of Kaspar Hauser's opponents not only to hinder the carrying out of his mission through his imprisonment but, by eliminating his effectiveness, to entangle the progress of mankind more deeply and strongly in the ahrimanic forces than was intended. The plot to get Kaspar Hauser into their power was undertaken by the ahrimanically oriented opponents with just such a far-reaching view of humanity as that which was possessed by the leaders of humanity—to place Kaspar Hauser into the evolution of mankind with a definite impulse.

In the auspicious events of the forties of the nineteenth century the grave absence of Kaspar Hauser's participation, which from this time on could and should have been developed in line with his prenatal decisions, played a leading part. Also the unhappy course taken by the German Revolution of 1848 is not least to be attributed to the fact that an example of the social structuring of society which should have been set by Kaspar Hauser as a spiritual signpost and stimulus to strengthen man's powers was lacking. And in this study it must not be forgotten what a rousing force can be exerted by an individual such as this who has a world-wide mission to fulfil. There were many people who in the hidden depths of their soul-life were yearning for Kaspar Hauser, who needed him for their own development and who felt abandoned and paralysed by his not being there. They were painfully aware of the spiritual lack on earth and became 'homeless' souls.[71] One is reminded of the saying of Lessing: 'Genius is only kindled by genius'.

1878/1879

If we look at the year 1878 the first thing that strikes us is the fact that, through his birth on Michaelmas Day in 1812, Kaspar Hauser had been so placed into the world that his life and activity took place twice 33 years before the beginning of the Michael Age, 1879.

The Berlin Congress in the summer of 1878 can be taken as an outstanding example of the effects which Kaspar Hauser's absence was to have in Europe. Bismark, as chancellor to the Hohenzollern Emperor, being a practical and pragmatic person, avoided the threatened European armed conflict. He thought of himself as the 'honest broker' who succeeded in engineering a balance of power and interest between Turkey, Russia and Great Britain by his skilful diplomacy. The territorial demands in the Balkans were settled, the spheres of influence were circumscribed. Peace was certainly assured—it would be better to say that war was avoided—but at what a price! Nations or national groups, landscapes, languages, religions were all ultimately figures in a game carried on under the aspect of power; they were used as exchangeable goods which could be offset one against another. By this arrangement on the physical plane it was no longer of any importance whether one were dealing with human beings or with historical or cultural realities. Bismark took his start from neither a real knowledge of conditions in the Balkans, nor from an idea of the necessary future form of these relationships. The outward success in the sphere of power blinded him to the fact that the real questions of the individual and national development of the Balkans had not been dealt with. Certainly Bismark and his associate politicians had not set themselves this task—but that is just the sad thing about it, because the unrecognized and unsolved questions necessarily led to ever more serious problems in the further progress of history. War was avoided in 1878, but the cost was that, in the course of the next generation, especially through Russian influence, a situation was created which unleashed the First World War about 33 years later. The consequence of a policy which believes it can

dispense with ideas which bring understanding and organization into historical reality has to be recognized. The practical
politicians have entangled mankind in ever more insoluble
conflicts. For the year 1878 it can be felt that at a critical
moment of European development the strength was lacking to
direct things in a healthy direction. Kaspar Hauser, as the
'Child of Europe', would have been able to intervene and
could have brought this strength into the constitution.

Diplomacy has ever since that time been following the
example set by Bismark at the time of the Berlin Congress. The
technocrats of our day, who only enquire about what is
practicable, have perfected this technique, as a result of which
mankind stands at the edge of an abyss from which only a
fundamental re-thinking can save it. One might interpose that
diplomacy was also decided by power-politics even before
Bismark. That is certainly correct. But the development of
mankind in the nineteenth and twentieth centuries is ever less
suited to this way of working, because the spirit wants to have
a say in all affairs of the world and because the spiritual world
has changed its attitude towards the physical. The discrepancy
between the development planned by the spiritual world and
the actual behaviour of man causes the greatest upheavals to
the social structure.

The time previous to 1878 can be characterized by other
events. First of all in 1875, the year of Daumer's death, came
the founding of the Theosophical Society, which took place
about 33 years after the 'epochal year 1841' (commencement
of Michael's battle in the spiritual world) which was to direct
man's attention again towards spiritual things. This founding
(of the Theosophical Society) which followed higher principles
arose from the belief that spiritual knowledge must be given to
the world to counter materialism, the enemy of progress.
Secondly, through the course of events in Germany, Nietzsche
felt himself obliged, in 1875, to characterize the development
in Central Europe as 'the extirpation of the German Spirit, in
the interest of the German Empire'. With these words
Nietzsche sharply outlined the catastrophe, which had
meanwhile become reality and which Kaspar Hauser would

have had to face: the tearing away of outward government from a spiritual task and content, from a truly all-human goal. It was Kaspar Hauser's task to put active spiritual content into a government structure as far as it was possible at that time, and one can visualize the despair that Nietzsche felt at the course things had taken.

The meaning which the lack of spirituality had for Central Europe is described by Rudolf Steiner in his article 'Die geistige Signatur der Gegenwart' (The spiritual mark of the present time) (1888). In a later lecture given on 1 January 1920 he refers again to this article with the words: 'An open mind for the striving towards the loftiest heights of the world of thought, an understanding for that soaring of the spirit which in the realm of science went parallel with our classic period of culture—this is lacking now. The serious side of this phenomenon only appears when we take into consideration that a persistent turning-away from that spiritual goal implies for the *German people* the loss of their own *Self*, a breaking away from the Spirit of the Nation. For that striving sprang from a deep need in the German nature.'[72] The spiritual forces which spoke through many of the cultural representatives of the German people at the turn of the eighteenth to nineteenth century prepared the impulse in many kinds of artistic creation and philosophical striving-after-knowledge to give structure to the social life on the basis of ideas rooted in the spirit, and thereby built a bridge between the sense world and the world of the supersensible. The classical epoch of German culture developed in the social sphere as far as bringing the beautiful form of friendship. The step to give structure to larger human organizations could not yet be taken. This is where the activity of Kaspar Hauser could have intervened and taken part; this is where the decisive next step should have been accomplished, in which the bridge between the spiritual self of the nation and social reality should have been made. The mission of Kaspar Hauser to try to build this bridge would certainly have helped to counter the loss of the German people's identity. The tragic development of Germany runs parallel in this sense to that of Kaspar Hauser. Daumer—as was shown in Chapter 2—

sensed this connection between the destiny of the German nation and that of Kaspar Hauser. The effect of the ahrimanic forces is always directed towards disturbing or preventing the connection with the self. For the German people the lack of a living connection to their real Folk-spirit has become an all-encompassing destiny.

In his 'Appeal to the German nation and the Civilized World' ('Aufruf an das deutsche Volk und an die Kulturwelt') in 1919, Rudolf Steiner refers to this situation from the opposite point of view. He there says that knowledge must be kindled in the German people to show them that 'it had founded an Empire half a century ago but had neglected to provide it with a task growing out of the inner content of the German Folk-character.'[73] Here, as elsewhere, the connection is made between the real cause of the First World War—out of which all later catastrophes arose—and the disturbance, or lack of a proper relationship, between the Folk-body and the Folk-spirit. It should be recognized, and will ever again be confirmed, that in this fact lies the true reason for the Central European conflicts and that a mastery of these difficulties has to start with a knowledge of the facts.

To sum up one can say that the years immediately prior to the beginning of the Michael Age are characterized by an unusual darkness, a most painful estrangement from the spirit.

At the beginning of the Michael Age in the autumn of 1879, within the 33-year rhythm, the youthful Rudolf Steiner becomes 18 and two-thirds years old. He has lived through his first moon-node—about which more will be said later. At the beginning of the Michael Age, Rudolf Steiner—for whom the spiritual worlds always lay open to his conscious awareness—learns about the secret of the threefold human organization which had been guarded by the Being of Michael.[74] The Christ activity, unfolding between Lucifer and Ahriman, which is the hidden source of all that is human, stands before his understanding gaze as he experiences the beginning of the Michael Age. The recognition of the Christ Being and its significance for the earth evolution matures in his soul from this time on. Rudolf Steiner himself stresses in his 'Autobiography' that he did not change his opinion about the Christ; that it was present with him from early times, but then withdrew for a time for karmic reasons.[75]

We dare here to voice our opinion that the result of Christ's activity, as described by Rudolf Steiner in his lecture-cycle *From Jesus to Christ* given in October 1911,[76] had been living in his soul since 1879. An evolutionary rhythm which was of decisive importance to Rudolf Steiner and the fulfilment of his mission links up at this point with the effects of Kaspar Hauser's suppressed mission. From 1879 onwards the activity of the two individualities work together in the flow of time. 33 years later Rudolf Steiner gives the aforementioned lecture-cycle out of a sense of 'esoteric duty'.[77]

1911/1912

The lecture-cycle *From Jesus to Christ* was held exactly 99 years after Kaspar Hauser's birth in his birthplace Karlsruhe, remarkably enough during the very days in which Kaspar Hauser lay in his mother's cradle.* It is deeply moving to see how the initiate Rudolf Steiner shares in and partakes of a higher kind of existence in the sense that on the one hand he fulfils all the objective obligations of life on earth and on the other, in a Christian sense, can defend and support another individual and his destiny. The deeds of an initiate spring from sources which are inaccessible and not immediately understandable to someone who is not an initiate.[78] For this reason it can occur that at particular times and in certain places there may be hidden grounds for what he says and does to which far too little heed has been given in the past. Many an enigmatic relationship in the life and work of Rudolf Steiner can be made clear by observing such connections.

An attempt will now be made to specify in detail what Rudolf Steiner reveals in this lecture course about the secret of the Kaspar Hauser individuality and his birth in Karlsruhe, although no allusion is directly made to Kaspar Hauser himself. In carrying out the earthly deeds themselves, the servant of the world-spirit acts in such a way as to resolve this difficult problem through his acts and words. To this there certainly belongs the fact that in so doing the real underlying spiritual background of the crime against Kaspar Hauser is revealed and the mighty struggle taking place behind the scenes of history is made plain.

As the lecture-cycle in question gives the basis for solving this riddle it is necessary to go more deeply into statements of Rudolf Steiner. After an introductory public lecture Rudolf Steiner speaks in the course in Karlsruhe, especially in the first two lectures, in a detailed and special way about the Jesuit training. In this attention must be directed primarily to the effects that are to be achieved. The first lecture, given on 5 October, ends with the words:

'King Jesus must become the Ruler upon earth, and we who belong to His army have to employ every means to make Him Ruler of the earth. To this we pledge ourselves, we who belong to His host assembled on the plain of Jerusalem, against the host of Lucifer assembled on the plain of Babylon. And the greatest disgrace for a soldier of King Jesus is to forsake the standard.'

This, gathered up in a single resolution of the will, is something which can undoubtedly give to that will immense strength. To characterize it we must ask, what then had been directly attacked in the soul-life? The element that ought to be considered as immediately holy, that which ought not to be touched—the will-element. In so far as in this Jesuit training the will-element is laid hold of, because the Jesus-idea seizes the will-element completely, in so far is the concept of the dominion of Jesus exaggerated in the most dangerous way, dangerous because through this concept the will becomes so strong that it can work directly upon the will of another. For where the will becomes so strong through Imaginations, that is to say, through occult means, it acquires the capacity for working directly upon the will of another, and hence also along all the other occult paths to which such a will can have recourse.

Thus we see how in the last centuries, among the many currents that meet us, there are two special ones, the one which has exaggerated the Jesus-element and sees in 'King Jesus' the only ideal of Christianity, and the other which looks only and entirely at the Christ-element and carefully distinguishes whatever could go beyond it. The latter view has been much calumniated because it maintains that Christ has sent the spirit so that, indirectly through the spirit, Christ can enter directly into the hearts and minds of men. There is hardly a greater contrast in the development of civilization during the last centuries than that between Jesuitism and Rosicrucianism, because Jesuitism contains nothing of what Rosicrucianism regards as the highest ideal of our judgement concerning man's worth and man's dignity, and because Rosicrucianism has always determined to guard against every one of those influences which can in the remotest sense be called a Jesuitical element.

In this lecture I wished to show, in ordinary life, how even so lofty an element as the Jesus-principle can be exaggerated and then becomes dangerous, and how necessary it is to sink oneself into the depths of the Christ-Being if we wish to understand how the strength of Christianity must consist in esteeming to the very highest degree human worth and human dignity. Nowhere may we with clumsy strides grope our way into that which we must regard as man's most inmost sanctuary. That is why Christian mysticism is so fought against by the Jesuit-element—and Rosicrucianism even more so—because it is felt that true Christianity is sought elsewhere than merely where 'King Jesus' is the actor. Through the Imaginations here indicated, the will has become so strong that even spiritual protests in opposition can be overcome through this will which has been acquired by the prescribed exercises.[79]

The Jesuit training is here characterized as a path for strengthening the will forces, which in this way become dangerous occult working-tools. The occult effect of this is that the will becomes so strong that it can work compulsively directly upon another human being without the consciousness being involved. The one who is thus surrendered to the will of the other person knows nothing, and is not supposed to know anything, about what is actually happening to him. He is *unconsciously* a slave of impulses which are impressed upon him by an occult act of will in which ideas occur in his consciousness which have nothing to do with what is going on in his will. In reality the person is torn apart and thrust into the abyss, but he does not notice anything of this, because his will, stupified in this way, hardly has the incentive to wake up.

In the same lecture Rudolf Steiner points expressly to hypnotism as a forbidden but extant means of influencing the will. 'The only healthy way to gain influence over the will of the other is through cognition'.[79] On another occasion Rudolf Steiner emphasizes concisely: 'The overpowering of a human being by means of hypnotism is a still stronger killing, for it destroys the will. The occultist therefore never intrudes into a person's freedom; he only relates facts.'[80]

Rudolf Steiner always defined as *the* Jesuit principle the gaining of power over another person's soul beyond or outside of the person's consciousness—and thereby without regard to human freedom. The process remains fundamentally reprehensible and unworthy of a human being irrespective of whether one thinks one is serving a higher purpose or not. In consideration of the inviolability of human freedom, no end can justify any means. The reason for the far-reaching effects of the Jesuit principle lies in the fact that a misuse of higher knowledge is being practised. The spiritual law that is here misused is described in short in Rudolf Steiner's book, *Knowledge of Higher Worlds*: 'It is a natural law among all initiates to withhold from no man the knowledge he is entitled to possess; but there is equally a natural law which lays down that no occult knowledge shall be imparted to anyone not qualified to receive it. And the more strictly he observes both these laws, the more perfect is an initiate.'[81]

Those who follow the Jesuit principle contravene the first part of this law, because they believe that man is not entitled to make research on his own. With them knowledge that is conceded to an individual is not measured according to that person's maturity but according to the purpose which the one who possesses knowledge wishes to achieve by giving it out or withholding it. Through that a deliberate retention of knowledge gives power over the other person. Usually it is the intentions of groups of people that are followed. The commitment to the *progress of humanity*, which was an essential motive in the heyday of German culture around 1800, was disregarded; but because the opponents of the Christian progress of humanity, as shown in the case of Kaspar Hauser, were in possession of important occult knowledge, the power which they exercised through the retention of this knowledge over those who were serving them is not to be underestimated. The members of the practising occult groups let the power they acquire be made use of by their leaders. This will, which remains hidden, acquires a tremendous strength through the fact that it is never consciously recognized or irradiated by feelings from the heart. In order to illustrate what is meant by the might of will thus acquired, we shall here again refer to the already quoted words of Rudolf Steiner: 'Through the Imagination here indicated, the will has become so strong that even spiritual protests in opposition can be overcome through this will which has been acquired by the prescribed exercises.'[79] The outrageousness of this statement quite exceeds all that has previously been assumed and thought of by mankind. It is easy for people to believe that the impulses coming from the spiritual world will be able to cope with every hostile attack against humanity. But here it is emphatically stated that the power of the spiritual world to counter the efforts which work against human progress can be compelled by the will-forces that have been increased by occult methods.

One has to imagine that the method which such occult groups as the Jesuits employ is that the knowledgeable ones among them, those who stand at the top in the hierarchic order, only confide a portion of their knowledge to those of the lower grades and intentionally conceal their true knowledge and motives. As this process is repeated in principle at every stage, the ultimate servant has really no consciousness at all of what he is actually serving with the powers which he has acquired by his spiritual exercises. Thereby this humanly most undignified labour in the spiritual realm—that is outside normal consciousness—becomes extremely effective.

It is only out of the motives of these groups that the tremendous effort which was exerted in this case can be explained. The motive that was here employed was such that the physical plane and those living upon it were to be controlled by a group of people through their luciferic-ahrimanically directed aims. An ancient pre-Christian form of control was to have been preserved here. This was justified as long as the contact with the spiritual world had still to be maintained and guided by the Mystery Centres for the ordering of the social life.

Lastly, we are dealing here with something which is archetypally presented in the sentencing and putting to death of Christ. If one looks at what Rudolf Steiner has to say on this subject it becomes plain that Christ was condemned to death by the Pharisees and Sadducees because he had infringed an old law. He had performed Mystery deeds in public. The Mysteries were presented openly by Him on the physical plane and are available in the future progress of mankind to everyone individually who has the readiness and maturity to receive them, who has succeeded in raising himself up to the New Mysteries. *Therewith, however, the power of one person over another has come to an end.* The impulse of brotherliness was deeply experienced in early Christian times and in Christ the Son of God becomes the Son of Man. He has become man's brother. The Pharisees and Sadducees turn against this development inaugurated by Christ Himself, because according to tradition they necessarily get the impression that a blasphemy is there being enacted. They become enemies of Christ because what is new, the impulse towards the free individual human being, is, in their opinion, a boundless conceit.

In contrast to Jesuitism and Rosicrucianism, as characterized by Rudolf Steiner, the continued enmity of the Pharisees and Sadducees towards what Christ brings into the world can also be experienced. If one calls to mind the description given in Chapter 1 of the crime against Kaspar Hauser which was at least twofold, one can notice that this crime was committed according to the Jesuit principle. A significant occult degree is required to recognize the place and time of Kaspar Hauser's incarnation. The true motive—namely, to hinder Kaspar Hauser from fulfilling his earthly mission—was not known to those in the foreground of history, the Imperial Countess of Hochberg and her helpers. They were following their dynastic views which were of importance to them. What concepts had been instilled into those taking part to make Kaspar Hauser's imprisonment understandable to them must remain an open question at this point. At any rate it did not accord with the truth.

If the directors of the crime, who remained in the background, acted in accordance with Jesuitical methods, that does not mean that they themselves have necessarily to be sought in the Jesuit circle, for this method is also used in principle by other groups of people. The instigators of the crime on Kaspar Hauser are, however, certainly the Jesuits themselves. Rudolf Steiner said this twice to Count Polzer-Hoditz, namely in November 1916 and on 3 March 1925.[82] 'Those circles which conceal everything and today still try to conceal what happened in connection with Kaspar Hauser's destiny, are those members of western Lodges and Jesuits who have worked together in their leading organizations for more than 150 years, but demonstrably since January 1802. The latter therefore do not want to have exposed what they have staged as an experiment, as an elaborate attempt to separate the individual in question from his mission and to hold him in a twilight zone, not completely spirit and not altogether a man on earth, but diverted from his mission and kept as though in spiritual exile; that is to say, build a body, but not be able to take hold of it as an individual ego. This experiment, however, did not succeed and that is the reason why Kaspar Hauser had to die. The people concerned were forced to experience that their experiment achieved just that which they had tried to hinder: the awakening of the individuality, yes, even that he became conscious of reincarnation and karma. But that was just that which should not have been.' Though it may seem irrelevant, we shall here allude to an intended co-operation between the Jesuits and the western Lodges—that is to say the Freemasons—from a point of time onwards of which we shall speak later (cf. p.145).[83]

From a deeper, spiritually inspired feeling for the truth, Jakob Wassermann, in his novel *Caspar Hauser*, saw in Lord Stanhope the connecting link between those working from the western Lodges and the so-called 'Grey Eminence'. The connection between Lord Stanhope and the 'Grey Eminence' corresponds in all details with the above described setting up and running of an active occult group. Through that it becomes certain that Lord Stanhope—as a result of his destiny and his weaknesses—half reluctantly and half willingly worked for the 'Grey Eminence', or rather was obliged to work, whereby it is necessary to know if he himself was being made use of for aims of which he was ignorant, or of which he was not allowed to know. The humanly distressing side of this relationship was characterized by Wassermann in the fact that—contrary to the historical sequence of events—he makes Lord Stanhope hang himself.[84]

The significance of Kaspar Hauser's imprisonment, from the point of view of human science as is here characterized by Rudolf Steiner, has been dealt with in Chapter 1. The question of to what extent Kaspar Hauser was aware of reincarnation and karma is reserved for the last chapter.

In the conversation of 3 March 1925 Rudolf Steiner further stated: 'Always bear in mind that the Jesuits have robbed man of his religious piety, they [the Jesuits] are quite identical with the might of the Roman State; the battle—that is to say the sin—against the spirit is the means by which they enforce their rule; it is the only sin which the scriptures say cannot be forgiven, and yet the spirit cannot be entirely extirpated, but only a few people will carry it forward into the future.'[82] The unsurpassable, testamentary severity of this statement made by Rudolf Steiner in the month of his death, refers us back to the already quoted passage about the Jesuits in the lecture-cycle *From Jesus to Christ* and underlines the latter in a special way. Whereas in that cycle the method used by the Jesuits is explained through the fact that the will is transformed into an occult weapon, here the 'sin against the spirit' is described in all cogency as the means of attaining world-supremacy. One must reckon therefore, in all seriousness, that this signifies: The truth is attacked because it has been recognized as the truth.[85] As the Christ lives in truth, so the battle against the truth is at the same time the battle against Christ.

After having described the opponents of Kaspar Hauser and their methods of working, we can now go deeper into the question of what it actually is that the people with knowledge in these circles are fighting against and we shall have to show that this is connected with the appearance of Kaspar Hauser.

In his lecture-cycle *From Jesus to Christ* Rudolf Steiner describes the deeds performed by Christ through His freely offered sacrifice. The significance of these deeds is described from both a cosmological as well as a microcosmic point of view. All-inclusive and all-supportive thereof is the knowledge of Christ's cosmic nature. From the cosmic point of view the development of man's physical body is traced through the planetary stages of the Earth from Saturn, Sun and Moon evolution, as Rudolf Steiner explains in detail in his *Occult Science*.[86] From that it can be learned that man's physical body, having passed through a fourfold process of embodiment and disembodiment, is the oldest member of his being and the most highly developed part of him. At the same time we are given to understand that the physical body of man (the form or shape of which has permanent existence) and its active power is of a spiritual nature. It is referred to by Rudolf Steiner as the 'phantom'.[87]

Here a common mistake is easily made, owing to the fact that the physical body, as it is experienced today, is onesidedly taken to be a visibly apparent object which is subject only to the laws of gravity. Rudolf Steiner tries step by step (in lecture 6) to show us how man presents us with a deep riddle in that he is visible at all, for all his members are of a spiritual— that is invisible—nature. He goes on to add that it is only now that the complex circumstances of the fourfold nature of man on earth is made visible. But this visibility, which is generally looked upon as something present from the start, is actually the result of a process whereby man was led into the material sense-world by the activity of the luciferic and ahrimanic beings. Through His deeds Christ would free mankind from the entanglements of this world.

During the Lemurian epoch of earthly evolution Lucifer worked upon man's developing being in such a way that independence and the will to be free were roused in him prematurely. The intentions of the beneficial Gods were to a certain extent frustrated by that. Owing to this attack by Lucifer the human being was not able to retain the spiritual height to which he had been predestined. This event, described in the Biblical account as the Fall of Man and the eviction from Paradise, led to the fact that man's being now also fell into the sphere where the ahrimanic spirits were at work to produce spiritual darkness and earthly gravity. Thereby the previously invisible physical body of man was filled up with the weight of matter and man's whole body was led in this way to become visible to the senses. The 'phantom', the spiritual-physical form-body of man, which was to have received the ego on the earth from the substance of the spirits of form, could therefore only be used indirectly for this reception of the ego. Man was torn away from the spiritual world and became a citizen of earth, whose nature it is to move further and further away from the spiritual world. The change which took place in man's whole organism caused death to enter in. Through becoming and remaining visible to the senses, death has been planted in man. The original phantom was designed to endow the ego, developing in the lap of the Gods, with a consciousness—albeit one dependent on the Gods—of both the spiritual and the physical worlds. Two conditions of consciousness, like those of waking and sleeping, would then have evolved. In place of this, two forms of existence developed: life in the spiritual world alternating with that in the sense world. Through the damage done to the phantom by the luciferic and ahrimanic beings, not only this was impaired—and this was undoubtedly the aim of all these actions from the start—the ego was diverted to another line of development. One can describe this action by saying that the ego, in consequence of the damage done to the phantom, was drawn ever deeper into the sense world, and when the weakened physical body was no longer able to support the ego—that is to say after death—the spiritual world was experienced ever fainter and shadowier. On account of its too strong connection with the sense world the ego was unable after death to fully awaken in the spiritual world. With every new incarnation the ego distanced itself further from its spiritual home. In addition to that, owing to the mistakes and seductions of the ego, the phantom itself was brought still lower. This path taken by the ego would inevitably have led to its self-destruction in a world ultimately estranged from it. The ego consciousness of its spiritual home would finally have become extinguished.

Novalis in his *Hymns to the Night* portrayed this human situation, later transformed by Christ, in the following verses:

There was but one thought: a ghastly phantom
Which monstrous to the merry tables strode
And wild with terror spirits there instilled.
The gods themselves despaired of means or mode
Whereby taut hearts with solace might be filled
Mysterious was the monster's shadow-road
Whose rage no gift or supplication stilled.
Its name was Death, who could that revel vanquish
With mourning and with sorrow and with anguish.

For ever parted now from all that taught
The sweet sensations that the heart may know,
Bereft of loved ones who on earth are wrought
By futile longings and by lengthy woe,
Within a languid dream the dead seemed caught
And strengthless struggle there to undergo.
The wave of all delight was shattered, spent
Against the rock of ceaseless ill-content.

(translated by Charles E. Passage)

All pre-Christian civilizations, in so far as they were informed about the spirit, have attempted to come to terms with this increasing loss of the spiritual world. Buddha, the last great teacher of the wisdom of antiquity, through his impulse of withdrawal from the earthly world, did the only thing possible to enable man to come to terms with the four-fold impairment of human nature: death, illness, old age and separation. This was a heroic attempt on the part of Buddha to save mankind for the spiritual world. It was he who gave man the impulse to free himself from the degrading influence of the earthly realm.

The Greeks, who experienced the tragic shadowiness of the world of the dead most acutely, saw their salvation, in contrast to that of Buddha, in clinging to the beautiful illusion of the senses, in which they still experienced the spirit. But they were unable to rid themselves of the feeling that the after-death relationship to the spiritual world could not thereby be improved. 'Bold with sensuous ardour man invested the grisly spectre with a beauteous guise' says Novalis in the 5th 'Hymn to the Night'. In the background of Greek civilization stands the insurmountable question—therefore banished to the edge of consciousness—of the existence of the ego in the spiritual world. Also the pre-Christian Mysteries which, from the background of history, would have been able to suffuse a spiritual influence ever and again into earthly life, had very largely fallen into decay by the corrupted human nature.

One must be quite clear about the fact that pre-Christian humanity found itself in a truly hopeless situation, because it actually had no possibility of doing anything about it which was of any importance. No ego living in a physical, etheric or astral body could prevail against the lucerific and ahrimanic powers in order to halt or even to alleviate the disintegration of human nature. Mankind faced the effects of superhuman deeds, for Lucifer and Ahriman, on their part, were divine-spiritual beings far advanced above humanity. It was, so to say, an uneven contest that was taking place.

If mankind were not finally to succumb to Lucifer and Ahriman a cosmic Being would have to enter the combat.

With the coming of Christ a divine-spiritual Being came from the cosmos, from the region of the sun to the earth, and incarnated in a body in order to restore the original human nature through a new act of creation—by His free act of love to implant even more into man than was originally intended. When Christ suffered death at the Mystery of Golgotha as a result of the earthly development brought about by Lucifer and Ahriman, He raised up the ever more downwards-inclined effect of the depraved human corporeality. That is the meaning of the words *'Christ died for all mankind'*, because, by this process, an objective change was brought about in human nature, in which, since then, all mankind actually shares. In the Easter Event, which in truth is the only starting point for any Christian development, Christ creates a new phantom, the resurrection body, which displays in full view its spiritual-physical, but immaterial, nature. In the 5th 'Hymn to the Night' the corresponding verse runs as follows:

> Thou art the youth who through the length of years
> Stood on our gravestones lost in thought immense;
> A sign of solace in the dark of fears,
> Thou didst the highest race of men commence;
> What plunged us into misery and tears
> Draws us with sweeter yearning now from hence.
> In death was life eternal first revealed:
> And thou art Death, who makest us be healed.

Rudolf Steiner describes the basic knowledge of these facts in the following words: 'But there came the Event of Golgotha, an Event which brought about complete reconstruction of the lost principles of man's evolution. If man takes unto himself that which in the preceding lecture was designated the "incorruptible body", and which has now been placed in greater detail before our souls—if man clothes himself with this incorruptible body he will attain to a clearer and clearer illumination of his ego-consciousness, and more and more to the recognition within his own nature of that which draws him on from one incarnation to another.' And a little later he

summarizes it as follows: 'His Resurrection is the coming to
birth of a new member of human nature—the incorruptible
body'.[88]

In the resurrection body, which can only be created by a
divine cosmic Being, new possibilities are made available for
man's post-Christian development. Those egos which recognize Christ's deed and receive His impulse into themselves
exert an ever stronger power of attraction towards the
reconstructed phantom, which—once it had been created—
can be reproduced in the spiritual world according to the law
of spiritual economy. Through that it becomes possible for
every ego to receive an individual spiritual-physical body,
specially adapted to its needs, arising out of the common
substance of the resurrection body, whereby a unifying soli-
darity is achieved in full accord with individualization. By
means of this new spiritual-physical body man will in future
become a true citizen of both worlds if, through Christ, he
gains for his ego the power to attract this new body to himself.
'The essential characteristic may be stated as follows: that
through such a process of mystic feeling [the feelings related to
the Christian initiation with its seven steps], we work right into
our physical body. When we do this, we do nothing less than
make ourselves ready in our physical body to receive the
phantom that went forth from the grave on Golgotha.
Consequently we work into our physical body in order to
make it so living that it feels a relationship—an attractive
force—towards the phantom that arose out of the grave on
Golgotha.'[89] Only as a result of the Mystery of Golgotha has it
become possible for an ego really to live on the physical plane,
i.e. for an ego to be born. True though it is that Christ's deeds
affect everyone, it is also true that the second process we
described, which presupposes the first, can only be accomplished through the free decision and work of the ego.

After having spoken, to begin with, about the divine-cosmic
aspect of Christ's deeds, we shall now speak about their effects
on man. The havoc wrought on human nature was, as already
mentioned, experienced in its archetypal form by Buddha.
Death, which proceeds out of the material-physical side of

man's nature, is an expression of the fact that man with his ego has entered a world over which he is not in control. *Ageing* comes about because the withering, consuming forces of the physical body overpower the eternal wellspring of the etheric body. *Illnesses* are the necessary consequence of the fact that man, influenced by Lucifer, tears himself away from the perfect harmony of the astral world and becomes entangled in the material world of Ahriman. By suffering illness a balance is established to the seductions and errors to which he succumbed. *Separation* from those we love is what the ego experiences when, during incarnation—bound to the physical body—the consciousness of the natural connection between one ego and the next, which is not conditioned by space and time, fades and apparently disappears. With this the whole of human nature displays a lamentable deterioration.

Christ appeared as the Healer, as the cosmic World-Physician who, through three acts of healing, which took place before the Mystery of Golgotha, harmonized the ego in the sense-nature, the astral body in thinking, feeling and willing, and the etheric body in the life processes.[90] These deeds of Christ differ from His act of incarnation. The significance of the latter lay in the fact that Christ was ensouled into the Jesus Body, as Rudolf Steiner put it. As these three sides of His nature were of a supersensible kind, Christ did not need to forsake the spiritual world in order to perform these acts of healing. The descent of Christ into the sense-material world, His incarnation into flesh and blood, is at the same time a unique and by far the most difficult task which He undertook. Christ, in His descent, followed the pathway into matter taken by man, in which the main difference lay in the consciousness with which the cosmic spirit followed this path.

The Mystery of Golgotha is the moment in which Christ suffered the human-physical experience of loneliness in the Stations of the Cross. The necessity of suffering grew out of the past development of mankind on the earth. The balance was restored through the Divine Suffering. In order to understand such suffering we have to imagine the gap which exists between the region of the sun and the dark world of matter in which man has become involved. This gap was experienced consciously by Christ with immense pain. His consciously-willed loving devotion brings about the balance. Just as the suffering of God points back into the past, so does the Easter Event, through which Christ as cosmic spirit in the realm of earth restores the physical body, point to the future and ultimately to the end-time of earthly evolution. By restoring the physical body's original nature the three previous Christ-deeds can for the first time become truly effective and fruitful. The Mystery of Golgotha and the Easter Event are the crowning deed of healing performed by Christ on human nature.

From now onwards it can only be a matter of making this work effective by means of devotion. The task of post-Christian humanity is to discover this devotion, against which the whole strength of 'the Old Adam' within man is pitted. By the four sacrifices of Christ—the last of which was the Mystery of Golgotha—the whole of man's fourfold nature has been set an example which, if taken up and acted upon, will be able to work in a healing way.

At this point the opportunity is once more given for us to direct our attention to the 33-year rhythm of post-Christian history. The 33 years' life-span of Jesus from conception to His death on Golgotha,[91] is impressed upon the whole of earthly development and earthly destiny because a cosmic spirit takes over the spirit-forsaken sphere of earth and puts it in order. That does not contradict the fact that it was only in the 30th year of the life of Jesus that Christ entered *into* this human being at the time of the Baptism in Jordan. His connection with the Jesus Being, whom He had ensouled on three previous occasions, was a factor from the beginning. This development was planned and purposefully guided and it is only a question of being directed at first more from outside, and later grasped and penetrated from within. The 33-year rhythm is the impression left behind of the union of the cosmic spirit with the earth. For the first time in human history Rudolf Steiner made it possible through his lecture-cycle *From Jesus to Christ*, which in effect is the account of a deed performed for the whole of humanity, that a then small circle of people could realize the essential significance of Christ's appearance on earth. The basis for this is offered by the scientific comprehension of the supersensible world as it is portrayed in his work as a whole, but especially in his book *Occult Science*.

Even though one can say that these secrets are already known in esoteric circles (the Rosicrucians, for instance), nevertheless their publication out of an 'esoteric sense of duty', as Rudolf Steiner expressly states,[92] out of the will of the spiritual beings who lead mankind, denotes a definite turning point. The publication of this essential Christ-secret, if it is taken up seriously and effectively by more and more people, will ultimately result in all that comes from ancient pre-Christian forces and conditions gradually losing its power and influence.

It is one of the sad things in human history that this turning point was immediately recognized by the opponents in all sharpness and clarity. From the Karlsruhe lecture-cycle onwards the 'fight against Anthroposophy' began, as Rudolf Steiner stated on 7 May 1925.[92] This was not because the content of the lectures was considered to be untrue, but because its truth was recognized and the opponents had every reason to fear the effect of the truth. It is this fear which motivated the opponents to take immediate occult measures on the physical plane, which have since demonstrated their historic effectiveness.

One should again be reminded of the fact that these deeds of enlightenment of Rudolf Steiner were given to mankind 99 years after Kaspar Hauser's birth in his birthplace in Karlsruhe. In his exposition of the training and working methods of the Jesuits he pointed to one decisive source of criminal actions against Kaspar Hauser. In giving forth his knowledge of the renewal of the phantom he points to the deeper secrets which lie behind the being of Kaspar Hauser and his appearance (in Nuremberg). This he does in response to the will of the spiritual beings whom he serves in his work for all mankind.

In turning one's attention once more to the individuality of
Kaspar Hauser, one can sense his deep connection with the
Christ impulse, as became apparent at his death. Whoever
perceives the child-like purity and innocence of his nature,
which prompted Tucher to remark that in Kaspar Hauser we
have a human being as he was without sin before the Fall,*
and whoever seriously considers Rudolf Steiner's statement
that, apart from Christian Rosenkreutz, no one ever shared so
deeply in the sufferings of Christ as did Kaspar Hauser, then
that person will be able to sense that this Being, who clearly
belongs in closest proximity to Christ, was armed and equipped for his earthly task—for the healing of mankind—with the
highest attribute that Christ created on earth: with the resurrection body. He will be one of the first to share in the effect of
Christ's deeds for the salvation of humanity.

From this point of view a revealing light shines upon many
extraordinary things in Kaspar Hauser's life, in particular on
the remarkable and therefore oft-disputed fact that during the
time of his imprisonment he was literally only nourished on
bread and water. Heyer tried at first to explain this by the fact
of the good quality of the bread and only lightly indicated
other deeper points of view.[93] We can justifiably point out that
according to the usual opinion concerning human nutrition
this presents us with an almost unbelievable state of affairs.
We know, however, that Kaspar Hauser showed no desire for
anything but bread and Daumer considered it his only mistake
to have changed Kaspar Hauser's diet to the usually accepted
one, because through that a fundamental change took place in
his original faculties.[94] In his later statements, for instance on
the occasion of the detailed sworn interrogation of 6
November 1829,[95] Kaspar Hauser emphasized that he only
ever partook of bread and water for as long as he could
remember. The mystery of Kaspar Hauser's diet can be solved
if one thinks of him as being connected to a higher stream of
life which is able to maintain the living coherence of the
organism with a minimum of earthly substance. One might
also say that in Kaspar Hauser the grace before meals—' 'Tis
not the bread which feeds, we are by Him through bread, with

His eternal Word, with Life and Spirit fed'—has become realized. The bread which nourished him can be felt imaginatively as the Body of Christ.*

Further facts are to be found in the unusual sense qualities of Kaspar Hauser. The twelve senses are parts of the physical body. The ego makes use of them in a twelvefold way.[96] The experiences which man is able to have in the sense world depend upon the quality of his organs as well as upon the faculties of his ego. The corrupted senses acting as organs of the physical body cause the illusion to arise in the ego that one is only confronted by a material reality in the sense world, whereas the effective qualities of the latter world are actually of a spiritual nature and origin. The spiritual reality is certainly present in the sense world; sense perception can be raised to supersensible insight.[97] The possibility of raising and purifying the senses, by which means they become capable of assessing the world as it truly is, to really get to know it, can be looked upon as a characteristic of the resurrection body. In Kaspar Hauser's sense-perceptions phenomena appear which can be interpreted in the above sense. The faculties of his senses far exceed the usual limitations; they extend to the comprehension of quality and the experience of what effect the perceived substances have. Daumer reports, for instance, on Kaspar Hauser's sensitivity to metals, by which he was able to feel metals covered by a sheet of paper and describe their different qualities.[98]

In the case of the sense of smell, too, corresponding observations were made. Thus, the apprehension of a minimal scent of alcohol had an effect upon him comparable to that of indulgence in alcohol.[99] Certainly these observations must be considered in the light of the fact that, through his imprisonment, Kaspar Hauser's childlike nature had been preserved to a greater degree than was compatible with his age. Rightly understood, however, this argument supports what has just been said, for the chief characteristic of a child's nature is that the luciferic-ahrimanic powers can exert the less pressure on it the younger the child is. The child's nature itself can be looked upon as something from which the luciferic-ahrimanic forces have been excluded by Christ.[100] Thus we can understand how it came about that, shortly after his arrival on the scene, Kaspar Hauser was given the name 'the Child of Europe'.

As the last point in this connection our attention should be turned to the mortal wounds inflicted on Kaspar Hauser on 14 December 1833. When the autopsy was carried out the doctors established a fourfold cause of death in wounds to the heart, stomach, diaphragm and lungs.[101] This would ordinarily have meant that the grievously wounded person would have been unable to move. Nevertheless, after the fatal blow, Kaspar Hauser walked from the orangery to Meyer's house and from there, with the disbelieving Meyer, to the orangery where Kaspar Hauser finally collapsed, although he still managed the walk back home with some support.[102] Does not this astonishing feat point to a more than human life-force, as though it were gathering up all its strength, which had been intended for a long and active life, to counter this most threatening danger? Yet the death intended by his enemies could not be avoided and, after 76 hours, this precious life was ended.

We might now ask why Rudolf Steiner did not directly refer to Kaspar Hauser in his lecture-cycle in Karlsruhe in 1911 as he did years previously, though certainly in different circumstances.[103] This question can be answered in two ways—outwardly historically and spiritually with reference to destiny.

It would have been impossible in Karlsruhe in 1911 to speak publicly about Kaspar Hauser, because the ruling Grand-Duke Frederick II, descended from the Hochberg line, had succeeded to the throne as a result of the crime committed against Kaspar Hauser in 1830. For social and political reasons a public discussion would not have been practicable, because it would have served no purpose in the prevailing circumstances. It would also have been purposeless at this moment to have accused the Jesuits of inciting the offence against Kaspar Hauser. Rudolf Steiner was certainly able to support his arguments derived from his own spiritual research, but there was no group of people around him who would have backed him up in the results of his investigation.

Primarily, however, there were spiritual reasons for Rudolf Steiner's reticence. These lay in the fact that at that time Kaspar Hauser's destiny was still in the process of unfolding, as will be shown in later accounts. It will also be shown how Rudolf Steiner himself was involved in this destiny, so that this too was another reason why it could not be openly discussed.

With regard to the year 1911 it should be emphasized that for a small circle of people—albeit an intimate one—one of the most important spiritual deeds for mankind was performed by Rudolf Steiner when he revealed the knowledge concerning important secrets of Christianity. And this act stands in close connection with the destiny and nature of Kaspar Hauser.

In connection with the question of the evolution of man, in 1911 Rudolf Steiner published the booklet *The Spiritual Guidance of Mankind*.[104] The importance of this publication at that time can be gauged by the fact that the lectures given in Copenhagen were prepared for immediate publication by Rudolf Steiner himself. This was something which happened very rarely with Rudolf Steiner.

In close connection with the year 1911 we have to consider the year 1912—in retrospect of the years 1878/79 and in prospect of the years 1944/45. Rudolf Steiner and his friends had to leave the Theosophical Society in 1912 because the teaching was spread abroad within the Society that the Christ was to be reincarnated in Krishnamurti. Rudolf Steiner, on the other hand, upheld the view of Christ outlined above and emphasized the uniqueness of the incarnation of a God. The definite and unreserved affirmation of this knowledge about Christ led in 1913 to the founding of the Anthroposophical Society in which he served as its spiritual leader. This historical step deserves to be remembered, because through it the spiritual science which was represented in Rudolf Steiner acquired its own social surroundings for the first time. The founding of the Anthroposophical Society led to the laying of the foundation stone of the First Goetheanum in Dornach in 1913, of which more will be said later.

A further noteworthy event is the publication of the anthroposophical *Soul Calendar*, 1912/13[105] through Rudolf

Steiner. With the words on the title-page of the original issue: '1879 years after the birth of the ego', Rudolf Steiner points to the 33-year rhythm and how it began and likewise to the year 1879 as the beginning of the Michael Age. To understand the significance of the 52 weekly verses in this connection one must consider that the course of the year is governed by the passage of the sun through the zodiac and therewith represents the rhythm of the physical body, whereas the months represent the etheric, the weeks the astral body and the days, in their interchange of light and dark, bear the rhythm of the ego. The ego, which desires to experience the course of the year, is enabled through the *Soul Calendar* to unite, in a hitherto unknown way, with the rhythm of the physical body. The mysterious lemniscatory structure of the *Soul Calendar* can become a source of strength for the physical body when it is used as it was intended. It is self-evident that the *Soul Calendar*, which concerns the whole human being, also includes the other rhythms of the supersensible organs through its monthly and weekly divisions and through that it connects everything together. The *Soul Calendar* is a jewel in itself, a treasure given to mankind at a crucial moment and waiting to be carried forward into the future.

A further historically important deed of Rudolf Steiner is the development of eurythmy, the new art of movement, in 1912. Once more it is necessary, with a few lines, to indicate the importance of this act. Human evolution has brought it about that the movements performed by people in the course of their working lives and in their works of art have become more and more caught up in outward or purely physical-bodily considerations. People's movements have gradually lost their connection to supersensible-cosmic reality for reasons stated above. From Rudolf Steiner's *Study of Man* it can be understood[106] that man in movement is the spiritual man, that all movement proceeds from the spirit. In so far as movement is enslaved by material existence it is torn away from its spiritual origin. Man loses his spiritual existence. This process is of the greatest importance to man in so far as, through the impulses that work unconsciously in the nature of the limb movements, man seeks and finds his destiny. A disturbance in this region must necessarily lead to karmic aberration. It was essential to move on to direct application of the spirit. In eurythmy Rudolf Steiner showed mankind how to put back into movement the supersensible, invisible, creative form. The spiritual element is reintroduced into the flow of man's movements and, into the human body thus mobilized, the seed of the liberating spiritualization is laid.

This has all been briefly shown in order to demonstrate how Rudolf Steiner in 1911/12—a hundred years after Kaspar Hauser's birth—performed definite actions in order to permeate the physical plane with the spirit of Christianity and to impart to it the impulse of deepest change, namely of spiritualization. In 1911, after Rudolf Steiner had divulged the knowledge of the healing powers given by Christ, he took the next step in 1912 by leading this over for the first time into the practical work. The founding of the Anthroposophical Society created a new possibility of awakening the soul powers through the cultivation of spiritual knowledge. Through his *Soul Calendar* he provided the meditative way for the individual to use the physical body as a tool to bring his ego and the cosmos together. With eurythmy a bridge was built for the human being in action to regain his connection with the etheric forces and to rejuvenate the dying body out of the spiritual fount of inspired movements. Thus through Rudolf Steiner the physical plane was taken hold of by the powers which aim to bring about a change in all earthly conditions. The opponents of this Christian development, who were likewise the opponents of Kaspar Hauser, noted with horror that by this means something was taking place which would radically shatter their power. One can understand how they immediately summoned all the occult forces at their disposal to prevent the decline of their authority. Here is the place to point out that, in the most favourable circumstances, only traces of these opposing activities will be historically preserved. The most important part of it will not be proved by documentary evidence because these events are not written down. One would underestimate the awareness of the opponents were one to suppose that they would leave any evidence of their activity behind. The science of history will have to content itself with accepting such facts and widen their former method of observation if they do not wish to miss the opportunity of grasping decisive motives of modern history.

1944/45

A century after Kaspar Hauser's birth, what had been intended as the goal of his existence was realized by Rudolf Steiner in metamorphosed form through his recognition of it and the deeds he performed. From 1878/79 Rudolf Steiner already joined the current which was to work into history through Kaspar Hauser. In following up the 33-year rhythm we arrive from 1911/12 to the year 1944/45. Normally the catastrophes of that time are not associated with the events which happened in the course of history in 1911/12. The cataclysmic, world-historically incisive events reveal the disastrous extent to which the opponents of Christ were willing to go in answer to Rudolf Steiner's spiritual deeds of 1911/12. The 33-year rhythm makes visible the secret activities of the opponents of the spirit. It is able—if understood correctly—to bring to light the doings of these practising occult groups.

Wherein lay the greatest danger for the occult organizations striving for world domination? It lay in the unrestrained activity of Rudolf Steiner in his service to the Rosicrucian impulse. His opponents saw as a direct threat the fact that Rudolf Steiner developed Anthroposophy in Central Europe, by which he restored to Central European spiritual life the task which had been allotted to it in the course of world-historical evolution: the building of a bridge between the sense-world and the world of the supersensible. This bridge-building was what Rudolf Steiner's own activity stood for. His most significant deeds in this respect in the years 1911/12 have just been the central theme of this discussion. The impulses described had as their aim to nullify the spiritual deeds of

Rudolf Steiner. In order to succeed in this aim they needed to unleash forces which would tear apart and destroy the area of Central Europe. It was above all necessary to allow foreign powers to interfere strongly in Central Europe to terminate its independence. The influence that Western powers would exert on Central Europe was characterized by Rudolf Steiner in 1917 in his 'Memorandum to the Imperial Government' as follows: 'He who understands the underlying cause of this war cannot but reject in the strongest possible terms the points in the Wilson programme agreement. For the true prospect of this programme—apart from its morally blinding effect—lies in the fact that it wants to make use of the instincts of the Central and East-European peoples to bring these people into economic dependence on Anglo-American policies by moral and political surprise tactics. The spiritual dependence would then merely be the necessary outcome of it.'[107]

One must accustom oneself to the idea that the Second World War was started in order to create chaos in Central Europe and to make the body of the German people unfit for the carrying out of their spiritual mission. For that it was decisive that this area should be occupied by people from East and West to divide Germany and to apportion the parts between the Allied Powers so that the autonomous tasks between East and West could not ultimately be fulfilled.*

A sad reflection on the loss of a sense of mission is the haste with which the politicians from both sections of Germany have served and continue to serve these ultimately alien impulses. In future the only salvation will be to have no illusion about the fact that in 1944/45 the real enemies of the living spirit won a tremendous victory. One must not fail to realize that the possibility is there for the Federal Republic of Germany to strive towards the mission of Central Europe. This possibility has certainly only been taken hold of to a very slight degree up till now and has led to some public activity here and there, but not to any historical consequences. A spiritual dependence, such as Rudolf Steiner described, has largely emerged as a consequence of economic dependence or, rather, a merging with the Western world.

A special tragedy lies in the fact that the failed coup of 20 July 1944 resulted in just those people being killed who would have been the likeliest to have served a future development along the lines laid down by the Folk-spirit. Their resistance, however, sprang from a feeling of moral responsibility and an insight into the abysmal deviation from the normal. If this coup had succeeded, the final consequences of the disruption would not have taken place. This had to be, however, also in order to prevent a new myth arising of a 'stab in the back'. Through this action the inner reputation of Germany was saved, but it was not directly effective historically.

If the one danger for the occult groups working against human progress lay in the waking up of Central Europe, the greatest danger lay in the knowledge about the Christ-Being disseminated by Rudolf Steiner. As already mentioned, the opponents had to acknowledge that the dawning understanding about the phantom in the sense of it being the resurrection body was gradually undermining their claim to dominance. They recognized at once—as perhaps no others did—the basic world historical importance of what Rudolf Steiner was developing. They decided therefore to fight against it in the most acute way. Nothing was more suitable for this purpose than to make use of powers inherent in radioactivity. The exploitation of this force had started 33 years earlier (1911) as a result of experiments carried out by the Englishman Rutherford (1871–1937) which inspired his model of the atom. This was referred to in a report made by G.Glöckler.[108]

In 1905—33 years before the splitting of the atom was envisaged by Hahn in Berlin—Rudolf Steiner, speaking about radioactivity in the same city, expressed himself as follows: 'In earlier times these atoms became more and more solidified; now, however, they are becoming increasingly separated. Radioactivity did not exist in earlier times and could not therefore be discovered. It has only existed for a few thousand years, because now the atoms split up more and more.'[109] This can be understood to mean that in the one part of earth evolution matter becomes more and more dense; the atoms, as Rudolf Steiner says, are more attached.

During the other part of earth evolution the spiritualizing effect of the ego causes the inner structure of matter to disintegrate again and start to become radioactive. The turning-point of this development came about at the time of the Mystery of Golgotha—evolution brings with it the necessary devolution; 'coming into existence' is balanced by 'passing out of existence'; consolidation by dissolution. According to a verbal account, Rudolf Steiner once said that radioactivity, contrary to all the beliefs of natural science, started to come into effect at the moment of Golgotha.*

When matter started to become radioactive a process began which will eventually lead to the dissolution of the earth-planet in the course of earth evolution. This also is part of the ageing process of the earth which necessitates an increasing detachment of the Earth Spirit, the Christ, from bodily nature. That corresponds with the fact that man has to strive to achieve a greater independence from his bodily processes during the second half of his life. Both of these processes, for earth and man, can only take place in a healthy way in and for the future if release is sought through the power of Christ. The power here referred to emanates from the resurrection body.

In the members of man's being the effect is primarily a loosening of his whole structure; in the body of the earth it results in radioactivity. Understood in this way, radioactivity can be seen as a phenomenon necessarily connected with the evolution of the earth and as such presents no great threat to mankind, especially not if the meaning of it is understood and is met on a soul-spiritual level.

A special technique employed by the forces of evil is to tear an ephemeral truth out of the course of evolution. Lucifer attacks mankind by binding it to an outlived impulse from the past; Ahriman attempts to gain power over humanity by snatching something from the future and introducing it too early and too quickly into the evolutionary current. The opponents of human Christian development have used the latter technique to unleash atomic power. The luciferic counterpart to this, in the above mentioned sense, lies in the wave of world-wide nationalistic movements, in which Central Europe played a specially tragic role.

We must also consider the question as to how far the asuras influence mankind when we deal with and make use of atomic power. Rudolf Steiner has only rarely spoken about this third evil power. The following statement about the asuras can be very illuminating: 'The asuras will generate evil with a far mightier force than was wielded by the satanic powers in the Atlantean epoch or by the luciferic spirits in the Lemurian epoch ... For these asuric spirits will prompt what has been seized hold of by them—namely the very core of man's being, the consciousness soul together with the 'I'—to unite with earthly materiality. Fragment after fragment will be torn out of the 'I', and in the same measure in which the asuric spirits establish themselves in the consciousness soul, man must leave parts of his existence behind on the earth. What thus becomes the prey of the asuric powers will be irretrievably lost. Not that the whole man need become their victim—but parts of his spirit will be torn away by the asuric powers. These asuric powers are heralded today by the prevailing tendency to live wholly in the material world and to be oblivious of the reality of spiritual beings and spiritual worlds.'[110]

Is this not the same as that which is otherwise called 'the sin against the Holy Spirit'—the only sin which cannot be forgiven? That means it is not a case of luciferic temptations or ahrimanic errors which can be set to rights again in the course of karma, but of effects which, as it were, go beyond karma and affect the ego directly during incarnation. It is evidently connected with the fact that the asuric spirits mainly affect the physical body and in such a way that the support of the latter is partly withdrawn from the ego, which consequently plunges down into the abyss. In normal circumstances the ego is engaged in transforming the physical body, whereby the consciousness soul is developed. The asuras work against this activity in order to prevent the ego developing in the direction of Christianity. The asuras, as retarded beings of the Saturn evolution, are connected with the creation of the physical body.[111] These 'evil Saturn spirits' therefore have a certain effect upon the ego by way of the material-physical. But it must also be considered in what way the part-destruction of the ego is manifested outwardly, that is, where it has its material counterpart. Does not the partial break-up of the ego in a hidden sense correspond to the partial destruction of what is outwardly apparent? The ego, which received its substance from the spirits of form, is supported by the physical body, which derives its substance from the spirits of will. If this relationship, which expresses a hierarchical harmony, is disturbed, a double effect is produced on the ego, one affecting the ego (in a hidden way) and one affecting the physical-material substance (in an outwardly apparent way). One can certainly think of the unleashing of atomic energy as being connected with this disturbed relationship. One can also see from this whole context that the ego, by concentrating its whole metamorphosing energy upon the physical body, can form an attraction for the phantom while at the same time the ego is violently attacked by the material world. Because the ego seeks to transform the physical plane which it enters and takes hold of, it becomes involved in a terrible struggle. One of the ways in which this struggle was manifested was the unleashing of atomic energy in 1945.

People will be drawn, by those who commit the sin against the spirit, into a life which will darken and destroy their supersensible nature and make it into something one-sidedly earthy. Through the atomic explosions both culprits and victims alike were plunged into happenings the dimensions of which have still not been comprehended. It was certainly to be expected after the discovery of nuclear fission, and the consequent destruction attendant thereon, that this would also be further exploited. This, however, could not be more quickly or effectively done than by the starting of the Second World War by Hitler. The latter played the role of the willing and outstandingly efficient tool, characterized by Johannes Tautz as someone possessed or led.[112] We shall refer to Hitler again in another part of this account. In order to develop the atomic bomb a situation had to be brought about which appeared to be life-threatening, especially for the western countries. The preliminary success of the German army made the situation more acute and accelerated the development that was mainly borne by Jewish scientists, who were excluded from Europe by Hitler. At tremendous pecuniary, technical and personal expenditure (at times 400,000 people were at work on the atomic bomb project) it soon came to the detonating of the first atomic bomb, which made a deep incision into mankind's history and brought about a turning-point in life on earth.

The ageing process of the earth is made more acute by its having happened too early. The gradual releasing of the spirit from matter was replaced by a process in which the spirit is dragged down into the abyss owing to a premature material degeneration. The body of Christ, the earth, is to become estranged from the effects of the Resurrection. A cosmic battle for the earth is being waged, in which the ahrimanic, and also the asuric powers and their servants, are consciously directing their wills towards eliminating the possibilities of the Resurrection. This holds the dimension of a second Crucifixion, born out of cosmic hatred and human despotism, intended to cancel out the effects of the first Crucifixion, which was a free deed of sacrifice. The physical bodies of human beings, which are intimately connected with the earth-organism, are drawn into this battle, the effects of which also spread to the etheric bodies of earth and man. The impairment of the forces of the human blood and reproductive systems through nuclear radiation shows that it is the etheric organization that has been taken hold of by the ego which is especially affected (see section dealing with 1932/33).

If the destruction of Central Europe is to be regarded as a significant victory for the forces of the opponents of mankind, the use of atomic power and all its consequences must also be reckoned as such. This terrible aspect of things is highlighted by the fact that in the further course of events the atom bomb has become the single most universal means of domination, whereby the atomic stalemate that has been brought about by reciprocal intensification has only aggravated the situation. The destruction of civilization is thereby technically possible today. Life on earth can be immensely and incalculably damaged.

Who can doubt that power and domination on earth today are derived from the atom bomb? Who does not see that the general fear for one's life works throughout the world as a soul-dominating force that paralyses all human activities? Fear, however, is the mighty power which Ahriman instils into human souls from the earthly material where he rules, hoping thereby to draw them down to serve his purposes. His servants, 'who in a heinously wicked hour, planned destruction for the human race,'[113] succeeded in making fear not only their prime weapon, but—in reversal of the truth—called it the basis of 'peace'. To call shrinking back from universal annihilation 'peace' is one of the most terrible perversions of a most deeply Christian impulse. In actual fact peace in man's soul—and, from that, peace in the community—springs from the activity of Christ within it. The only way that peace can be introduced into a wicked world is for the individual soul to allow itself to be penetrated by the power of Christ, whereby fear is overcome. This peace that fills the soul not only overcomes evil but also counteracts estrangement from the world, which arises as the luciferic counterpart to fear.

To summarize what has just been said, those people who tried to gain world rulership through the 'sin against the spirit' gathered their forces for a tremendous attack against the spiritual work of Rudolf Steiner in 1911/12 which, among other things, came to expression in 1945 in the atomic explosions. By this means a necessary power of dissolution of earth's evolution was turned into its opposite by excessive concentration and premature technical application, and became a drastic means of spreading fear and shock. By this means the enemy seeks to oppose what was to have been brought down to earth by Kaspar Hauser in the nineteenth century and by Rudolf Steiner in the twentieth century. The titanic efforts become understandable because for them it was a matter concerning nothing less than world domination. This aim was pursued with complete disregard for human needs and—if necessary—with an almost unlimited wish to destroy.

Schiller, with gifted historical insight, has characterized such a personality, pursuing hidden but decisive aims, in the figure of the Grand Inquisitor in his *Don Carlos*, who expresses what is here referred to as 'putrefaction rather than freedom'.

We have tried to explain how the historical course of pre-war times, the Second World War and the post-war period, has been directed by an overriding impulse which involved the nations concerned—including Germany—in the single aim of destroying Central Europe. On the other hand one could argue that serious discrepancies existed between National Socialism and the western democracies and that ultimately the insatiability and excesses of Hitler led consciously to the outbreak of the Second World War. One could also point out that it was only with the greatest difficulty and with the help of many nations that the world threat of National Socialism could be overcome.

On closer examination, however, it is clear that these arguments can be invalidated. The leading western politicians actually encouraged Hitler in his ever more arrogant exploits during the thirties by their excessive indulgence and sheer incomprehensible laxity. The successes that were conceded to Hitler enticed him ever further. It does not need a great deal of psychology to see that there could be nothing more seductive for the irresponsible nature of Hitler than constant success. Why did the western democratic powers wish to have Germany changed into such a state and then allow an obvious dictator, who should have been fought against on principle, to have every imaginable concession? Where was the adherence to principle and morality on which so much had been built after the First World War? Hitler's strength resulted not least from the real—or feigned—weakness of his adversaries. Can we not see that everything was aimed at allowing him to be the cause of the calamity which resulted in the outbreak of the Second World War?

This view includes the thought that for the cold-blooded possessors of knowledge who directed Hitler and his seeming opponents, a world war could only lead to the downfall of

Central Europe and to the alteration of all power relationships in the above explained sense.

Already at that time there were people who—without being able to penetrate to the underlying causes—turned against the violence and lack of judgement. When in 1938 Colonel General Beck, as General Chief of Staff, opposed Hitler's plan of campaign, it was not only on grounds of moral responsibility, but also from a conviction of the futility of such a war. A modern war, as a technically economic venture over which ultimately the powers of production are decisive, could never be won by Germany and its allies against the whole of the rest of the world. This view was also supported by the later General Chief of Staff Halder, who, in 1942, at the height of military prowess, realized that the war had been lost for Germany because the human and material loss, in spite of successes, had pushed the balance of power hopelessly in favour of the enemy. The facts basically vindicated the clear prediction of Beck. It is characteristic of the whole situation that the outbreak of war was not the outcome of planned and purposeful thinking taking into account the economic and technical realities, but was the result of megalomaniacal blindness. The latter, proceeding from Hitler, spread to the surroundings and paralysed its clear judgement to a wide extent.

If one remembers that a certain effect was envisaged for 1945, then the known facts appear in quite a different light. They serve these intended aims since 1911/12, partly as a means to an end, partly as an effective far-reaching illusion.

It is in no way suggested here that the leading western politicians acted in conscious agreement with those whom Rudolf Steiner calls 'the background figures'. One cannot speak of a conscious thought-directed control of the situation by any of the personalities involved. In the historical events of the thirties a dim and clouded consciousness is to be perceived, a fact upon which a significant light will later be thrown.

It may be regarded as self-evident—but must nevertheless be especially emphasized—that on no account is it a question of shifting the blame from Germany on to some other nation.

The nations as such are to be regarded as the victims in this connection, whereby, however, the single human being as a member of his nation cannot escape co-responsibility. Those who started and directed these events, which misused innumerable people as willing tools, carry a paramount responsibility for it owing to their conscious participation. It is a matter involving small international circles of people whose nationality is of secondary importance. It is only a confusing and distracting point of view if one speaks of the guilt or innocence of nations.

The events of the years 1944/45, which are here considered as the fulfilment of deeds consciously set into the stream of history by the opponents of human evolution in 1911/12, certainly represent an end to the domination of National Socialism—which had fulfilled its appointed task. As far as that goes, however, they do not represent the end of an era, but introduce a further development which lands humanity still more firmly into the hands of those who wish to gain control of the world for their anti-spiritual purposes. In the already quoted conversation between Rudolf Steiner and Count Polzer-Hoditz at the end of November 1916 about Kaspar Hauser, there is expressed what has largely come to pass in 1945. 'From that time onwards [at the turn of the eighteenth to nineteenth century], the range of tasks was clearly defined, but in their aims they were all the more effectively directed towards world domination. The ideological and spiritual concerns had been exclusively placed into the hands of the Jesuits; the economic affairs had been entrusted to the Anglo-American Lodges, the Lodges of the West. These plans, however, will lead more and more to tragic conflicts and catastrophes, because all these plans fail to reckon with the human being and with human evolution. What was intended for Kaspar Hauser was shattered by human beings.'

The character of the year 1945 as the turning point has been formulated by Solzhenitsyn with pregnant brevity: 'From Adam till 1945'.[114] The impulses which were introduced at this turning point into the three spheres of the social organism in order to obtain, or to maintain, world rulership will be described in what follows. The calamitousness of these impulses was not noticed because neediness was so prevalent and victory over the Hitler regime distracted the mind from everything else.

To economic life, which formerly directed and controlled the whole social organism, was added the impulse of unlimited growth of the powers of production, which, in the course of a generation, led to the soul-life of countless people becoming paralysed or tied up by affluence and to earth-forces being polluted or destroyed to a disastrous extent. This growth— which wrongly bears this lovely name—must of necessity be recognized as a cancerous formation which is liable to badly damage or even completely wreck the whole social organism. The cancerous growth, which is antisocial in the deepest sense, becomes visible in the poverty and misery which the affluence and riches of the industrial nations bestow on the so-called Third World countries. Rudolf Steiner, in his main rule for the social life, which works in the social organism with the compulsion of a natural law, has understood the connection between egoism on the one hand and poverty and misery on the other.[115] Egoism, in which most people today see the only effective motivation in commercial life, belongs together with cancerous growth. Egoism, which wants to gather to itself more and more things, does not see that the social life is thereby deprived of the basis provided by the fact that all work is directed towards the other person.

The destructive process of economic growth is universally strengthened by the gigantic armament efforts. At present these exceed by far everything that was produced in this direction during the Second World War. To that is added the fact that since 1945 atomic weapons were introduced, the unimaginably destructive potential of which can only be produced by tremendous economic achievements.

The process of economic growth here mentioned, active since 1945, characteristically unites during the course of the years with the so-called peaceful use of nuclear power. This connection of economics with nuclear energy which should permanently sustain growth culminated in recent years in the motto of political economics: 'Growth only through nuclear power!' What is to be expected from this 'marriage' will ensue from the temporal and spiritual origin of its partners.

In 1945 international judicial life, too, was seized by an impulse that was decidedly opposed to development. It consisted of the fact that all human rights were only seemingly based on the freedom of the individual. Under the name of 'the liberation of the people' this idea was introduced by [Woodrow] Wilson into international circles in 1917, but only after 1945 did it acquire universal acceptance and produce alarming results. As the principle of non-interference in the internal affairs of other nations, this impulse served the universal suppression of the individual. It is actually the enemy of human rights.

It is thanks to Rudolf Steiner that the disastrous historical character of this impulse was immediately recognized and countered by him in the sharpest manner. Rudolf Steiner writes already in 1917: 'The freeing of the nations is possible. It can only be the *result* of the freeing of the individual, not the *basis* upon which the freeing of the individual takes place. When individuals have been freed then the nations become free through them.'[116] In another place he makes clear what is meant by the freedom of nations in Wilson's view: 'If this is understood then it will straightaway become apparent why this war has come about and why, under the false ensign of "a war to free the nations", it is being waged in order to suppress the German nation and in a wider sense to suppress all independent national life in Central Europe. If one unmasks the Wilson programme according to the latest coded version issued by the *Entente* powers, one will realize that to carry it out would signify no less than the destruction of Central European freedom. But this does not prevent Wilson talking about the freedom of nations; for the world does not run according to words, but according to facts which arise as a result of these words. Central Europe is in need of true freedom, but Wilson is not speaking about true freedom. The whole of the western world has not the slightest understanding of the true freedom which is needed by Central Europe. One talks about the freedom of nations and does not thereby have the true human freedom in mind, but a chimerical collective freedom of human relationships as they have developed in western European countries and in America.'[116]

With reference to the single human being, Rudolf Steiner summarizes it as follows: 'The all-human aspect and the relationship of the nations to one another today and in the future demands that the individual human being must be free. A person must be allowed to belong to a nation, to a religious community, or have other commitments according to his general human aspirations without being prevented by political or commercial considerations from state regulations.'[116] Today everyone can see what devastating consequences the wrong principle of the liberation of nations, advocated by Wilson and gullibly accepted by others, has had on countless numbers of human beings. When will this wrong principle, the devastation of which has been historically demonstrated to excess, be finally abandoned?

The United Nations Organization (UNO), founded in 1945 as the successor to the League of Nations, had certainly put the Human Rights Charter at the forefront of its striving, but as a combined activity of various nations it had neither the insight not the will to really and truly defend the rights of individuals against the outrageous misuse of civic powers. The impossibility of its composition led for more than a generation to endless cant and unbearable deceit. In most recent times this world-organization had to admit that by far the greater number of its members violated the human rights clause to which they had solemnly sworn allegiance. This catastrophic malignant process, arising out of the fundamental error regarding the human right to freedom, cannot be more clearly described than that. The overcoming of this error entails a considerable curtailment of civic powers and therefore can never proceed from the state, but only from individual human beings who develop a sufficiently strong spiritual life.

With that we become aware of spiritual existence. Ultimately the catastrophe of 1945 is the result of the collapse of spiritual life—especially the exclusion of that pertaining to Central

Europe. In order to avoid misunderstandings it should be emphatically stated here that by spiritual life is meant that power which supplies a contact with the supersensible world in a humanly appropriate manner and thereby becomes the moving and shaping element in all public matters. To grasp the spirit in this way and to apply it effectively in the shaping of history was one of the main tasks allotted to Kaspar Hauser. The direct connection between Kaspar Hauser's birth and imprisonment in 1812 and the world-wide catastrophe of 1945 will be explained more fully from a different aspect later on.

When Rudolf Steiner states that the Jesuits have robbed mankind of religiosity, he means by that the loss of living contact with the supersensible worlds, as this, for instance, should have been brought into being through Kaspar Hauser. The Jesuits are opposed to this spirit because it would nullify their claims to world dominance. The lack of strength and imagination of the spiritual life intentionally paralysed in this way is also demonstrated by the fact that it can neither find the possibility of curbing the degenerate economic process, nor can it create a foundation to rightly liberate the individual human being. In this way we can understand the indication of Rudolf Steiner to the effect that a healing of the social organism can only come about if a new spiritual life is developed by man in freedom. The events of 1945 and the impulses which have been working since then to the detriment of the social organism mean that such an exhortation calls upon all our human forces.

The survey of the years 1944/45 cannot of course be concluded without raising the question as to the results of Rudolf Steiner's acts of recognition which have been described according to their world-wide historical significance; for it is a fact that 'all deeds in the course of history undergo a metamorphosis according to the 33-year rhythm', not only the evil deeds.

One positive outcome of Rudolf Steiner's indications can be seen in the fact that the forbidden Anthroposophical Society and all the institutions working from the same principles in Germany and its occupied territories during the time of the

Nazi regime have experienced remarkable progress since 1945. In spite of many opposing circumstances and some inner difficulties, an astonishing spread and increase in the number of institutions has taken place. Spiritual scientific work has brought fruitful results in many fields of research. Especially in practical activities anthroposophical endeavours have received a much wider acceptance than heretofore. This process could be observed since the centenary of Rudolf Steiner's birth in 1961, and then to an increasing extent in the early seventies.

In still another, twofold, way the spiritual events of 1911/12 stand in relationship to those of 1944/45. At that time there were apparently only very few people who grasped the truly worldwide importance of Rudolf Steiner's ideas. The opponents, however, as he often emphasized, have understood him quickest and best. The intervention of the adversaries was to counteract the danger by which they were confronted. It prevented Rudolf Steiner's spiritual impulses of 1911/12 from taking immediate effect in the historical course of events. If there had been a sufficiently large number of people awake to this knowledge then the First World War could have been avoided. The fact that these spiritual impulses were prevented from taking effect did not, of course, abolish their importance or force in any way. These impulses had to take another route to mankind, they had to change their form. This metamorphosis can be understood by means of a kind of spiritual rule, according to which that which has been presented to a human being or a group of human beings by the spiritual world at a particular moment, if not taken up by them and acted upon— for whatever reason—will have to be experienced by them through pain and suffering.

The catastrophes, which are so necessary for mankind, cause great harm on the one hand. On the other, however, a compensation for the lost opportunity is given through grief and pain. The evil principle here meets its limit when it drives mankind into pain and suffering—for through pain man is able to experience the proximity of the spiritual world and the reality of his own higher nature.

In connection with the fact that the impulse towards the Threefold Commonwealth was not taken up by mankind in 1919/20, Rudolf Steiner once said that people would have to learn through 'blood and tears' what was needed by the social organism. A connection such as this can be experienced in the immeasurable pain, sorrows and sacrifices of innumerable people of many races in the years 1944/45. Through that a meaning can be discerned in the tragic happenings in the face of which all words fail us. Innumerable human beings have met an early untimely death. Through a sacrificial death the soul is enabled to meet the Christ to Whom in life the way was barred. This threshold experience which man has as he crosses over in death has been admirably captured by Albrecht Haushofer in one of his Moabite Sonnets. In his poem *The Resurrected One* Haushofer reshapes in memory the resurrection picture by Matthias Grünewald (on the altar in Colmar), his experience of the Christ event at the present day, which will be dealt with later on.

The Resurrected One

I have beheld Him in a thousand ways.
As Judge of Worlds, both wrathful and sublime,
As crowned with thorns and as Madonna's Babe—
Yet none of these will wholly bide with me.

Now do I feel that only one is true
As He is shown by Master Grünewald—
But not the pale One, hank'ring after death—
The Light-enhanced One, this One is the Christ.

Man's skill alone was not the artist here,
Lightly arising from sepulchral gloom,
His head with golden splendour wreathed about.

Bathed in the spirit-light of all the colours,
Substantial still, and yet unlimited,
God's Son ascends towards the lap of God.[117]

In other poetical works something of this event has been preserved, for instance in the *Requiem* of Max Frisch composed in January 1945: 'Now they are singing again', and in the Autobiography of Jacques Lusseyran, *And There Was Light*, in the chapter called 'Life and Death' describing his experiences in the Buchenwald concentration camp in the years 1944/45.[118]

The results for those who have undergone a death of sacrifice will only be able to be worked out in a succeeding life. But for the earth and for humanity as a whole the incalculable sacrifices will also be of direct significance; they will counteract destructive egoism and will constitute the strongest forces of healing and blessing. Humanity is seen from the spiritual world as a unity, as a great coherent whole. The greatest imaginable damage is caused by spirit-enmity, by the battle waged against the spirit. This damage, inflicted by the spirits whose wish is to drag mankind down into the abyss, will have to be compensated for if the destiny of all mankind is not to be thrown off balance. It is the innocent victims of sacrifice claimed by the catastrophes which make up the bitter, but unavoidable, means of compensation.*

Whoever would prevent the sacrifices caused by the catastrophes must do all in his power to overcome spiritual enmity. It is only by such an endeavour as this that the catastrophes which bring pain and suffering can be made superfluous.

The destiny of Kaspar Hauser, through his sacrifice in the world of the nineteenth century, which was so opposed to the spirit, is seen by the inner eye as forming a link between the physical and the spiritual world. The already quoted statement by Rudolf Steiner: 'It should not have happened like this, but what has happened was necessary' (cf p.63), holds good for the events of 1944/45.

With this thought one approaches very nearly the secret of evil, which is so difficult to fathom. The healing comes about as a result of evil in the sense of that power 'which ever strives after evil but ever causes good'.[119] A boundary is thereby set to evil, a factor which eludes mephisthophelian calculation, for all its cunning.

In the world-historical scene, recorded in the 19th chapter of the Gospel of St John, the boundary set to evil is portrayed in an exemplary way. Pilate reminds the captive Christ that he has power to either condemn Him or to set Him free. Christ's reply to this was: 'Thou couldst have no power over me, except it were given thee from above'.

1977/78

In looking at the years 1977/78 it is possible to check what was said about the years 1944/45. Because now the first 33 years thereafter have been completed. It seems necessary to point out that, according to the law of the 33 years, the time of the Second World War (1939/45) is expressed in the events of the years 1972 to 1978. Two events take their start from this time and come to a kind of conclusion in 1978, but they are and remain something belonging to the future.

Through the visit of Nixon to Peking in 1972 a first meeting between the USA and China came about. The mutual efforts to find common ground led in 1978 to the acceptance of the official diplomatic and economic relationships. The world-historically incalculable significance of the destruction of Central Europe in 1945 can thereby be imagined. The loss of the Centre leads inevitably to the commencement, after 33 years, of a co-operation between the Far East and the Far West. This alliance could prove to be a fatal constellation, for from the start it is only motivated by the interests of commerce and power politics. China supports the world supremacy of the USA; it has chosen the way of the consumer society and is therefore united in treading the path of commercial growth as characterized above.

Added to this is the fact that China and Japan entered into an alliance of friendship and trade in 1978. A procedure of this kind is characterized by Solovieff at the beginning of his story called *The Antichrist* as a moment of awakening of the Yellow Race.

In 1973 the oil-producing Arab States used their oil as a weapon against the industrial nations for the first time. The greatly increased price could be met at first. Through the Mohammedan revolution of the Shiite leader Khomeni in Iran, the question of quantity was added to that of price. The revival of archaic powers created a situation which inclined people towards the use of nuclear energy, just as Hitler, by unleashing the Second World War, made the precipitate building of the atom bomb appear necessary. Anyway, it is certain that during these years the destructive power of atomic weapons was perfected and the commercial use of nuclear energy was accepted worldwide. In spite of many efforts running counter to this trend there was ultimately no country, with the exception of Austria, which spoke out against atomic energy as such. In this case it was not all just a matter of being for or against atomic energy. What is disastrous for mankind's future is above all the ever more obvious trinity of state supremacy, striving after commercial expansion and the application of nuclear power. This trinity has the tendency to control the whole of the social organism, or, as the case may be, to take its place and to create conditions, the irreversibility of which will make future progress impossible. The impulses which were implanted into historical evolution in 1945 have now become a terrifying reality. At the World Summit meeting for Commerce in Bonn in the summer of 1978 the seven leading industrial nations agreed to tackle the existing problems, particularly that of unemployment, by means of increased industrial development for which the further development of atomic power would be needed. A decision of this nature is certainly consistent with the wishes of those who base their world dominance on a perverted economy. One is deluded about this state of affairs by the suggestion that circumstances allow no other solution. This, however, only applies so long as the spirit is condemned to ineffectuality.

Not to be overlooked is the fact that civilization finds itself on a downward trend and that the forces which would drag man down into the abyss have grown stronger. Inherent necessity from without, paralysis of soul from within would like to put an end to the initiative being of man. This is an expression of the fact that spirit-enmity has become an integral part of the reality created by man. In the relationship of man towards the spiritual world there is the greatest possible contrast between credit and debit.

That also has to do with the character of the Michael Age which has lasted already for 100 years. The Michaelic Spirit of the Times waits for the free deeds of man proceeding from spiritual knowledge. Through Rudolf Steiner Michael has placed Anthroposophy with man in order to make it possible for him to understand the spiritual world; Michael speaks to man through the events of the time and the rhythmical course of history, but he does not directly intervene, because what he wants is the recognition of the individual. Thus everything depends upon striving after knowledge, whereby solemnity and strength are acquired to participate in reality. True knowledge will become reality in the course of time, if human will, through which it comes about, makes itself worthy to be filled by the will of spiritual beings. True progress of humanity cannot be acquired through human option, for man stands in far too intimate a relationship to the spiritual world during this age of light, even though this is not sufficiently well recognized consciously. In the process of making the human will into a vessel for the spirit by striving after knowledge, communities will also develop in order to carry humaneness into the future.

Looking back on the 33-year periods starting with the birth of Kaspar Hauser in 1812, it can be ascertained that at all stages traces can be found which more or less point to the gaps which have been left by the elimination of Kaspar Hauser. And it can be a significant experience for us to become aware of Kaspar Hauser's mission which still continues to this day and to realize that what can be done towards steering this mission to a beneficial conclusion depends upon the free enlightenment of as many people as possible.

The death series from 1833

After having dealt with the sequences relating to Kaspar Hauser's birth according to the 33-year rhythm, it now behoves us to investigate the same rhythm in connection with his death. For that we have to take into account that in the course of events a kind of double aspect is apparent in this series: the results of Kaspar Hauser's murder as it stands over against other world-shaking events. The latter are of especial interest in so far as they have to do with the suppressed mission of Kaspar Hauser.

In connection with Kaspar Hauser's murder in December 1833, there is an allusion to the 33-year rhythm in the quoted passage by Rudolf Steiner that 'the heads of the western Lodges and the Jesuits have worked together for 150 years— demonstrably so from January 1802 onwards' (vide p.108). It is not known wherein Rudolf Steiner found confirmation of this co-operation, whether he based it on historical facts or on the results of spiritual investigation. If we look at the turn of the eighteenth to nineteenth century from the aspect of the united attack by these two organizations seeking world supremacy, we shall find the obvious confirmation of this in the murder of Kaspar Hauser 33 years later. The 33-year rhythm is probably more precisely adhered to than at first appears from Rudolf Steiner's reference, for the definitive act of union and co-operation must certainly have been preceded by deliberations and decisions to arrange and prepare for it. The first disastrous consequences of this fatal union is certainly the violent death of Kaspar Hauser. The endeavour to commit therewith the perfect crime, as was described in Chapter 1, illustrates the amount of consciousness and ruthless will with which the proceedings were carried out.

If the 33-year rhythm is used to explain the events of 1833, then it might be argued that Kaspar Hauser's murder was necessitated and made inevitable by the setback which his opponents experienced when they released him. If they did not wish to see all their plans miscarry they would have to decide to kill him. Without doubt they would have found it preferable if Kaspar Hauser could have disappeared and perished in some inconspicuous fashion. But there was a power in his appearing at Whitsuntide 1828 which prevented that happening. (cf pp.14 et seq.)

The argument rests on the fact that people think linearly from one year to the next. One year is usually explained out of the preceding one. From a purely earthly aspect as it is understood by the intellect, this is justified. However, it does not exclude the possibility that in the facts themselves other connections can be discovered. If one regards the outward aspect and looks at it with the 33-year rhythm in mind, one can see what was intended here by the union of the two organizations in about 1800—the elimination of Christian activity on the physical plane. It was *this* which necessitated the murder of the youth who was the expression of pure humanity and goodness. Through the power which is latent in the 33-year rhythm, the murder of Kaspar Hauser leads to the unmasking of the impulses working against what is human.

It would, of course, have been in the interest of humanity's progress to have kept Kaspar Hauser safe, but for that it would have been necessary to have debilitated the strong powers that were intent on preventing the fulfilment of his mission. As this did not succeed, the opposing impulses had to run their course.

What the plans and intentions of the leadership of humanity had been, which the murder of Kaspar Hauser frustrated, has been made clear to us through the statement which Rudolf Steiner made in his conversation with Count Polzer-Hoditz, quoted in Chapter 2: 'South Germany should have become the new Grail-Castle of the new Knights of the Grail' and the cradle of future events. The spiritual ground had been well prepared by all those personalities whom we know as Goethe, Schiller, Hölderlin, Herder and others. Kaspar Hauser was to have gathered around him, as it were, all that existed in this spiritual ground thus prepared. But that was not wanted by those circles (the western Lodges and the Jesuits). They could not tolerate a centre which was awakening to consciousness if they were not to relinquish their power and designs for power. 'A spirit such as Goethe's frightened them. Napoleon forced them to unite and form a league for the aspired-to world domination in the sphere of ideology and commerce. Napoleon had already thwarted their effort; it was he who fundamentally forced the two currents into union.' (The text quoted on p.278 continues from here. It is necessary to keep the various statements in mind.)

Southern Germany, which includes Baden, Württemberg, Bavaria and also Austria, was also the region selected to take the main role in the initial realization of the spiritual-social impulses. Had this plan been fulfilled in Kaspar Hauser, the mission of Rudolf Steiner, which was set to occur later in this region, would have been more consciously prepared and people would thereby have been instructed how to meet the decisive events of the twentieth century in a more conscious and understanding way.

Rudolf Steiner emphasized the fact that the preparatory work for Kaspar Hauser had mainly been done in the spiritual and cultural field. But on the other hand this preparatory work called forth the strongest opposition on the part of the enemies of progress: 'A spirit such as Goethe's frightened them'. This is a statement which one cannot take seriously enough, for it explains much of the subsequent happenings. The Goethean spirit is characterized by the fact that through it the individual human being seeks and finds a living connection to the supersensible world. By this Goethe gives to every personality the possibility of partaking in this development; in this sense he can be seen as the great forerunner of Anthroposophy. From the fact that this work of preparation was already opposed in the strongest way possible, one can gauge with what distaste the rise and spread of Anthroposophy itself was greeted by those circles. The discussion of the years 1911/12 already hinted as much.

Rudolf Steiner points to Napoleon as a personality standing in close connection with the events of the turn of the century. One might be surprised at first at the role Rudolf Steiner assigns to Napoleon. His historical deeds—springing out of his very nature—reveal a dangerous lack of cohesion. Napoleon holds allegiance to a progressive, forward-looking principle in contrast to the powers which would wish to fetter mankind to what is ancient in order to win dominion over them. From the remarks made by Rudolf Steiner it follows that, apart from the existing family ties and the founding of the Grand Duchy of Baden, Napoleon had inner ties with Kaspar Hauser. This was described by Heyer in the first place as a polar relationship, as a Mercury-Mars polarity.[120] Apart from that, Napoleon should have been the one to prepare the way for Kaspar Hauser's activity. This only came about in an outward way, not in the realization of inner impulses. That is connected with the fact that Napoleon himself 'forgot' his own true pre-natal mission, which would have been a contribution towards the peaceful uniting of Europe.[121] By forgetting his real mission, Napoleon lived out his life according to the Mars impulse in its old form. Although the transformation of the Mars forces, as Rudolf Steiner describes in a lecture on 18 December 1912,[122] had been experienced by Napoleon in his pre-natal life, it became clouded over for him on his way to earth. For that reason he was unable to gather around him the representatives of German spiritual life—they had to become his opponents, like Fichte, Beethoven and Schiller.

The task of preparing the way for Kaspar Hauser was fulfilled by Napoleon in so far as he upset the plans of the Jesuits and the members of the western Lodges. But the opposition which he thereby raised and which drove these organizations to unite, was responsible for making the carrying out of Kaspar Hauser's mission impossible. The latter is certainly the result of the split in Napoleon's nature, of his 'forgotten task'.

1866

The year 1866 shows the first stage of the repercussions resulting from Kaspar Hauser's murder in the region destined for his activity. The Austro-Prussian conflict, which was an expression of the north-south antagonism, came to an end with Prussia finally gaining supremacy. South Germany was unable to take over its predestined role and so the leadership necessarily devolved on Prussia, on Bismarck and on the Prussian King. Without direct reference to the Civil War of 1866, Rudolf Steiner says in his conversation with Polzer-

Hoditz regarding Bismarck and his relationship to Kaspar Hauser: 'On these "planned" ruins [he means the result of the exclusion and ultimate murder of Kaspar Hauser] the black-and-white principle gained ascendancy. The black-and-white principle, however, is something constructed, something exclusive. This is also the tragedy of Bismarck himself who was quite well able to construct the model for a Federal State, the constructive idea of a true Central Federation, but could not supply the supporting idea, that which would have made a State construction of this kind appear necessary and justified. It was that which Bismarck was seeking in Frankfurt, too, the Goethean spirit, that which Kaspar Hauser could have developed in the region of South Germany, but did not live to accomplish. It was in Frankfurt, actually, where Bismarck encountered the principle of black-and-white and all which then bound him to the King of Prussia. It was from then on that the era of the lawyer began, but politics is not a legal problem.'

By black-and-white Rudolf Steiner apparently means that which results from the union of the Jesuits and the western Lodges. This principle involves social life in a polarity between commercial and apparently spiritual tasks which, because they are not balanced by a third principle, do not uplift but paralyse society. If this contrast is seen as a luciferic/ahrimanic polarity, the unfruitful and paralysing effect of this swing between opposites is easier to understand. Human beings are torn—without knowing what is happening to them—from one pole to the other and become entangled in the 'company affairs of Lucifer and Ahriman' as Rudolf Steiner once expressed it.[123]

The transition from what should have come about through Kaspar Hauser in Southern Germany to what then developed in Prussia took place to begin with in Bismarck himself. Bismarck, too, needed the spirit-inspired activity of Kaspar Hauser in order to awaken him to his higher mission. But as he was unable to find what he needed, his life necessarily took another turn. He now had to take a course for which he was not predestined because there was no alternative.

On this example one can very well study the methods employed by those who arrange things from the background. Their masterpieces are always successful in cases where situations can be contrived in which things are forced upon people without any other possibility being available.* Polite reticence can then be practised. A direct, even compromising, action is unnecessary. The 'realities' effect what has to be done, 'common sense' decides the only right action to be taken. And nobody asks who created the situation which arose. The point of view which makes it impossible for the supersensible Christian impulse to take effect is always victorious. The aim of all these events is to separate earthly and human development from these impulses altogether.

It is essential to take Rudolf Steiner's advice seriously when he says that the principle of black-and-white leads to the 'era of the lawyer'. Whoever knows even a little about present day political and social reality knows also how very much legal thinking has in the meantime become predominant and decisive to the extent that everyday life is almost intolerably burdened by it.

The founding of the Empire in 1871, which followed soon after the events of 1866, raises a problem with regard to the German Folk-spirit,[124] because of the fact that it occurred after a military victory. In characteristic fashion it raised the Prussian King of the Hohenzollern dynasty to be the German Emperor. This line of development, which was wrong because it was inconsistent with the spiritually objective impulses, led with a certain inevitability to the First World War, as was mentioned above in discussing the period around 1878. What was decisive for this inevitable result was the fact that only very few people realized that the wrong way was taken. Most people were dazzled by renown, success and progress.

The year 1866, with its shift from south to north, led to the fatal line of development which was only revealed in its true dimension 66 years later. Never before in German history has the discrepancy between what happened in history and what was needed by the spirit been so great. The illusion that was created in people's minds, coming out of the unknown murky background, was well nigh complete.

1899

It becomes only too plain from the political events around 1899 that something took place in 1866 that was, and still is, directed against the true interests of Central Europe. Bismarck was able, at least outwardly, to provide influence and gain worldwide acceptance for his newly founded Empire as a great power. But through and around William II, when Bismarck was no longer the political head of Germany, powers were at work which could unfold their malignant influence on Central Europe without hindrance. A spiritual emptiness and estrangement came about as a result of imperialistic colonial policy, commercial competition with England and the building of the fleet. At the turn of the century—66 years after the murder of Kaspar Hauser—the powers of Central Europe became so superficial that they were dissipated wrongly into the world and work in an erosive way. Thus the decisive infection of Central Europe was prepared, which showed up 33 years later. The inner process of erosion prepares for what happened in 1933. This has nothing to do with the fulfilment of the German character, but with an emptying out of the same. Into this vacuum utterly different powers from outside stream in.

That which takes place at the turn of the century in Central Europe is met from outside by the encirclement policy of England, against which no effective future remedy could be found by Germany. It was Edward VII, closely united with the English Lodges, who was behind this policy. Just as in the life of Kaspar Hauser it was Lord Stanhope who introduced the element from without, from the West, which brought about Kaspar Hauser's downfall, so on a historical level it was Edward VII who played the corresponding role in this case. The attacks levelled against Germany reach their first climax in 1907 with the coalition of England and France in the

Entente Cordiale. The attitude of the western powers during the thirties, delineated above (p.132), appears once more in a different light if it is looked at from the point of view of the 33-year rhythm and in connection with the encirclement policy of England at the beginning of the century. These events lead to such a spiritual vacuum in Central Europe during the thirties that, as a consequence, forces which seek to destroy the Centre are sucked in from outside.

What is indicated here becomes more explicable if one asks what the real aims were behind the unleashing of the Second World War in 1939. According to the 33-year rule the year 1939 would find its fulfilment in 1972. In that year the four-power treaty over Berlin and the territorial agreement between the two German states was signed. These events were merely the keystone to a development by which the separate states in Central Europe were forced to recognize, as a consequence of the Second World War, that a nationally coherent human community in Central Europe no longer existed. The final stage in the destruction of Central Europe had thereby been achieved. Not only was the old system of separate states finally and legitimately done away with, but the new German states, which had grown up in the meantime, were both placed, and still remain, in the greatest dependence on the spiritual and material powers of West and East which, in the long run, seriously hamper the effectiveness of Central Europe, or even exclude its activity. What was displayed on the world-stage in 1972 was the same that was secretly sowed in 1939. The destruction of Germany in the Second World War was not an unintentional result, but the aim of these martial practices to cause and achieve the obliteration of Central Europe. That seemingly contradicts what lived in the consciousness of those who arranged this war on the part of Germany, but that says nothing about the unconscious impulses which motivated these people. Misled by Hitler, most of the leading personalities accepted the vague ideas of raising Germany to the ranks of a Great- or World-power. Through that, however, the power which Hitler wielded over the spirit of Central Europe is shown to be hostile.

In Chapter 2 we quoted Schiller's poetic fragment *Deutsche Grösse* in which he warns against the inner enemies: 'That is not a German's greatness that he conquers with the sword'. The inner enmity against the true spiritual impulse of Central Europe, carried by a mighty will, became reality and is now easily recognized by everyone. There was, *from the very beginning*, no intention of making Germany great, but of destroying it.

The state of consciousness of those taking part on the side of Germany can be symptomatically characterized by pointing to the fact that Hitler, on hearing of England's guarantee on behalf of Poland signifying war, merely asked: 'And what now?' That which was to be reckoned with and, after what had already taken place, every responsible person expected would happen, was met here with paralysis and petrification as an expression of confusion and thoughtlessness. The loss of ego-conscious reasoning cannot be more clearly demonstrated than by that.

This exposition, which has for the sake of clarity dealt with certain things out of their true order, must now return to the year 1899. The death sequence coincides in 1899 with the end of Kali Yuga and with the ascending forces at the beginning of the age of light.

The end of Kali Yuga, the so-called 'Dark Age', is of world-historic significance. The meaning of this era, which lasted 5000 years from 3101BC to AD1899 was to darken the spiritual world ever more and more for the consciousness of men on earth, until finally the impression could arise that no spiritual world existed. Through this far-reaching dimming of con-sciousness it became possible for man to become a citizen of the *earth*. It was of special importance for man, who in ancient times possessed an instinctive knowledge of reincarnation and karma, of rebirth and destiny, that he should lose this knowledge in order to learn to value the single earth-life to its full extent. It is true that, up till the beginning of the new age, supersensible impulses played into the soul-life of mankind. In some ways people were led through these in a dreamlike fashion. It was not intended for man to know the supersensible world consciously at that time, and so he was not able to determine his own position with regard to it. With the end of Kali Yuga the relationship of the spiritual world to the physical world was radically altered. An expression of this fact is the appearance of Anthroposophy, the life's work of Rudolf Steiner. One of the fundamental spiritual changes consists of the fact that the description of spiritual facts is made public and is directed to the understanding of everyone. Rudolf Steiner began his spiritual work to this end in June 1899, exactly at the time that Kali Yuga ended. Through his activity he fulfilled a mission thousands of years old. His work united with a cosmic point of time and at the same time also with a rhythm which began with Kaspar Hauser's exclusion. The close relationship which exists between Rudolf Steiner and Kaspar Hauser will be clarified in the next chapter.

Rudolf Steiner writes about the start of his spiritual work in his autobiography at the beginning of Chapter 30: 'The decision to speak publicly about esoteric life from my own research and experience impelled me to write, on the occasion of the one hundred and fiftieth anniversary of Goethe's birth (28 August 1899), an article for the *Magazin* on Goethe's fairy tale, *The Green Snake and the Beautiful Lily*, under the title *Goethes geheime Offenbarung* [Goethe's Secret Revelation]. This essay, it is true, was not very esoteric, but to say more would have made too great a demand on my public.'

In the same year he was asked by Countess and Count Brockdorff to hold a lecture for their group. During his first lecture (about Nietzsche) he remarked that 'among his audience there were personalities who had a great interest in the spiritual world'. He then reports further: 'I therefore suggested, when asked to give another lecture, to speak on the subject of "Goethe's Secret Revelation". And in *this* lecture I became quite esoteric in talking about the fairy story. It was an important experience for me to be able to speak in words which were stamped with the seal of the spirit, whereas formerly, during my time in Berlin, I had been forced by circumstances to only let the spirit shine through my descriptions.' A beginning was thus made in harmony with

Rudolf Steiner's predestined preoccupation with Goethe. Goethe had developed the spiritual life of Central Europe in such a way as to prepare it for the coming spiritual revelation. Rudolf Steiner's decision to speak openly about his knowledge of the spiritual world wherever it was asked for was not so much the result of his own intention or his own will—it sprang from the recognition of the spiritual needs of the time. This is exemplified best by an extract of a letter to Marie von Sivers in which he writes: 'I can only say that had the Master not convinced me that, in spite of all this, theosophy is necessary for our age, I would only have written philosophical books and lectured on literature and philosophy even after 1901.'[125] With this remark a light is thrown upon those individualities, here called 'Masters', who, whether incarnated or not, seek to guide the destinies of mankind from the spiritual world and for that purpose have to find people who are willing to take this sacrificial task upon themselves. It denotes the highest kind of freedom to do what is required out of knowledge, for in the process nothing arbitrary or personal is involved. It is in this sense that Rudolf Steiner's decision must be understood.

It was through the Brockdorffs that Rudolf Steiner got to know the Theosophical Society of that time. Immediately afterwards Rudolf Steiner reached the age of 40 (1901), 'before which time . . . no one, in the view of the Masters, is allowed to teach as an occultist. (Wherever this takes place earlier it is the result of an error.) Now I was able to devote myself publicly to Theosophy.'[125] With that the possibility was given to Rudolf Steiner to work in harmony with the spiritual leaders of humanity to make the beginning of the age of light a reality within the life of the spirit. Whereas Kali Yuga had deprived mankind of the knowledge of reincarnation and karma, it was Rudolf Steiner's particular task—as he proclaimed on various occasions—to give mankind an insight into this knowledge, through which he linked to the time before Kali Yuga. Now it is a very remarkable thing that Rudolf Steiner, in his earlier-quoted remark about Kaspar Hauser, points to the fact that the latter knew about reincarnation and karma and it was this which induced the opponents to kill him. This fact clearly reveals the inner connection between Rudolf Steiner and Kaspar Hauser, but it also shows that Kaspar Hauser has to do with the future. In all realms of life the realization of the knowledge of reincarnation and karma will bring an upheaval with it, a 'transvaluation of all values' (Nietzsche). Through that the spiritual world will play an increasingly big part in the life of the individual; he will be strengthened in his inner being. A person who is really able to understand the teaching of reincarnation and karma comes into relationship with the spiritual world in a manner which is humanly worthy, individual and independent. This is the goal of the whole of spiritual evolution of the West and at the same time the only way by which mankind can avoid the loss of individuality. Because this is the case, the opponents of ego-development fight against it with all the means at their disposal and with all their might. Their activity becomes glaringly obvious through the events of 1932/33.

1932/33

In the literature about Kaspar Hauser there is one place which, in a strange, almost prophetic way, points to the year 1933. 'Had I the fully valid proof, which is still lacking, I would lock it away in an iron casket and write upon it: "To be opened on 17 December 1933".' This is what Henriette von Feuerbach, the daughter-in-law of the famous criminologist, wrote on 2 January 1884.[126] In the main, of course, she is concerned with finding out the identity of Kaspar Hauser and all the questions connected with that. On the other hand it seems that she is in possession of some secret and believes that she must not divulge it. 'I know more than what the books tell us and I have written it down and put a black seal upon it in my writing desk' she writes on 5 February 1884.[126] These notes were not discovered! It is questionable whether they ever contained anything that goes beyond what we know today. One has the feeling that she is deeply connected in her soul with Kaspar Hauser, sometimes to the point of agony and satiety, as one can glean from the letters. The genius of history, which is a good spirit of humanity, has inspired her from subconscious depths to write down: 17 December 1933. One hundred years after Kaspar Hauser's murder there will be revealed what really happened—thus might the unconscious impulse be expressed that led to her prophetic utterance.

It is staggering to note that, exactly 99 years after the murder of Kaspar Hauser, events take place which then came to a head on 30 January 1933 in the seizure of power by Hitler. In connection with what we have to say about Kaspar Hauser, there comes up for the second time with conspicuous exactness the 99 years as a trebling of 33 years: 1812–1911, 1833–1932/33, and in the case of the latter span an important inner connection is revealed. In Hitler we see the counter image, the opposing force to Kaspar Hauser. This counter force arises as the historic consequence of Kaspar Hauser's murder which was wantonly committed. The effect of Hitler upon Europe—nay, upon the world at large—was as destructive as the blessing would have been that the 'Child of Europe' could have brought. (How it came about that Hitler was made into a tool for these powers will be dealt with in Chapter 4.) The pain arising from the catastrophe in Ansbach is intensified in experiencing the consequences that came about 99 years later. The enormous amount of suffering that occurred gives us the responsibility to point out the recognized causes and the real culprits.

The contrast between Hitler and Kaspar Hauser goes far beyond what is outwardly perceptible to history. Only on the spiritual level can it be seen that Hitler was to have finally eradicated all that was to have been built up by Kaspar Hauser for the twentieth century. A consideration of the 33-year rhythm can once again help us to understand this. The significance of the end of Kali Yuga, as a unique event of history, referred to by Rudolf Steiner at a decisive moment in his work in Berlin, will be revealed after 33 years. Rudolf Steiner spoke only once about the year 1933 and its significance, and that astonishingly enough in Karlsruhe on 25 January 1910. This observation becomes more than just a hint if one remembers that Rudolf Steiner gave the results of two important pieces of research about Christ in Karlsruhe in 1910 and 1911 (*vide* his lecture cycle *From Jesus to Christ*), both of which were not delivered in Kaspar Hauser's birthplace by accident. This is a striking example of the fact that in Rudolf Steiner's words a deed of a higher order is fulfilled.

The above mentioned lecture given in Karlsruhe deals with 'the greatest mystery of our time: the mystery of the reappearance of the Christ.'[127] These utterances of Rudolf Steiner must be quoted and studied singly, as also those of the cycle *From Jesus to Christ*, because of the special importance attached to them.

Would it not also be possible today for something of infinite importance to take place without people being aware of it? Might not our contemporaries fail to have the slightest inkling of the most important happening in the world at the present time? It might well be so. For something of supreme importance is taking place, although it is perceptible only to the eyes of spirit. There is a great deal of talk about periods of transition; we ourselves are actually living in a very important one. And its importance lies in the fact that the Dark Age has run its course and a new age is beginning, when slowly and by degrees the souls of men will change and new faculties will be developed.

The fact that the vast majority of people are entirely unaware of this need not be a cause of surprise, for it was the same when the Christ Event took place at the beginning of our era. Kali Yuga came to an end in the year 1899 and we have now to live on into a new age. What is beginning is slowly preparing men for new faculties of soul.

The first indications of these new faculties will be noticeable in isolated souls comparatively soon now, and they will become more clearly apparent in the middle of the thirties of this century, approximately in the period between 1930 and 1940. The years 1933, 1935 and 1937 will be particularly important. Very special faculties will then reveal themselves in human beings as natural gifts. Great changes will take place during this period and biblical prophecies will be fulfilled. Everything will change for souls who are living on earth and also for those who are no longer in physical bodies. Whatever their realm of existence, souls are on the way to possessing entirely new faculties. Everything is changing—but the happening of supreme importance in our time is a deeply incisive transformation of the human soul.

Kali Yuga is over and the souls of men are now beginning to develop new faculties. These faculties—because this is the purpose of the epoch—will of themselves draw forth from souls certain powers of clairvoyance which during Kali Yuga had necessarily to be submerged in the realm of the unconscious. A number of souls will experience the strange condition of having ego-consciousness but at the same time the feeling of living in a world essentially different from the world known to their ordinary consciousness. The experience will be shadowy, like a divination, as though an operation had been performed on one born blind ... Through what we call esoteric training these clairvoyant faculties will be attained in a far better form. But because human beings progress, they will appear in mankind in their very earliest beginnings, in their most elementary stages, through the natural process of evolution.[127]

From 1933 on, therefore, deeply incisive changes in man's soul faculties will become more evident and also more frequent than before 1930. In the present account we have already dealt with the cataclysmic events that came about through the domination of National Socialism. The strange state of mind and the kind of consciousness which has already been characterized for the thirties becomes much more understandable if one takes into account that the events so described were experienced unconsciously by people, but could not be understood because the conditions for that had not been created. The question of the fulfilment of the biblical prophecies will still have to be gone into. It is of primary importance that this change comes about for the whole of

mankind, both for the living and the dead, and that the new
faculties appear in the form of a natural gift. They will appear,
they must come, because Kali Yuga is over and now the effect
of the greatest event during Kali Yuga, the Mystery of Golgotha, can and must be revealed in supersensible, etheric form.
The event itself cannot be influenced by human whim—it is
bound to happen! A human understanding of this Christ-
appearance, which is of the greatest importance for the whole
future evolution of the earth and mankind does not, however,
come about of its own accord. That is why Rudolf Steiner
concerns himself with the question as to how this event may be
made acceptable to man and how man can be prepared to
receive it. He says:

> But it might very easily happen—indeed, far more easily
> now than at any earlier time—that people would prove
> incapable of grasping this event of such supreme impor-
> tance for humanity, incapable of realizing that this denotes
> an actual glimpse into a spiritual world, although still
> shadowy and dim. There might, for example, be so much
> wickedness, so much materialism on the earth that the
> majority of people would show not the slightest under-
> standing, and regard those who have this clairvoyance as
> lunatics, shutting them up in asylums together with those
> whose minds are obviously deranged. This point of time
> might pass people by without leaving a trace, although
> today we too are letting the call of John the Baptist, the
> forerunner of Christ, and of Christ Himself, again resound:
> A new epoch is at hand when the souls of men must take a
> step upward into the kingdoms of heaven!
> The great event might very easily pass by without being
> understood by people ... If between the years 1930 and 1940
> the materialists were to say triumphantly: True, there have
> been a number of fools but no sign whatever of the expected
> great event ... this would not in the least disprove what has
> been said. But if the materialists were to win the day and
> mankind were to overlook these happenings altogether, it
> would be a dire misfortune. Even if people should prove

incapable of perceiving them, great things will come to pass.'[127]

It is the task of spiritual science to prepare the understanding of the Christ event. It is a Johannine clarion call to awake. But one can also become aware of the great anxiety expressed in Rudolf Steiner's words of how endangered is the conscious apprehension of this event. Are we not forced to admit that this anxiety was justified and that the malice and materialism *were* so great that the majority of mankind did *not* show the least understanding of this happening and that it *passed* them by without a trace? Did not the materialists triumph in the years 1930–1940? In another lecture Rudolf Steiner astonishingly says '1930–1940/45.'[128] Must we not say: Not even the lunatics have appeared who, on account of their natural clairvoyance, had to be shut up in asylums?

The beginning of the age of the new etheric clairvoyance was dazzled by the powers of opposition through the well-known events of the thirties and forties. To that was added the fact that the experiences in the soul were so delicate, so intimate and inconspicuous, and the alert powers of comprehension so weak, that the fleeting impressions on the soul were not clearly enough observed. Everything was planned in such a way—and to that belongs not least the murder of Kaspar Hauser—that by means of a great, dazzling historical event attention was drawn away from the spiritual happenings. This was highly successful.

In the further course of the lecture Rudolf Steiner speaks about the length of time that man has been given to develop an understanding of the true course of events and to deepen and make more explicit its consequence for the individual.

What can happen is that it will be possible for people to acquire the new faculty of perception in the etheric world—a certain number to begin with, and they will be followed by more and more others, for mankind will have 2,500 years during which to develop these faculties in greater and greater perfection. This opportunity must not be missed. If it were, this would be a tragic misfortune and mankind would then be obliged to wait until a later epoch in order to retrieve the lost opportunity and subsequently to develop the new faculty. This faculty will consist of people being able to see in their environment something of the etheric world which hitherto they have not normally been able to see. Man now sees only the human physical body, but then he will be able to see the etheric body at least as a shadowy picture and also to perceive the connection between deeper happenings in the etheric world. He will have pictures and premonitions of happenings in the spiritual world and find that in three or four days' time such happenings take place on the physical plane. He will see certain things in etheric pictures and know that tomorrow or in a few days' time this or that will happen.

The faculties of the human soul will be transformed. And what is associated with this? The Being we call the Christ was once on earth in the flesh at the beginning of our era. He will never come again in a physical body, for that was a unique event and will not be repeated. But He will come again in an etheric form in the period indicated. People will learn to perceive Christ inasmuch as through this etheric sight they will grow towards Him. He does not now descend as far as the physical body but only as far as the etheric body; men must therefore grow to the stage where He can be perceived. For Christ spoke truly when He said: 'I am with you always, even unto the end of the days of earth'. He is present in our spiritual world . . . and those especially blessed can always see Him in this spiritual, etheric world.

A man who was with particular intensity convinced through such perception was Paul—in the vision at Damascus. But this etheric sight will develop in individual human beings as a natural faculty. In days to come it will be more and more possible for men to experience what Paul experienced at Damascus.

We are now able to grasp quite a different aspect of spiritual science. We realize that it is a preparation for the actual event of the new Appearance of Christ. Christ will appear again inasmuch as with their etheric sight men will raise themselves to Him. When this is understood, spiritual science is disclosed as the means of preparing people to recognize the return of Christ, in order that it shall not be their misfortune to overlook this event but that they will be mature enough to grasp the great happening of the Second Coming of Christ. People will become capable of seeing etheric bodies and among them, too, the etheric body of Christ; that is to say, they will grow into a world where Christ will be revealed to their newly wakened faculties.

It will then no longer be necessary to amass all kinds of documentary evidence to prove the existence of Christ; there will be eye-witnesses of the presence of the Living Christ, people who will know Him in His etheric body. And from this experience they will realize that this is the same Being who at the beginning of our era fulfilled the Mystery of Golgotha, that He is indeed the Christ. Just as Paul at Damascus was convinced at that time: This is Christ! ... so there will be people whose experiences in the etheric world will convince them that in very truth Christ lives.[127]

A little later on Rudolf Steiner explains the consequences of the comprehension or non-comprehension of this event, which goes far beyond a mere historical understanding.

Christ is ever-present, but He is in the spiritual world. We can reach Him when we rise into that world. All anthroposophical teaching should be transformed within us into an indomitable will not to allow this event to pass unnoticed but in the time that remains to us gradually to educate human beings who will be capable of developing these new faculties and therewith to unite anew with Christ. Otherwise, before such an opportunity could again arise, humanity would have to wait for long, long ages ... indeed, until a new incarnation of the earth. If this event of the return of Christ were to be overlooked, the vision of Christ in the etheric body would be restricted to those who are willing to fit themselves for such an experience through esoteric training. But the really momentous fact of these faculties being acquired by humanity in general, by all men, of this great event being understood by means of faculties developing naturally in all people ... that would be impossible for long, long ages.

Obviously, therefore, there is something in our age that justifies the existence and the work of spiritual science in the world. Its aim is not merely to satisfy theoretical needs or scientific curiosity. To prepare people for this great event, to prepare them to take their rightful place in the epoch in which they live and with clarity of understanding and knowledge to perceive what is actually present but may pass men by without being brought to fruition—such is the aim of spiritual science[127]

We must ask whether Rudolf Steiner means the years from 1930 to 1945 in connection with the events which mankind must not allow to pass by without a trace, or whether he means the whole span of 2500 years beginning with 1933. From the wording '... in the time that remains to us gradually to educate human beings who will be capable of developing these new faculties' one can assume that it is the decisive importance of the years of the thirties and forties that he means. This agrees with the fact that Rudolf Steiner says that spiritual science will *prepare* humanity for the event which will come about during these years. This time of preparation seems to refer to the first 33 years after the end of Kali-Yuga. After that time other conditions will naturally prevail because by then the return of Christ will have affected all other happenings. With that the task that spiritual science has to fulfil will also have changed. The possibility for the *whole* of humanity to acquire the faculty of perceiving Christ in the etheric body and the ability to understand this by naturally acquired means has not been realized during the thirties and forties.

In the interest of humanity one can only hope that through the spiritual scientific work of as many people as possible devoted to this state of affairs it might be possible, over this great length of time, to make up for what has been lost in order to avoid the inevitable consequence of having to wait for a new embodiment of the earth. Strangely enough, it is only in the lecture in Karlsruhe that Rudolf Steiner refers to this consequence, as he also does to the restriction of the vision of the etheric Christ to 'those who are willing to fit themselves for such an experience through esoteric training'.[127] The significance exerted by a small group of spiritual trainees is hereby demonstrated. The question remains open as to whether, through the present experiences of individuals—to whom Rudolf Steiner alludes—all mankind will be prepared for and introduced to etheric insight. These experiences and the spiritual work of individuals, or small groups of people, could have built an inner sanctuary for the greatest event of our epoch. Through a special dispensation of destiny something of this experience has appeared in poetry. This could be demonstrated when the events of 1944/45 were discussed with examples of personalities such as Albrecht Haushofer and Jacques Lusseyran.

Our consideration must now return to Kaspar Hauser, however. It has been pointed out, especially in discussing the years 1845 and 1878, that materialism was only able to maintain such a strong influence in the nineteenth century because Kaspar Hauser had been excluded. This excessive materialism results in the twentieth century in mankind witnessing the greatest happening without being aware of it. Conversely, we may conclude that through his preparatory activity Kaspar Hauser had the task of overcoming materialism to such a degree that this happening would have been experienced by everyone as a natural event. The mission of Kaspar Hauser, directed towards the whole of mankind, is here revealed. At the same time an important feature of German spiritual life is inherent in this mission. Kaspar Hauser appears in this connection as a preparer of the Christ impulse.

In connection with the far advanced materialism of our time, Rudolf Steiner points out that an error will become associated with the reappearance of the Christ in the etheric that will have a terribly seductive effect upon mankind. 'Materialistic thinking will conceive of this event as a descent of Christ in the flesh, as an incarnation in the flesh. A number of persons in their boundless arrogance will turn this to their own advantage and announce themselves to men as the reincarnated Christ. The near future may therefore bring false Christs, but anthroposophists should be so fully prepared for the spiritual life that they will not confuse the return of Christ in a spiritual body, perceptible only to higher vision, with a return in a physical body of flesh. This will be one of the most terrible temptations besetting mankind and to lead men past this temptation will be the task of those who learn through spiritual science to rise in the true sense to an understanding of the spirit, who try not to drag spirit down into matter but to ascend into the spiritual world themselves. Thus we may speak of the return of Christ and of the fact that we rise to Christ in the spiritual world through acquiring the faculty of etheric vision.'[127]

One might think that people who proclaimed themselves to be reincarnations of Christ have not yet made their appearance. But that would be to interpret Rudolf Steiner's words too narrowly. Through the seizure of power by Hitler in 1933 a man was placed at the head of the German State whose opinion of himself as the 'Führer' must be seen in connection with Rudolf Steiner's statement. The long superseded principle of a 'Führer', which was characterized above in its antagonism to Christianity, works upon people through Hitler with such a degree of fascination that due to that—and, of course, owing to lack of preparation—they are unable to recognize the Christ event (*vide* also p.232 et seq.). The arrogance of the superman, his self-ordained deification, becomes frighteningly evident in word and deed; strangely enough it was very little realized as such and repulsed. This can only be understood if one sees the underlying dimming of consciousness as the work of a superhuman event as described by Rudolf Steiner. The dark powers succeed in creating a *counter-image* on earth of what should take place spiritually. Through that the awakening faculties in man work in the opposite direction or are reversed. This large-scale attack on mankind is reinforced by special forms of materialism. Whereas actually human beings have the task of freeing themselves more and more from the forces of the blood and avoiding the danger arising from the decadence of the blood, the 'Blut und Boden' (the linking of landed property to the family) becomes the basis of so-called 'renewal' in the ideology of National Socialism. The national community is conjured up in the ancient sense, which has long ago ceased to have any meaning. The impulses of German spiritual life were directed towards the individuality of man, which ultimately has nothing to do with nationality or race. The goal of individualization was forgotten, was sacrificed. An erroneous idea of nation is turned into an enemy of the individual person.

The tremendous effect of the pseudo-religious movement, which gained a decisive success in 1933, achieved this by managing to seize the will element in man. The individual is rooted in the spiritual world with his unconscious will-nature. Through this he seeks and finds his destiny. He participates in what happens in the spiritual world without knowing anything about it in his day-consciousness. The events which Rudolf Steiner said would necessarily occur in the thirties and forties, would be shared in by human beings in this region of the will. That is why, on the part of the opposition, the attempt was made to get hold of this element, without, of course, supplying man with the necessary spiritual knowledge. Through the controlled activation of the will, for example by sports events, the mass gatherings, the famous parades and the pseudo-sacred nocturnal open-air festivities—that consciousness-befogging fascination was aroused in man which has wrongly been called enthusiasm. Dulled by the materialism which haunted people's minds and unable to consciously recognize the spiritual happenings through thinking, the will-system, bound up with the physical body, took control of the human being. Through that people were empowered by a force arising out of dullness of soul; they got on to a track in which, in the truest sense of the word, they did not know what they were doing.

At this point we should think of Kaspar Hauser who, by his Christian name, points to the sacred element in the will. The will element, associated with the name Kaspar, can be found by the heart and senses of man; it leads him aloft to the supersensible realm of the etheric, whereas the other way leads inevitably into the abyss (see Chapter 2).

It has been mentioned above that with the end of Kali Yuga the spiritual world will again take up direct contact with mankind. This wish of the spiritual world to communicate with man directly lives in Anthroposophy. Rudolf Steiner himself, through his research into reincarnation and karma, saw it as his task to lead people to a conscious understanding of their own destiny and equip them with knowledge to deal with this situation where it might arise. This experience is linked to that of the supersensible-etheric nature of man. Rudolf Steiner has the following to say about it:

> But still other faculties will appear—for example, a faculty that a person will notice in himself. After he has performed some deed, there will appear before his soul a kind of dream-picture which he will know to be connected in some way with what he has done. And from spiritual science he will realize: when an after-image of my deed appears in this way, although it is essentially different from the deed itself, it reveals to me what the karmic effect of my deed will be in the future.

> This understanding of karma will develop in certain individuals during the middle of our century. The explanation is that Kali Yuga has run its course and that from epoch to epoch new faculties appear in people. But if no understanding is developed, if this particular faculty is stamped out, if those who speak about faculties of this kind are put away as if they were insane, disaster is inevitable and humanity will sink in the morass of materialism. Everything will depend upon whether understanding is awakened for spiritual science, or whether Ahriman will succeed in suppressing its intentions. Then, or course, those who are choking in materialism may say scornfully: They were fine prophets who stated that a second man will be seen beside the physical man! Nothing will be apparent if the faculties for seeing it are crushed out. But even if these faculties do not become evident in the middle of the twentieth century,

this will be no proof that the rudiments of them are not within man, but only that the seed of the young buds has been crushed. The faculties that have been described today exist and can be developed, provided only that mankind is willing.[128]

Attention is here drawn to two things. Firstly: reincarnation and karma are here portrayed as fundamental supersensible experiences which gain more and more meaning when they are understood through spiritual science. Secondly: Ahriman, the opposite materialistic current, fights against spiritual science in order to make an understanding of the newly-awakened faculties impossible. But by that an important light is thrown upon the events of 1933. Kaspar Hauser was the one who knew about the newly-arising experiences of how karma is formed and was predestined to prepare for it, as Rudolf Steiner tells us. The ideology of National Socialism could never have gained any great importance if the fact that man incarnates in various nations and races in the course of evolution had been more generally known through the teachings of reincarnation and karma. If it had not only been Rudolf Steiner who had spread the teaching of reincarnation and karma by his solitary and often misunderstood efforts, but also Kaspar Hauser before him in a form corresponding to his time, then undoubtedly there would have been a far greater possibility for an understanding of the new soul-faculties. A similar task united Rudolf Steiner and Kaspar Hauser in this way. The National Socialist movement—first correctly assessed by Karl Heyer as anti-anthroposophical—fights in spirit against both these things. Nothing is more conducive to extinguishing the feeling for destiny than the ideology of blood and family inheritance of land. It must be looked upon as a pre-eminent ahrimanic weapon. What Rudolf Steiner foresaw with great anxiety became reality in the thirties. Ahriman's retaliation succeeded very largely in driving the new spiritual faculties into the background. This spiritual background consists of the fact that three important currents of spiritual life unite in man.

The newly-awakening faculty of spiritual experience which came at the end of Kali Yuga combines with the effect of the Mystery of Golgotha, the power of which makes the spiritual ascent of man possible in the first place. In addition to this the ego was enabled by means of the Resurrection to incarnate as a spiritual being and by that to recognize itself consciously as such in its destiny and repeated earth-lives. This threefold current of the spiritual life of mankind exists: the Mystery of Golgotha, the new soul-faculties and the ego-experience of reincarnation and karma. Whoever raises himself to the knowledge of these is able to share in them. Something of the healing impulses which Rudolf Steiner gave to mankind and which Kaspar Hauser also would have brought can be fulfilled.

The events which took place in Germany from 1933 were understood and expressed with unique spiritual genius by the 18-year-old poet, Hermann Kükelhaus (b. 4 August 1920 in Essen, d. 29 January 1944 in Berlin) in his school-leaving examination speech of 1938. The youthful poet, to whose peculiar destiny it belonged to be educated in a National Socialistic school, characterized the Hitler movement as a 'cosmic cancer'. His brother, Hugo Kükelhaus, reported the understandably unpreserved speech as follows:

> The blind power and its adherents were analysed as (literally) 'cosmic carcinoma', as a sickness of the earth-body, from which the conclusion can be drawn that man and his setting-to-rights of this calamity is unable to defend himself by any direct means, either by attack, or by sufferance. Only the spiritual intensity of Holiness, the Divine Sacrifice, can bring about the change: it 'irradiates the cancerous growth'. At the end of his report, which he was unable to finish reading, he called for an extension of anthropology, of civil- and social-science, to include the idea of the demonic as an empirical quantity.[129]

The reference to the cosmic-demonic power of destruction, against which no human method of either attack or sufferance can prevail, is short and pithy. The mysterious irresistibility, the human incomprehensibility, can now be made more understandable if it is seen as a 'sickness of the earth-body', that is to say an event which takes place between the earth and the cosmos. Only the Holy One, that is He who raises Himself to the spiritual-cosmic through sacrifice, can bring about the change for the good. His spiritual intensity 'irradiates the cancer' as the dreadful, unforgettable formula expresses it.

More has been accomplished by this in the way of understanding and mastering National Socialism than in countless books which, with many words and facts, are unable to grasp the main point, because this—itself of a spiritual nature—can only be understood from a spiritual point of view. It is comforting to find in Hermann Kükelhaus a person—living immediately at the time of the events—whose consciousness was able to follow and interpret with understanding what was happening.

On the basis of this unfinished speech to the school community, Hermann Kükelhaus was sent as a punishment to a mine in Kattowitz—he himself experienced it as an enormous blessing to be underground during daytime. As a soldier in Russia he developed an anticipatory clairvoyant love for this country, to which he was constantly drawn. He returned to Berlin with a severe head injury which he received in Russia and had a fatal accident while putting out a fire in Berlin on 29 January 1944.

The National Socialist movement can truly be overcome when its significance is seen in this considerably widened context. It gains its importance through its connection with the conscious battle against the spirit, which it has served without its adherents being aware of it. It is rooted in the criminal assaults that were made against the Christ principle and those who served it in the nineteenth century. Also what happened through the outer destruction of this regime has helped the cause of spirit enmity, as this was described when the events of 1945 were being discussed.

1965/1966

If we follow the 33-year rhythm of history further, we see that

mankind was shaken in the mid-sixties by an inner jolt which
was connected with the end of Kali Yuga and the acquisition
of the new soul-faculties. In itself this process was hardly
noticed consciously because the thoughts of spiritual science
were not sufficiently well known for people to understand how
the supersensible takes effect. The resulting mainly unconscious process, however, clearly played a part in the awareness
of life and even in historical events. The awareness here
referred to rests on the inner impression that everything that
mankind had achieved during Kali Yuga was worthless by
comparison with the new spiritual enlightenment. In this light
all values have to be reassessed; they have to show that they
can maintain themselves in the light. But what finally results
from such a test seems to be less than what was desired. So one
gets the feeling that all values cease to exist, that one plunges
into the abyss along with all traditions and all established
things. Everything that does not share in the new and immediately present life of the spiritual worlds, which has lost its
progression and become inwardly rigid, ceases to exist for the
soul. Such an end as this is the necessary step for the freeing of
souls from that which would hinder the comprehension of
what is new. This process takes place largely in the unconscious part of man. The forces which arise out of unconscious
depths—that is to say, those connected with prenatal existence
and the nightly connection with the spiritual world—meet
with a day-consciousness confused by intellectuality and
materialism that does not know how to deal with the reality of
soul-experience.

A deep rift is present in the attitude of mind of those citizens
of the spiritual world who experience the dawn of a world
epoch open to the spirit to which the ahrimanically restricted
day-consciousness cannot find access. This unbridgeable gap
becomes agony of soul and the spiritual experiences which,
through the working of Ahriman, become too deeply fixed in
the subconscious, create fear in mankind as the terrible shadow of the light. For that reason man clings all the more
tightly to what is old, or even believes that he must fight
against what is new.

An example of this inner process can be seen in the development of the youth movement of the sixties. If one also bears in mind the year 1933, one then perceives the principal connections between the work of Kaspar Hauser and that of Rudolf Steiner. In order to get to the root of these events, further explanation is necessary. Over against the appearance of Christ in the etheric world, which sought to be revealed to mankind from 1933, events have taken place on the physical plane which stand in stark contrast to this because they are rooted in the opposite impulse. The aim which those fighting against the spirit ultimately wish to serve is the coming incarnation of Ahriman among western humanity. Rudolf Steiner spoke, mainly in October and November 1919, about this result of his spiritual research, which is so important for an understanding of present-day and future development. His first allusion to it was in the lecture in Zürich on 27 October 1919. He says there:

> Just as there was an incarnation of Lucifer at the beginning of the third millenium BC and as there was an incarnation of Christ at the time of the Mystery of Golgotha, so there will be a western incarnation of Ahriman some time after our present life on earth in about the third millennium AD. It is thus only possible to properly understand the course of modern man's development throughout nearly 6000 years of history if one interprets it so that the incarnation of Lucifer stands at the one pole, Christ's incarnation is in the middle and the incarnation of Ahriman stands at the opposite pole.[130]

In the history of the last centuries Ahriman's power is becoming increasingly active as he attempts to arrange for his incarnation in the best way possible.

> The ahrimanic powers prepare man's evolution in such a way that, when one day Ahriman will appear in human form in western civilization—which will then hardly pass as civilization in our sense of the word—just as Lucifer once appeared in human form in China and Jesus Christ

appeared in a human form in the Near East, so will mankind be liable to succumb to Ahriman. It does not help to
give oneself up to illusions about this. Ahriman will appear
in human form. It will only be a case of how he finds people
prepared: whether his own preparation enables him to
ensnare the whole of humanity which calls itself civilized
today, or whether he finds humanity in a condition to offer
resistance. It does not help at all today to give oneself up to
illusions about these things. These days it is as though
people flee from the truth, which cannot be given them in a
plain unadorned fashion, because they would ridicule,
deride and scoff at it. But if one offers it to them in the form
of the Threefold Social Order, as we try to do at present,
then—at least most of them—also will not accept it. But,
from the fact that most people will not accept it, that is just
one of the ways in which the ahrimanic powers are best
served, so that when Ahriman appears in human form he
will have the greatest possible number of followers on earth.
It is just this lack of consideration for the most significant
truths that will build the best bridge for Ahriman to
promote his incarnation.[130]

It cannot surprise us that Ahriman, as the spirit of untruth
and deception, does his utmost to undermine man's attitude
towards the truth. In this way lies have won a recognized
position in the political life of today. Whoever fails to make use
of lies only demonstrates his naïve ignorance of the realities of
life in the eyes of the worldly wise. The fact is overlooked that
this kind of truth is the very existence of Ahriman, by which he
seeks to destroy human beings. Compared with that the most
important task of spiritual science is to establish the truths
about the realization of the Christ impulse in the minds of men,
so that people may be enabled to order the conditions on the
physical plane in accordance with these truths. Rudolf Steiner
especially mentions the threefolding of the body social as being
one form of the truth. The connection of the threefolding of the
social organism with Ahriman's incarnation is clearly
emphasized in Rudolf Steiner's lecture of 2 November 1919.

All the things that people who 'live in phrases' aspire to are meaningless 'as long as they fail to realize that if the old unified state as such, whatever the constitution—whether a democracy, a republic or a monarchy or whatever else—when it is a unified state and does not become *threefold*, this is simply a way of helping Ahriman's incarnation.'[131]

The energetic endeavours of Rudolf Steiner to bring home to his contemporaries the importance of the Threefold Social Order becomes understandable in this context. It also belongs to the mission of Kaspar Hauser to introduce into the political system a development which leads away from the unified state. In contrast to that the National Socialist movement developed a particularly idiotic form of the unified state in which it was combined with the old leadership principle and, in addition, all the main offices were given into the hands of one person. The National Socialist state was the exact opposite of that society which could grow out of the threefold social organism. Karl Heyer is right when he describes it as a tool of the devil. This tool of the devil functioned in a way to promote the incarnation of Ahriman and was therefore particularly successful because, by falling back on ancient blood relationships, an effective method was being put to use in the sense of Ahriman. 'That is why in our day Ahriman, in order to confuse mankind, makes use of everything arising out of the old blood relationships, which man of the fifth post-Atlantean age has basically outgrown. Everything stemming from the ancient blood relationships is used by the power of Ahriman to set groups of people in disharmony against one another. Everything arising out of old family, racial, tribal and national differences is used by Ahriman to create confusion among mankind.'[130] The basis from which the 'blood and family-property' ideology, the emphasis on nationality and race, has drawn its disastrous and seductive power is here elucidated. Also racial delusion reveals its ahrimanic source through its humanity-destroying consequence.

A slightly different description by Rudolf Steiner throws light on the incarnation of Ahriman within a relatively short time:

From the spiritual world this ahrimanic power is preparing
for incarnation on the earth, is endeavouring in every conceivable way to make such preparation that the incarnation
of Ahriman in human form may be able to mislead and
corrupt mankind on earth to the utmost. A task of mankind
during the next phase of civilization will be to live towards
the incarnation of Ahriman with such alert consciousness
that this incarnation can actually serve to promote a higher,
spiritual development, inasmuch as through Ahriman
himself man will become aware of what can, or shall we say,
can *not* be achieved by physical life alone. But people must
go forward with full consciousness towards this incarnation
of Ahriman and become more and more alert in every
domain, in order to recognize with greater and greater
clarity those trends in life which are leading towards this
ahrimanic incarnation. People must learn from spiritual
science to find the key to life and so be able to recognize and
learn to control the currents leading towards the incarnation
of Ahriman. It must be realized that Ahriman will live
among men on the earth, but that in confronting him men
will themselves determine what they may learn from him,
what they may receive from him. This, however, they will
not be able to do unless, from now onwards, they take
control of certain spiritual and also unspiritual currents
which otherwise are used by Ahriman for the purpose of
leaving mankind as deeply unconscious as possible of his
coming; then, one day, he will be able to appear on earth and
overwhelm people, tempting and luring them to repudiate
earth-evolution, thus preventing it from reaching its goal.[132]

Everything depends upon people learning to take up the
impulses of Ahriman consciously and deciding for themselves
how they can turn them to mankind's advantage. The positive
side of Ahriman's incarnation—which in itself cannot and
should not be hindered—can only come about if human beings
are able to retain their consciousness through spiritual insight
in spite of what Ahriman does. That is conceivably difficult—
no one should have any delusions about that—for Ahriman

does everything in his power to dim and befog the consciousness of man. Ultimately, only those people will be able to stand up against these tremendous demands on human consciousness who can counter the deceptive power of Ahriman on the physical plane with the surety which comes from having experienced the reappearance of Christ in the etheric world. Rudolf Steiner indicates—as quoted above—that ever more human beings will have to have the supersensible experience of the Christ if something is not to be missed which can only be made good during the next, Jupiter, evolution of the earth. Over against this Ahriman sees it as his task to mislead mankind to such an extent 'that earth evolution is unable to attain its goal'.[132] The far-reaching consequences of present and future historical events are presented here in their cosmic significance. This broad connection must be taken into account if one is to understand the three steps: 1932–1965–1998.

Before their incarnation souls are living completely according to the facts spoken about by Rudolf Steiner. When people are born they are taught by their past lives and directly also by their pre-natal experiences whereby, of course, their individual connection to world-historical spiritual events can be the most varied imaginable.

The young people born in the forties experienced in the spiritual world what Rudolf Steiner describes as the events of 1933 and they were able to work upon these with their soul-forces for more than seven years. The cosmic attack of the ahrimanic powers, the 'cosmic cancer', was also experienced by them in pre-natal existence. Through that these young people bore within themselves an impulse of renewal which questioned the whole constitution of society. We can understand this to mean that in this impulse, hidden and unrecognized, lives the knowledge that Rudolf Steiner made known when he said that the state is a pre-eminent tool in the hand of Ahriman to prepare him for his incarnation. According to the feeling among the young people that the whole system ought to be radically altered, and in their endeavour to create a new social beginning independent of the already existing social organization, there appears, in a hazy and incomplete way, what the pre-natal, and at that time (1965/66) contemporary, spiritual impulse had been. The view was extant in an unclear form in extra-parliamentary opposition that a social change must be sought in a far more radical and elementary way than it had been up till then. These processes were in no way restricted to a particular nation. A sign of this is much of what led to the 'Prague Spring' in 1968 (the Prague freedom uprising). This hope-inspiring movement, which sought to introduce a humanitarian socialism bearing undoubted similarities to the threefold social order, was brutally suppressed.

What is so tragic and calamitous about this youth movement is only comprehensible if it is seen in the light of the spiritual law by which, in the age of the consciousness soul and since the end of Kali Yuga, all spiritual experiences, including pre-natal ones, are changed into destructive forces if they are not consciously taken hold of. It hardly need be mentioned that young people, fed extensively on Marxism and on materialism in psychology and sociology, were unable to grasp in conscious thought the spiritual experience which pressed upon them from outside and rose up within them. It could also be said that the spiritual-scientific concepts imparted by Rudolf Steiner, by which man's spiritual experiences could be made comprehensible, were far too little known and recognized for them to be of help in this case. Thus already in the thirties the National Socialist movement was able, through its own inherent ahrimanic powers, to turn to its own advantage much of what lived unconsciously within the young people. The spirit which, since the end of Kali Yuga, now wants to communicate with mankind in the rhythm of 33 years, must be redeemed by man through knowledge, otherwise the unconscious spirit will become a point of attachment for luciferic and, above all, ahrimanic powers. If man does not awaken to the spirit through his soul activity, then it could just be the spirit which will turn into senseless destructiveness. In a slightly more ahrimanic form this misguided spirit, which changes into its opposite, expresses itself by the use of force and terror. The ice-cold intelligence that combines with this destructive instinct must not be blinded to the fact that in the person in question the decisive process takes place in the unconscious. The less the soul is conscious of the soul-spiritual reality in which it lives, the more unconscious is the urge to commit a crime. The ahrimanic deception with regard to the nature of the soul delivers the latter into the hands of Ahriman who wishes to destroy mankind, whereby the soul through this fanatical obsession cannot gain a clear understanding of it. This fanaticism kills all understanding and human connection with the surroundings.*

The luciferically coloured form of the misguided spirit comes to expression in those parts of the youth movement that have recourse to intoxication in one or other form, whereby people more or less undermine the basis of their lives. Those, however, who set out on the long path through the institutions out of a kind of resignation and despair because no proper alternative to existing social life can be found, ultimately become the servants of the unified state, against which their innermost feelings had justifiably rebelled.

In 1967 the novel by Ira Levin called *Rosemary's Baby* appeared in London. It significantly became an international bestseller and was most successfully made into a film by Roman Polanski. In the novel, which tells of the birth of Satan on 25 June 1966, the 33 years are mentioned without any explanation being given. The soul-deceiving and fateful proceedings which happen to a young woman—Rosemary—on 4 October 1965 at the conception of Satan are even explained therein by a reference to a book by J.R. Hanslet that was published in Torquay in 1934, *All of Them Witches*.[133] ' "We are living in the year 1966," said Rosemary's husband. "This book was published in 1933," said Rosemary. "There were covens—that's what they called them—in Europe, in North and South America, in Australia. Do you think they've all died out in just 33 years?"'[134] This 33-year connection is still further emphasized by the fact that Rosemary's husband is himself 33 years old. It is highly symptomatic that wide circles—even if only in a novel—take account of the conception and birth of Satan, here called Adrian Stevens. In his Christian name a suggestion of Ahriman can be distinguished. A circle of people assists—with knowledgeable skill—at the birth of this satanic being. The conception takes place on 4 October 1965 during the Pope's visit to New York, strikingly on the same date of the year as the launching of Sputnik on 4 October 1957. During the conception the mother is in a state of unconsciousness, caused by alcohol and an ointment called 'chocolate mouse', which was administered to her by the circle of people who purposefully direct proceedings. The husband—himself very drunk—already serves the satanic crew consciously at this point, and is rewarded for it by being helped by them to a successful acting career.

This satanic community makes use of human beings for its own ends, in the same way as the occult brotherhoods applied their methods (see p.105 ff). Consciously and purposefully something is brought about of which the person concerned is not allowed to know or suspect anything, as is here preeminently exemplified in Rosemary herself. The seduction of her husband was so arranged that he came under the spell—unnoticed by himself—of a group of people and their intentions. This was brought about by the psychological trick of fully, but surreptitiously, meeting all his inclinations and interests and by that—unknown to him—gaining his sympathies. Destructive occult powers are ruthlessly and murderously employed against those who stand in the way of the group's plans being put into practice (as with Donald Baumgart who is suddenly struck blind) or those who begin to get wise to their plots and to recognize them for what they are (as with Hutch, who wakes up temporarily from his deep and unexplained state of oblivion before dying).

The birth of Satan is systematically evolved as a counterpart to the birth of Christ and therefore is so placed in the course of the year that it takes place directly after St John's, 'just after midnight on 25 June ... immediately after the end of the half year of you know what'. This date—25 June 1966—was allegedly prophesied by Edmond Lautréamont 300 years ago, that is in 1666. If one omits the thousand from this figure it is certainly not by chance that we arrive at 666, first named by John in the Apocalypse (Chapter 13) and about which we shall have more to say. This concealed hint about the number 666 is easily overlooked.

It is important to remember that 33 years after the cataclysmic events of Central Europe, the spiritual background of which is made clear by the indications of Rudolf Steiner, it is just in New York that the words are expressed: 'God is dead and Satan lives. It is year 1, the first year of our Lord! Adrian's year has started.'[135] With that the end of the century is prophetically alluded to, the time when Satan, born in 1966, will have reached the age of that Being against whom he believes he has to fight. It is not of much importance to ask if the things recorded here actually happened in this way. But it is decisive to be clear about the fact that such manipulations are basically possible and must be taken seriously. One can look upon this novel as a summons to overcome the dangerous blindness and irresponsible *naïveté* in face of such evil occult influences upon history.

It must remain an open question as to the source of the knowledge that Ira Levin uses and which, as a novelist, he is not forced to disclose. It is more important to ask about the impulse by which it was motivated. Is it by intention (and by what circles and to what purpose?) or by necessity, that in our day similar things happen, as it were, in public? The necessity can be understood from the course of history as here related because, since the end of Kali Yuga, the spirit reveals itself ever more directly to human beings. Included with this spirit, connected with human development, are also the evil beings opposed to humanity's progress, which inevitably hinder and obstruct man, so that by gaining knowledge of evil he can determine his own course out of freedom. Mankind today is much more deeply involved in the struggle to recognize evil than it cares to admit, because the spiritual-cosmic dimensions of this battle have hardly become conscious.

1998—the end of the century

'And in the course of the twentieth century, when the first century after the end of Kali Yuga has elapsed, humanity will either stand at the grave of all civilization—or at the beginning of that era when, in the souls of men who in their hearts ally intelligence with spirituality, Michael's battle will be fought out to victory.'[136] These are the words with which Rudolf Steiner (19 July 1924) prophetically characterizes the situation at the end of the twentieth century. The task for those who wish to serve the true Spirit of the Age in this Michael epoch since the end of Kali Yuga consists in 'not contesting Michael's rulership of human thinking! Here there can be no question of fatalism. Here it can only be said that men must work together with the gods. Michael inspires men with his own being in order that there may appear on the earth a spirituality consonant with the personal intelligence of human beings, in order that people can be thinkers—and at the same time truly spiritual. For this and this alone is what Michael's dominion means.'[136] In the time that remains between the end of the first century of the Michaelic Age (1979) and the end of the present century, the discernment of as many people as possible must have taken care that life on earth may not become altogether permeated and taken hold of by ahrimanic-materialistic powers. But for that, however, a knowledge of the historic moment in its earthly and cosmic dimensions is indispensable. One can do nothing if one does not know where one is. Man is faced with the fact that he stands in freedom in front of the cosmic Christ-Event guarded by Michael, and either understands it and accepts it—or sinks into the abyss of inhumanity through the powers which are connected with Ahriman's incarnation.

This means—as you might realize—that through Anthroposophy something must be introduced into the spiritual evolution of the earth, for all kinds of demonic, ahrimanic powers are taking possession of people. The ahrimanic powers in many a human body were exultant in their confidence that it would no longer be possible for Michael to take over his rulership of the Cosmic Intelligence which had fallen down to the earth. And this exultation was particularly strong in the middle of the nineteenth century, when

Ahriman already believed: Michael will not again recover his Cosmic Intelligence which made its way from the heavens to the earth. Verily, great and mighty issues are at stake.[137]

It was Kaspar Hauser's task to prepare mankind for the attainment of these mighty ideals. He would have been in a position to pit his Christ-devoted thinking against Ahriman's exultation on the physical plane and thereby maintain the connection with the spiritual world. In the Rosicrucian sense this devotion to Christ means that, through knowledge, a bridge is built to the spirit by which man can still remain man. All powers opposed to the spirit work in ever greater intensity to deprive man of his conscious resilience when, towards the end of the century, a cosmic decision has to be made. The means used by Ahriman to lead mankind astray are confusion, fear and despair.

The event at the turn of the century stands in the death-sequence of Kaspar Hauser. The year 1933 revealed for the first time in its true dimension the result of Kaspar Hauser's murder by those who committed the sin against the spirit. This coming event, which can be described as an attack on the Christ-Impulse, has predetermined history—in reversal of the normal sequence of events. There in the future lies the original cause of much that has already occurred.*

The struggle for the spirit on the physical plane, in which Kaspar Hauser was to have taken such an active part, is the hidden but essential motif of the history of the last two centuries, wherein the decision comes at the turning point of the twentieth to the twenty-first century. The uniting of the leading organizations of the Jesuits and the western Lodges, which was spoken about at the beginning of the death sequence (1933), was ultimately used by them to prepare, during the course of two centuries, for a decision in their favour.

Vladimir Soloviev (1853–1900) pointed in the year of his death to the significance of this century's end in his story *The Antichrist*.[138] This prophetic writing which describes the beginning of the twenty-first century—the beginning of the third millenium—tells, according to a fictitious retrospective account of the twentieth century, about the inescapable appearance of the Antichrist, who becomes the generally accepted world ruler with his headquarters in Jerusalem. Soloviev mentions twice that the decisive change in the man who became the Antichrist happened at the age of 33. 'He was still young, but, thanks to his great talent, at 33 years of age was widely proclaimed as a great thinker, writer, and social worker ... He believed in Good, but the All Seeing Eye of the Eternal knew that this man bowed before the power of evil when it offered him a bribe—not by the snare of the senses and lower passions, nor even by the superior attraction of power, but through his immeasurable self-love alone. Besides, this self-love was neither an unconscious instinct nor a foolish pretence. In view of his exceptional talent, his beauty, nobility of character, his supreme display of continence, his disinterestedness, and his active beneficence, it seemed that his enormous self-love was justifiable, and worthy of a great spiritualist, ascetic and philanthropist.'[138]

It is this self-love which was the source of the change. 'He had passed his 30th year and still another three years go by. Suddenly the thought flashes into his mind and pierces to the depths of his brain with a burning shudder, "But if? If it is not I, but that other—the Galilean. If he is not my forerunner, but the real first and last?" '

In the place of humility and veneration 'there grows up in his heart, at first a sort of horror and then a burning envy and fury which seizes and contracts all his being, a hatred which fills his soul. "It is I, and not He," he calls out. "No, he is not alive and will not be. He has not, He has not risen! He is rotting in the grave, rotting as the lost..." '[138]

Soloviev here describes the decisive moment in which this well-prepared person finally surrenders to the Antichrist. He recognizes the truth of Christ's resurrection—he must basically recognize it—but he intentionally denies such truth and, with all the means at his disposal, seeks to nullify and destroy it. This is the archetype of the sin against the spirit in which knowledge of the truth is consciously opposed. The recognition of the earthly-cosmic effect of the resurrection body, discussed earlier in such detail, lies at the basis of the decision of will which here entirely includes the Antichrist. At the same time it was emphasized that the Antichrist, in sinning against the spirit, ruthlessly opposes this with universal humanity-encompassing tactics.

When the Antichrist denies the resurrection for the second time, he throws himself into the abyss, but is stopped in mid-air and thrown back up. 'He felt a vibration as from an electric shock ... For an instant he lost consciousness.'[138] Through the 'electric shock' and the break in consciousness the Antichrist himself has the archetypal experience of that which Ahriman uses as the classical means of infusing the soul with his forces.[139]

After these episodes those forces enter the superman—in conscious reversal of the Baptism in the Jordan—which enable him in the shortest space of time to write his book *The Open Way to Universal Peace and Prosperity*. He can write the book in his *own* name, he does not need to obey or serve anyone. The book is written in such a way that it will suit everybody, everyone will interpret it according to his own fashion, for nothing will induce man 'to offer a sacrifice to truth itself, to *actually* raise himself above his "I" for its sake'. Actually it is not a matter of transforming the ego, nor of gradually absorbing the Christ-Impulse into the ego in order to truly change the nature of man, but it involves a resting or hardening of the ego itself.

'The wonderful author not only attracted everyone, but he was welcome to each, thus fulfilling the words of Christ: "I am come in My Father's name and ye receive Me not: if another shall come in his own name—him ye will receive." Of course, for the latter to be received he must be welcome.' These words reveal their prophetic character for our time. As the economic process is understood and practised nowadays it largely serves to make things comfortable and easy by rousing and satisfying new needs. One becomes increasingly aware that, in connection with the community of man, egoism and antisocial

behaviour in respect of the earth and its surroundings reveal
forces of destruction and exploitation.

Behind the Kaspar-Hauser-destiny the heads of the Jesuit
and Freemasonry Orders would be seen to be the deciding and
directing powers. As Soloviev describes it: 'The principle
directors of general European policy belonging to the powerful Society of Freemasons felt the lack of a common
executive authority... Then the "devoted ones" resolved to
institute a personal executive authority of one person with full
and sufficient powers. The principal candidate was a member
of the Order, "the coming man". He was the only person with
a great worldwide reputation. Being by profession a clever
scientist in the branch of ballistics, and by possessions a large
capitalist, he had friendly relations everywhere in financial
and military circles.'[138]

It has been shown how, especially since the events of 1945,
the economy and armaments have become the decisive factors
for life throughout the world. And should we not look upon
Soloviev's remark, 'by profession a scientist in the branch of
ballistics' as a pointer towards space travel? At the instigation
of the Freemasons the 'coming man' was the elected lifelong
president of the United States of Europe and finally, amid
general rejoicing, raised to the rank of 'Roman Emperor'. He
begins his rulership on earth by bringing peace—which is no
other than 'peace through force', and he solves the social-
economic problem through 'an equality of general repletion'.
The culmination of his accession to power was achieved
through the magician Apollyon, who was a master of the half-
scientific, half magical art of 'attracting and controlling
atmospheric electricity according to his will, which was com-
monly known as calling down fire from heaven'. Through
miracles and signs he became the great entertainer of the
nations of the world. Finally the Emperor wished to resolve
the religious question at a Council in Jerusalem. 'When the
Emperor entered, accompanied by the great magician and his
suite, the orchestra played the "March of United Humanity",
which served as the imperial national hymn.'

'The March of United Humanity'. Over against that was, in

the Christian sense, the choir of many nations with many different voices that individually served the community. The Emperor easily managed to win over most of the members of the Council to his way of thinking—Orthodox Christians, Catholics and Protestants. But he failed with the small remainder of Christians. To his question what he could do for them the venerable John replied: 'Confess now before us, Jesus Christ, the Son of God, Who came in the flesh, Who rose from the dead, and Who will come again.'[138] As the Antichrist could not give the appropriate answer he was unmasked. When the venerable John openly proclaimed in front of the Council: 'Children, it is the Antichrist!' he broke the spell. It is true, the magician Apollyon was able to prevent the immediate consequence of this unmasking through a seeming divine judgement, nevertheless the doom of the Antichrist has hereby been irrevocably sealed through his unmasking. Outwardly this was brought about by the Jews, who, having looked upon the Superman as the Messiah, noticed that he was not a Jew at all. He was imprisoned by a mighty earthquake and a volcanic eruption which engulfed the Emperor, the magician and all belonging to them.

Soloviev's story is not to be dismissed in a trivial way as a prophesy. It reproduces, as it were, the ideal plan for the Antichrist, the historical fulfilment of which is diverted, damped down and crossed by several other factors. The actual historical process, which takes place in a quite different period of time, presents a very much modified picture. In providing a knowledge of the evolutionary tendencies and the motives of the present day and near future which have to come to terms with the principle of evil, Soloviev's writing presents us with archetypal pictures that are of great importance and the reader will easily be able to verify how much in the course of history is based on such archetypal pictures.

Sorath—the Demon of the Sun and the number 666

The world-historic significance of the years immediately preceding the end of the millennium can be more profoundly understood if one takes into consideration that 1998 is also three times 666. What lies hidden in the number 666 is the most concentrated action of evil on mankind and the earth. This number is first mentioned in the Apocalypse of St John (Chapter 13). Rudolf Steiner explains it in two ways.

First of all one must bring to mind that pitted against the good Sun Spirit, the Intelligence of the Sun which calls forth all life upon earth, is an evil spirit, a Demon of the Sun, which also lives in the evil forces in man.[140] Rudolf Steiner further explains that the number 666 can be read according to Aramaic secret doctrine and that the numbers correspond to letters. 'These letters symbolize the four principles that lead people to complete rigidification if they are not able to transform them. Through Samech the principle of the physical body is expressed, through Vau the etheric body, Resh the astral body and Tau the lower "I" that has not yet raised itself up to the higher "I". The whole when read together is Sorath. This is the occult name of the Sun Demon, the opponent of the Lamb.'[140]

The dragging down and killing of man's inner nature is made clear—666 is the number of the human being who shuts himself off from the facts of Christ and can therefore receive no benefits from them.

Rudolf Steiner comes to speak more fully about the number 666 in the 11th lecture of his lecture cycle *The Apocalypse of St. John*.[141] To the anthropological aspect is now added the world-historical one which includes that of the whole earth evolution. Rudolf Steiner divulges the fact that by 666 a distant period of earth's development is referred to in which mankind will have already finally split up into an evil and a good race. Preceding this there will be decisions between good and evil which man will again be able to revoke while there is still time to turn back.

Even though these events are still far distant, Rudolf Steiner distinctly emphasizes that 'everything of the future is already being presently prepared'.

The evil referred to, which emanates from the Sun Demon, Sorath, the antagonist of the Sun Spirit, Christ, must apparently not be compared with the luciferic and ahrimanic powers. What proceeds from Lucifer and Ahriman has a necessary effect upon mankind. Man can only achieve his goal by using these powers. This is compensated for by his destiny in which the balance is restored by finding the Christ Impulse.

'To pervert man to immorality alone, as it is normally recognized among ordinary people, it is not necessary for the monster such as the Sun Demon to be involved. Only when the beings which bring salvation to mankind, when spiritual uplift is changed into its opposite and spiritual power is made subservient to the lower ego-principle, can mankind be brought to the point where the Beast described as having two horns gains control over them. The misuse of spiritual powers is connected with that seductive power of the Beast with two horns. And we call this misuse of spiritual power black magic in contrast to the proper use which we call white magic.'[141]

In describing the crime committed against Kaspar Hauser the misuse of spiritual powers was first alluded to. The sin against the spirit committed in this connection may therefore be understood to be an expression of the seduction carried out by Sorath. That is consistent with the fact that the sin against the spirit cannot be forgiven, that is to say, it cannot find compensation as can other sins or aberrations of a luciferic or ahriman nature.

In the historic fulfilment of Kaspar Hauser's murder in 1933 the hand of the Sun Demon, evoked by the actions of the Jesuits (and the western Lodges) against Kaspar Hauser, is discernible. In carrying this out the forces coming from the Hitler movement, which prepare for the end of the century in the sense of the Sun Demon, play into it. The revelations which the resurrected Sun Spirit wishes to show to mankind are opposed by the work of the Sun Demon who finds predestined, willing human organizations for it. The awakening spiritual powers of innumerable people were misused; the magical effect, the beguiling influence on the unconscious powers of the will-forces which—rooted in the spirit—ought to be kept sacrosanct, is for the first time explained against the background of the battle between the Sun Demon and the Sun Spirit.

In his lecture given on Hegel's 150th birthday anniversary, 27 August 1920, in Dornach, Rudolf Steiner discusses the Swastika.* He quotes from a news article which states that a 10,000-rouble banknote bore in the centre a finely and clearly drawn Swastika:

> This symbol, which a Hindu once looked upon when he spoke of his sacred Brahman, is seen today on a 10,000-rouble note! In the strongholds of politics, people know how to influence human souls. One knows what the victorious advance of the Swastika signifies, the sign which a great number of people in Central Europe are already wearing today—again based on other underlying reasons—one knows what it means; yet one is unwilling to listen to something that seeks to interpret the secrets of today's historical developments out of the most important symptoms.[142]

Retrospectively this pointer to the enigmas of present-day historical development can be put in its context, here expressed, whereby its correctness is confirmed.

The Sorath influence within the movement which bears the Swastika is further distinguished by the fact that the impulse of the being 'to make himself into a god', as Rudolf Steiner once said,[143] is feebly reflected in the 'Heil Hitler' salute in that a man demands divine recognition. This misplaced, senseless religious veneration really serves the Sun Demon. In the already quoted Karlsruhe lecture Rudolf Steiner emphatically states that in the thirties of the present century 'the Biblical prophecies will be fulfilled'.[127]

Through the second aspect of the number 666, its connection with the year 1998, and with that prospectively the whole century since the end of Kali Yuga, becomes immediately clear. We are told that the Sorath impulse tried to manifest strongly in the *year* AD 666.[144] But now the Sorath influence notably works in history—in weakened form—through the doubling and trebling of this number.* Three times 666 is 1998.

In the lectures given in October 1918 in Dornach and Zürich, Rudolf Steiner adds to knowledge he had already given about the number 666 the fact that Sorath had intended to corrupt mankind in AD 666. And this seduction was so great that it could not be prevented or diminished by human means, but only through the incarnation of Christ Himself and the Mystery of Golgotha. In face of Sorath, the Beast, only Christ, through His deeds on earth, could restore the equilibrium. Rudolf Steiner points to the connection here with the twentieth century: 'Our age is, in many respects, a renewal of those periods which took place partly through the Mystery of Golgotha, partly through what happened in AD 333, partly through what occurred in AD 666.'

What was to have happened around the year 666, but was prevented, or rather weakened, by the Christ-Impulse, was that the consciousness soul, with all its spiritual possibilities, would have been allowed to function much too early, that is to say directly and without human development taking place, so that the further development of mankind in the future would have been made impossible. Humanity was to have been deluged 'with the wisdom of the Beast'. It was planned 'by certain higher spirits, particularly by a being of ahrimanic nature who was to lead these spirits, that this being should appear, even if not on the physical plane—but he was to appear.'[143] All this 'was to have been instilled into man even in 666 through the ahrimanic-luciferic powers'[145] so that he would have become consciously aware of his own personality, whereby his ego would have become completely hardened within itself, completely suffocated.

This impulse was to have emanated from the Arabian Academy of Gondeshapur, which is the place where Manes was crucified as a Christian martyr. The writings of Aristotle were translated into Arabic there. The Aristotelian concepts served the sages of Gondeshapur, in a rather changed form, as their world outlook. 'Their endeavour ... was on behalf of an all-embracing knowledge which was meant to replace the exertions of the consciousness soul. It would have made of man a mere man of the earth and would have shut him off from his true future—his evolution into the spiritual world.'[146]

At the turn into the third millennium it is only too plain that a kind of renaissance of these efforts is strongly in evidence—a fact which has been confirmed in several details, 'even though that which was to have gone out from Gondeshapur was deadened through the appearance of Mohammed and his visionary religious teaching', nevertheless what 'the eminent teacher whose name is unknown, but who was the greatest opponent of Christ Jesus'[146] taught his pupils had a strong lasting effect; for from this actual leader of the Gondeshapur Academy two things, among others, have emerged, which are of great significance for the subject under discussion.

The first is that contemporary natural science, particularly in the form it has taken since the forties of the nineteenth century, has developed under the influences of Gondeshapur.[147] And this development resulted in the atom bomb in 1945 and later in nuclear energy with all its unpredictable consequences.

The second thing is that the influence of Gondeshapur, as opposed to the Spirit, was at work in the Catholic Church. 'The Roman Catholic Church, which was strongly under the influence of the remnants of the impulse of the Academy of Gondeshapur, decreed dogmatically at the General Ecumenical Council of Constantinople in AD 869 that we must *not* believe in the spirit, because the Church did not wish to enlighten everybody on the Mystery of Golgotha, but wished to spread darkness over it. In AD 869 the Roman Catholic Church abolished the spirit. The dogma which was decreed at that time reads: "We must not believe in the spirit, but only in body and soul, the soul possessing something of a spirit-like nature." But the fact that man really consists of body, soul and spirit was abolished by the Catholic Church under the direct influence of the impulse of Gondeshapur.'[145] This statement of Rudolf Steiner appropriately supports and bears out what we have here attempted to reveal: the battle of the Jesuits against the true spirit as it was intended to appear in Kaspar Hauser. This battle is at the same time a battle waged against Christ and the Mystery of Golgotha.

If one studies the end of the millennium with respect to the knowledge of evil, the question of the difference between Ahriman and Sorath must arise. Mankind experiences the intense preparation that Ahriman is making for his incarnation. The only way man can protect himself against it is through a knowledge of its world-historical necessity. Mankind must learn—in the age of the consciousness soul—to deal with such a fact and to decide how to act in accordance with it. This is not possible without a knowledge of the spirit.

About Sorath one can say that he is the actual evil principle itself, the Antichrist. According to Rudolf Steiner there is *no* question of Sorath incarnating. The activity of Sorath lies along the lines of the asuras, mentioned earlier, about which was said that whatever succumbs to them is irrevocably lost and that through them 'fragments of the ego' are torn off. As the Sun Demon, Sorath is the being who finally wants to drag mankind down into the abyss. He seduces man to commit the sin against the spirit which, because of this source, cannot be forgiven.

It is truly a very serious and difficult situation in which mankind is spiritually placed in that Ahriman and Sorath direct their development against the Christ-Impulse. Their activities are different, but nevertheless both aim in the same direction. Ahriman attempts to capture human intelligence in order, according to his intentions, to turn the earth and the cosmos into a mechanism. Through Sorath the will is attacked—which is more difficult for human beings to assess—and in that way, through a kind of magical intoxication, man is torn away from his spiritual home, the Sun.

In Soloviev's story of the Antichrist one is dealing with both. The Antichrist-impulse is first described in the sense of the Apocalypse of John, that is in the sense of Sorath. But then the moment of incarnation is added. Ahriman steps in and appears on the physical plane. At this juncture Soloviev describes two beings who ape the relationship between the Father God and the Son God. In order to make plain in a picture the difference as it is meant here and the existing relationship of the two, one could say that

Sorath represents the Father and the incarnating Ahriman the Son.

They are characterized by Soloviev in the following way: 'He saw these two piercing eyes and heard, proceeding neither from within nor from without, a strange voice, dull, as if smothered, and, at the same time, precise and entirely soulless, as if it came from a gramophone. The voice said to him: "My well-beloved son, all my affection is in thee. Why hast thou not sought me? Why honour that other, the wicked One and His Father. I am god and thy father. The other—a beggar and crucified One—is a stranger to me and thee. I have no other son but thee. Thou, my one, only begotten, equal to me. I love thee and ask nothing of thee. Thou art so beautiful, great and powerful. Act in thine own name, not in mine. I do not envy thee; I love thee. I am in need of nothing from thee. He, whom thou didst deem a god, demanded of His Son obedience and boundless subservience, even to the death of the cross, and He was unable to help Him on the cross. I require nothing of thee, and I shall help thee." '[138]

Survey and summing up

If one looks at the 33-year rhythm over the last two centuries from the time of Kaspar Hauser's birth and death, one can become aware of a language previously unknown in history, the language of the cosmic Christ-Spirit which—united with the earth—seeks to communicate with mankind through historical events. The language which sounds forth here is so new and unfamiliar that, to begin with, it is hardly audible. It is spoken by the great breath of the spirit, embracing a whole generation and in a tongue derived from the Mystery of Golgotha that will only become audible to the awakening spiritual faculties of man after the dark age has run its course. What is new must be comprehended by what is newest of all. All that is here attempted is to make audible the first note of a great future melody.

One could also say that our aim is to decipher an unknown

piece of writing. The first letters have hardly been recognized up till the present. Their sequence and arrangement into words must be found in thinking. Sense can be made out of the words. Haltingly and stammeringly one learns the first letters, the meaning of the first words is grasped, the sense is conjectured. In this kind of mood one can try to get a survey of the whole—and in particular the special features of each of the two series (the birth sequence and the death sequence).

In the birth sequence lies a force that seeks to let mankind participate in the healing deeds of Christ. The birth of a prepared, guarded individuality, worthy to bear the secret of Christ's deed on his very person, was predestined in the world-plan to help bring to mankind a new experience of Christ at the beginning of the Michael Age (2 × 33 years later) and after the end of Kali Yuga (1899). This secret remained almost hidden during Kaspar Hauser's lifetime, but the fact that it existed and continued to take effect is apparent through the knowledge of the 'phantom', the resurrection body, which was confided to mankind by Rudolf Steiner exactly 99 years after Kaspar Hauser's birth, and in his birthplace, Karlsruhe. This fact is based on the so-called 'hundred-year rule',* about which Rudolf Steiner came to speak three days after the first great explanation of the 33-year rhythm on 26 December 1917 in Dornach, quoted above.

'A human generation of 33 years brings the germ of a thought or a deed to fruition. Once it has come to fruition it continues to work on in history for another 66 years. One can also recognize the intensity of an impulse implanted by someone into the course of history by its effect throughout three generations, for a whole century.'[148]

In the present volume many things have been included in order to show the significance and strength of the impulse connected with Kaspar Hauser. If one is able to assess the intensity of this impulse with which the guiding spiritual powers themselves have placed Kaspar Hauser on to the earth, one can only be amazed at the consequential result which shows in history through the fact that a free spirit, Rudolf Steiner, could fulfil the compensatory deed 99 years later.

Rudolf Steiner placed himself consciously into this current of activity in 1911/12. Through that the possibility arose of belatedly fulfilling Kaspar Hauser's mission. Not least for this reason, it was a terrible and unavoidable blow dealt against everything that Rudolf Steiner bestowed on mankind in the way of spiritual gifts and knowledge, which then became effective in history in 1944/45. The events of 1944/45 bear determinative, incalculable consequences for the future. One can experience strongly how these are being fulfilled already in the immediate present (1978) according to the rule of 33 years.

One only has to think of the decisions with regard to the new atomic weapons, or the generally accepted sentence: 'economic growth only by means of nuclear power', and the petrification of state proceedings through terrorism, which has functionally taken over the task of the Hitler movement in this respect. For the latter fought from Central Europe against the whole world—concealing thereby the most significant events of that time. However, the whole world was not weakened, but extensively strengthened, in its dangerous tendencies. Thus the war against the world—paradoxically formulated—was quite to the advantage of the world. On the other hand a stronger awakening of consciousness for humanity's position and a strengthening of responsibility for the future is noticeable.

If one now looks at the death sequence, the year 1933 stands out conspicuously—again in accordance with the 'hundred years' rule'. The impulse expressed by the murder of Kaspar Hauser was so powerful that it could not be countered by the spiritual activity of Rudolf Steiner, which started to develop at the end of Kali Yuga. That does not mean to say that this activity was in vain. It provided the basis for understanding the situation and introducing the necessary future development.

In the foreground of the death sequence, understandably enough, is the attack by the evil powers, which took place at the beginning of the nineteenth century by the banding together of the heads of the Jesuits and Freemasons. For their own ends they needed to prevent the activity of Kaspar Hauser. Their widespread occult intentions, inspired by evil sagacity, only become clearly comprehensible to history in the twentieth century. In this trend the 'Lucifer-Ahriman-company' join forces with the activities coming from Sorath.

What they were ultimately aiming at was to get human and earthly evolution into their hands by the end of the twentieth century, as this had been planned already around the year 666. Dazzled by what was happening in the foreground, the events which followed the death of Kaspar Hauser—whereby the spiritual world itself sought to draw near to and communicate with those whom it found ripe—remain in the background in the 33-year rhythm. Thus with the turn of the nineteenth to twentieth century the spiritual world becomes accessible to the searchers after knowledge who, since then, led by Rudolf Steiner's deeds of spiritual enlightenment, have, through a progressive spiritual penetration of the world, been enabled to find security and meaning in life. During the course of this growing accessibility of the spiritual world since 1933, *that Being*, Who is the centre-point of man's physical and spiritual development—the Christ Being—approaches mankind in spiritual-etheric form.

The birth-sequence is concerned with the physical world and the transformation of its bad and good parts. The death sequence is concerned with the relationship between the sense world and the spiritual world and with the building of a bridge between the two. The cosmic background of earthly-human history directed towards the future is especially evident. We should remember that Jakob Wassermann describes the funeral of Kaspar Hauser as accompanied by a unique celestial phenomenon (see Chapter 1, p.57).

When one tries to find the connection between the birth-sequences and the death-sequences one is surprised to discover that the period of 12 years, which is the time the National Socialist rulership lasted, appears of its own accord in the time lying between these two sequences. This arises from the fact that the 21 years of Kaspar Hauser's life make up the 33 years when 12 are added. If one reckons 99 years ahead from Kaspar Hauser's birth, one arrives at the year 1911. The succeeding 33 years divide into a 21-year section (till 1932) and a 12-year section (from 1932 till 1944). In the year 1932/33 the death sequence necessarily joins this subdivision.* The 12 years in between the two sequences were a special incursion point for the ahrimanic and asuric powers. One must suppose that the perpetrators of the underlying deed had this in mind from the first. With this reference to the human perpetrators a difficult question of discrimination is raised.

Experience teaches that even people who recognize the good and evil influences of spiritual beings in human history are difficult to convince of the fact that human beings give themselves up to evil *consciously* knowing what they do. For a good reason the belief has been implanted in man's soul that spiritual knowledge can only be a strength and foundation for morality. Natural and healthy as this is, one should not generalize about it, otherwise it would hinder one from facing up to the terrible fact that people do not only come into contact with the principle of evil through presumption and error, but also intentionally and consciously. The tremendous significance of this fact follows from the consideration of the last two centuries as they have been presented here. There is no possibility of prevailing against the influence of such people if one is unable to gaze impartially into the abyss of evil.

Among other things that these circles of people put abroad is the opinion that there is no such thing as a cosmic spirit which works in history. In this sense they are supporters of modern science, to which materialism in all its branches is acceptable. Anyone who tries to draw attention to the shady actions of certain circles is, in their opinion, merely someone who from the outset affirms what is absurd and unprovable. In answer to that, one must firmly point out that everything spoken about in that way only serves the one who says it. The best and simplest way to protect their endeavours, is to deny the spirit as such. Who would want to protect himself against something that does not exist? A cunning disguise of evil is to deny that it exists.

Once again the whole seriousness involved in the situation must be made plain by a statement of Rudolf Steiner's: 'These brotherhoods of which I have just spoken, whose aim is to

banish the souls of men into materialistic spheres, are also
making it their aim to ensure that the coming of Christ should
pass by unnoticed in the twentieth century, that His coming as
an etheric Being should not be noticed by humanity. This aim
is developing under the influence of a very definite idea, a very
definite impulse of will, to win the sphere of influence which
should come to us through Christ in the twentieth and later
centuries, for another being—to conquer that sphere for
another being—of whom more will be said later. These
brotherhoods of the West do exist. They aim to thwart the
impulse of the Christ and to put in His place another individuality that has never appeared in the flesh—an etheric being
of a strongly ahrimanic nature.'[149]

Thus the battlefield is prescribed upon which the extensive
catastrophes that befall mankind occur. The catastrophes
themselves are by no means the worst part of it. Far worse is
the lack of understanding and the lack of will to really learn
from the events. The situation becomes impossible owing to
the way that Anthroposophy is ignored, rejected or attacked.
Therefore the majority of people have not got the slightest idea
of what is happening today.

If one is not to despair of ever overcoming the difficulties
that present themselves, the only remedy is to help to create a
new basis for the functioning of Central Europe by unreserved
recognition of what has taken place. Nothing of any value can
happen, unless the dimension of the battle is properly assessed.
'For mankind could bungle the whole arrangement,' Rudolf
Steiner once tersely stated,[150] whereby in this context the
whole of earthly activity was meant. That is the enormous
concern with which we are now faced. It is true, the whole
world cannot be unhinged, but the further development *might*
so run its course that it is ultimately justified to say that it has
been 'bungled'.

In this sense we can now speak of the fact that in the
future—perhaps only after centuries—the German nation
may still find the possibility of fulfilling its mission (in Chapter
2 in the section: 'Kaspar Hauser and the German Folk-spirit'
this question has already been dealt with from a different point

of view). The German nation has the world-historic mission of cultivating the ego within the consciousness soul. To that also belongs the task of taking up the Christ-Impulse into the ego. As this is at the same time a task for humanity in general, nothing is further from the truth than to regard this endeavour as being merely of national significance.

The German spirit could not adequately continue its path leading on from the time of Goethe. It got lost, not only on account of the massive activity of its opponents, but also due to the *naïveté* and weakness of those who should have fostered it. Linking to Goethe, Rudolf Steiner tried to rouse and succour this spirit in the Anthroposophical Society. Now, through the bitter knowledge of Central Europe's destruction—with outside causes, but inner blame—the strength must be found, trusting with patience and calmness in the efficacy of the spirit, to bring about a change for the better at the turn of this century.

What, on the other hand, the opponents of the spirit have been aiming at during the last two centuries, and also before, and what they still want to achieve, is to exclude from the physical plane the effect of the true spirit as it manifests in Christianity. According to this principle of exclusion they would like to conquer the physical plane for themselves. It is their ideal to sweep the earth clean of spiritual impulses in order to chain mankind to the earth and drag it along with them on their path of development—which is into the abyss.

The incursive, purposeful impulses of the opponents of the spirit are served worldwide—unwittingly and with the best of intentions—by most politicians. The latter merely have the possibility of swimming with the existing current, as their actions are held in check by 'realities' of which the origin and consequences cannot be seen. In no field of activity is the illusion that one can actually influence things spiritually oneself so great as in politics. It is only because one does not see the manipulating strings that one thinks one is moving events oneself.

The most blatant example here, too, is Hitler, who accompanied his deeds with all kinds of concepts that he also gave voice to, but which, in a peculiar way, served the principle of suppression, especially by means of the world situation which he himself brought about. The opponents of the spirit achieved their greatest success through Hitler being amenable to their influence. They only interfere directly themselves when they find themselves forced to do so by the facts—as with Kaspar Hauser's birth. The greatest danger for them is when a spiritually awakened human being—an initiate—begins to work concretely for the spirit on the physical plane.

The initiate is called to his mission by the will of beings above man acting from the spiritual world. If an initiate as such is attacked, the attack is also directed against these spiritual beings. This was the position in which Rudolf Steiner found himself—but more about that later. Through an initiate a bridge is built between the physical, sense world and the supersensible-spiritual world, but every contact made by a human being with the spiritual world is a bridge-building.

The picture of the bridge as used here is to be understood in the sense of the bridge in Goethe's *Fairy Tale of the Green Snake and the Beautiful Lily*. Goethe encompassed the most profound evolutionary principles of his own and future times in his imagination of the bridge-building. But his kind of spirit terrified the opponents of the spirit who saw it as their task to destroy the bridge and to prevent it from being built. They would regard it as a triumph if this led to the belief that the building of a bridge was vain and ineffectual. The opposite is the case. Everything carried out spiritually which reaches the spiritual world has its inevitable result as a bridge-building achievement (according to the 33-year rule). It is only a question of it not being merely a concept or an intention in the mind of those involved, but that a real objective contact is made with the spiritual world. The deed of man needs the approval of the spiritual world. Let us demonstrate what is meant here by the finest example in history closely connected with the destiny of Kaspar Hauser.

The conversation which took place in Jena in 1794 between Goethe and Schiller was the means of bringing about a friendship between two individuals who at first did not understand one another. Both had previously approached the spiritual world from their own angle—Goethe chiefly through his discovery of the archetypal plant (Urpflanze). This discovery was made in Palermo in 1787, seven years before the above conversation took place and formed its main topic. Schiller received an inkling of the spiritual world when, in 1791, he lay critically ill at the threshold of death and made the initial step towards an understanding of the threefold human being. In the letters which he wrote to his patron, the Duke Karl Christian of Augustenberg in Denmark, the deeply-rooted idea of 'threefoldness' first took shape (cf. his dissertation: 'Concerning the connection between the animal and spiritual nature of man'). Man's freedom is not seen as something bestowed on him, but as something which can only be obtained by his own effort. In the playing of children—observed by Schiller on his eldest son—can be found the model which points the way for human beings. The artistic process fulfils the requirements of play through the spirit being made perceptible to the senses and material things made spiritual. Only when what is artistic in this sense is achieved by man, does he enter the realm of freedom. With that a firm basis is established for future aesthetics, in which art is shown to be a necessary requirement of the human state, even the fulfilment of man's striving for freedom.[151]

In the conversation between Goethe and Schiller both the archetypal plant as well as the aesthetics propounded by Schiller had a part to play. Reinhard Buchwald has clearly proved how Goethe and Schiller could find one another in the realm of aesthetics because Goethe felt himself understood by Schiller in this realm. And Schiller gradually gained access to Goethe's way of looking at nature. The friendship between Goethe and Schiller was based on their free and independently achieved views of man, which proved to be essentially the same in both. This mutual experience, that their views were not opposed but had an inner affinity, not only unlocked their souls to one another but also allowed the spirit to enter into this human encounter through which they could dimly participate in the events of the spiritual world.[137] In this way their friendship became a deed of world-historical importance that proved its fruitfulness on every hand in that each of them could continue to work with increased ability. This joint work of theirs was published in 1795, when in Goethe's magazine *Die Horen* there appeared 'Die Unterhaltungen Deutscher Ausgewanderten' (Conversations of German Emigrants) to which the Fairy Tale belongs, and the 'Briefe über die ästhetische Erziehung des Menschen' (Letters about the aesthetic education of mankind) by Schiller.

One effect of this epoch-making event in the spiritual history of mankind is the fact that 33 years later, at Whitsuntide 1828, Kaspar Hauser appears in Nuremberg. He is led out of the darkness of his prison into the light. The motives which led to his release at this point of time have remained unknown up till now. It has often been remarked on or felt that his life in the world obviously did not go as his opponents intended. The attempted murder in October 1829, the appearance of Lord Stanhope in May 1830 and finally the murder in December 1833, speak a clear language. Whatever the opponents of Kaspar Hauser might have had in mind when they freed him, they very soon decided that this had been a mistake. On the other hand, however, mankind has to thank this appearance of Kaspar Hauser for the knowledge of his existence.

The spiritual strength which arose out of the friendship of Goethe and Schiller since 1794 (and through the publication since 1795) and with their building of a bridge into the spiritual world is seen here as something that takes effect in the depths of history which helped to free Kaspar Hauser. Whatever is rooted in the powers of the spiritual world itself comes to objective effect in the outer world. The work of Goethe and Schiller and their spiritual friendship prepared Central Europe for the activity of Kaspar Hauser. Dark intrigues hindered the latter in its effect, but the uniting in the spirit of two human beings, the friendship between Goethe and Schiller, creates the impulse which supports it. It is as though the language of history itself wishes to draw attention to this background, in that Kaspar Hauser makes his appearance in Nuremberg just at a Whitsuntide Festival, which is the element of Christianity connected with the future. For the uniting of mankind in the spirit, for the founding of a true human community, there must previously have taken place the winning through to freedom by the single human being in at least one sphere. In the friendship between Goethe and Schiller this is archetypally presented. Its significance for the future is immeasurable.

When we consider the darkness that attacked Kaspar Hauser, is it not a real consolation to know that the spirit achieved through the efforts of man works powerfully into history? Through this it can be recognized that what happens is not from the outset a question of fate, but something through which spiritual strength can be won by man against tremendous evil.

If we follow the 33-year rhythm further, we come to the amazing fact that 33 years after Kaspar Hauser's appearance, in Nuremberg, Rudolf Steiner was born. Thus Rudolf Steiner is placed into the series of important bridge-builders through his very birth date. The stream of spiritual connection and of a combined work for the spirit continuing objectively from generation to generation becomes noticeable. The question asked of the powers of destiny—not yet answered—is: Has the martyrdom of Kaspar Hauser provided Rudolf Steiner with a helpful and protective force?

The great event of the birth of one of the leading spirits of humanity on earth finds its spiritual counterpart 33 years later through the publication of Rudolf Steiner's *Philosophy of Spiritual Activity* in 1894. The inner connection of the whole series brought forward here is shown if one reckons that the *Philosophy of Spiritual Activity* was published a century after the publications of Goethe and Schiller in *Die Horen* in 1795.* That has inner justification. Through Goethe man's perception and observation was particularly enhanced and raised to the spirit (archetypal plant, Theory of Colour). Through Goethe a step was made to free man's powers of observation from Ahriman's tentacles, which give the erroneous impression that in the field of the senses there is nothing of the spirit, only material substance.

Through Schiller thinking is prepared to become an instrument of spirituality by his taking up the Michaelic impulse of threefoldedness. Schiller follows the path of the Christianization of thinking by overcoming the dualism which is given by Lucifer.[152]

Both elements are taken up and continued by Rudolf Steiner, who demonstrated how, in man's cognition, observation and thinking are so united that through the act of knowing, in restoring the unity of the world, man becomes an individually free being.

The mirroring-rule

The decisive importance of the year 1945 and the connection of the above described events of that year with Kaspar Hauser's destiny can be checked and confirmed from another angle according to the mirroring-rule. The rule here referred to was explained by Rudolf Steiner in Dornach on 14 October 1817 as follows:

Things go in cycles or periods. Anything which happens in the physical world is really a kind of projection, or shadow, of what happens in the spiritual world, except that it would have happened earlier in the spiritual world. Let us assume this line here [see sketch] was the line or plane separating the spiritual and the physical worlds. What I have just said could then be characterized as follows: Let us assume an event— for example the battle between Michael and the dragon— happens first of all in the spiritual world. It finally comes to an end when the dragon is cast down from heaven to earth. On earth, then, the cycle is brought to completion after a time interval which approximately equals the time between the beginning of the battle in the spiritual world and the time when the dragon was cast down. We might say: The dawn, the very beginning of this battle between Michael and the dragon, was in 1841. Things were particularly lively in 1845. It is 34 years from 1845 to 1879, and if we move on 34 years after 1879 we come to the mirroring event: you get 1913, the

1841 spiritual event

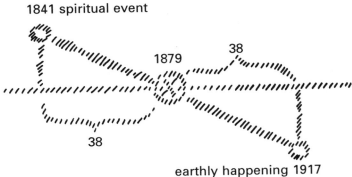

earthly happening 1917

year preceding 1914. You see, the developments which started in the physical world in 1913 are the mirror-image of the prime reasons for the spiritual battle. And now consider 1841–79–1917 ! 1841 was the crucial year in the nineteenth century. 1917 is its mirror image. If one realizes that the exertions of the crowd of ahrimanic spirits in 1841, when the dragon started to fight Michael in the spiritual world, are mirrored right now in 1917, much of what is happening now will not really come as a surprise. Events in the physical world can really only be understood if one knows that they have been in preparation in the spiritual world.[153]

Rudolf Steiner pointed here mainly to the connection between the years 1841 and 1917. The background to the year 1917 will be important for a later discussion. The year 1845, dealt with in the birth sequence for that year, was given prominence by Rudolf Steiner's statements and the tragedy of Kaspar Hauser's exclusion can also be seen in the mirrored image of the related outbreak of World War One.* Through not having Kaspar Hauser on the physical plane it was not possible to blunt the attack of the ahrimanic forces. The latter were able to spread confusion and paralysis in the minds of leading personalities, particularly in Germany. It was to this, in conjunction with the long prevailing spiritual vacuities, that Rudolf Steiner ascribed the actual outbreak of war.

The impression of the calamity connected with the exclusion

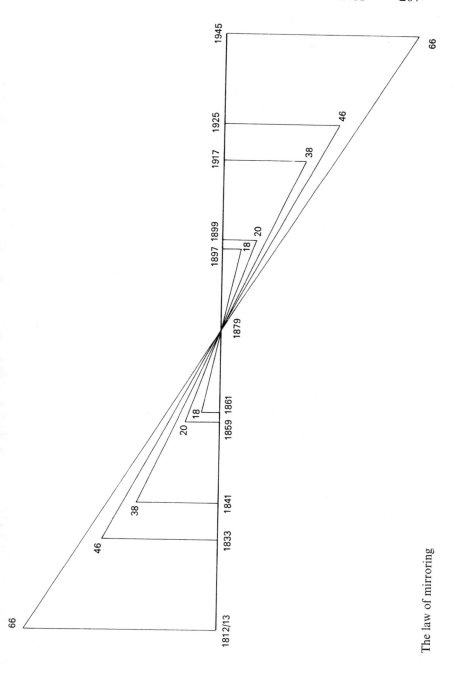

The law of mirroring

of Kaspar Hauser was considerably increased by the fact that
the years 1813 (Kaspar Hauser had been born three months
earlier) and 1945 are mirrored in the year 1879. Kaspar Hauser
was born and put into prison 66 years *before* 1879: 66 years
after 1879 Central Europe was destroyed and atomic energy
was unleashed. Both events are intimately connected with the
task and destiny of Kaspar Hauser.

The creation of a spiritually founded state in South
Germany should have made the impulse from the time of
Goethe so effective on the physical plane that through
Anthroposophy, due to come in the twentieth century, a
sufficient number of people would have been adequately
prepared to meet the spiritual events of the century. In spite of
the tremendous spiritual efforts of Rudolf Steiner, the arrears
brought about by the exclusion of Kaspar Hauser could not at
first be immediately made good. Without forgetting the malice
of the opponents it must be seen that the lack of understanding, seriousness and alertness prevented people, in union
with Rudolf Steiner, from making possible what, so to speak,
is impossible.

If Kaspar Hauser could have been in a position commensurate with his task, forces secretly connected with his
spiritual-physical phantom, which are the exact opposite of
atomic power, would have been able to unite with the physical
world.

An argument against the mirrored connection of the years
1812/13 and 1945 could be that Rudolf Steiner spoke of an
event in the spiritual world, which was then projected onto the
physical plane. One might think that the birth of Kaspar
Hauser was not such an event as this. Over against that one's
attention can be drawn to the fact that, particularly in the case
of the birth of a leader of mankind at an important moment—
Michaelmas 1812—this would be the result of an impulse
springing from the spiritual world. Added to that the kidnapping and exchange of Kaspar Hauser with a dying child
two weeks after his birth is the evil application of occult
knowledge. The imprisonment and treatment meted out to
Kaspar Hauser are the expression of a spiritual battle fought

out between the spiritual and physical worlds. One of the hallmarks of such a battle is that it takes place so secretly that it remains unknown to most people or appears unbelievable. The concealment of Kaspar Hauser's birth in respect of place and time is also a method of this occultly determined strife. How the doubt about Kaspar Hauser's origin can be overcome is demonstrated at the beginning of the first chapter of this book.

The application of the mirroring-rule can also reveal a deeply moving connection between the year 1833, the year of Kaspar Hauser's death, and a later event. Kaspar Hauser was murdered about 46 years prior to the autumn of 1879, the beginning of the Michael Age. Barely 46 years after 1879, on 30 March 1925, Rudolf Steiner was forced to abandon the physical plane. One is confronted by the shattering fact that the two greatest spiritual bridge-builders of Central Europe were driven from the physical plane in a mirrored relationship pivoted round the start of the Michael Age.

The hundred-year event from 1833 is the coming to power of Hitler in 1933. The mirroring is 1925, the death-year of Rudolf Steiner. Rudolf Steiner incarnated into a world-historic spiritual battle, partly as proxy for the suppressed Kaspar Hauser. His untiring work, especially in this century, was directed towards rescuing mankind from the plunge into the abyss. The observation of the mirrored relationship of the deaths of these two individuals raises the question of their mutual relationship to one another. This point will be dealt with in the next chapter.

4. Kaspar Hauser and Rudolf Steiner

The world is fain to blacken
what is bright and to drag into
the dust what is supreme.
Schiller on Joan of Arc

The mirroring-rule in the life of Rudolf Steiner

The rule of mirroring, revealing a hidden connection between Kaspar Hauser and Rudolf Steiner, can also elucidate a decisive moment in Rudolf Steiner's biography. Through his birth on 27 February 1861 he was co-ordinated into the stream of time in such a way that when he reached his first moon-node (at the age of 18 years and 8 months) it coincided exactly with the moment when Michael cast down 'the forces opposed to him from the spiritual world into the world of man'—that is to say that, since that time, they rule 'in the feelings, will and ideas of human beings'. Since November 1879—a moment that Rudolf Steiner especially points to—'these discarded spirit-beings of darkness unfold their activity among men'.[154] But also, at this same moment, Rudolf Steiner begins his Michaelic activity on earth.

The passage through the first moon node often manifests in the biographical development in such a way that the living individuality, hidden in the depths of the will, steps more clearly and actively into the consciousness of the young person, and, above all, the destined task of the present incarnation becomes more clearly envisaged. Often an aim in life, the choice of a career, the connection to other people is suddenly and perceptibly altered. In the case of Rudolf Steiner this step in development was marked—in complete harmony with the cosmic event of the Michaelic battle—by the beginning of his study at the Technical High School in Vienna in 1879 and by his soon-to-be developed friendship with Karl Julius Schröer and the herb gatherer. In the third chapter of his autobiography Rudolf Steiner tells about these karmic encounters.

Through Schröer he forms a connection to the world of Goethe, which becomes for him an important point of contact and his livelihood for many years. He also gets to know *Faust* for the first time through Schröer. In Schröer was living an individuality—deeply connected with Rudolf Steiner—which had to endure the tragic destiny of not being able to fulfil much of its deeper underlying spiritual and karmic impulses. He is one of those souls who—as indicated above—were unable to properly awaken to their destiny in the nineteenth century because Kaspar Hauser was not there and because their consciousness was clouded by the preponderance of materialism. From the time of his later Goethean studies, right up to the building of the Goetheanum, Rudolf Steiner quietly started—without wasting any words—to selflessly carry out the task connected with Goethe that his beloved teacher had been unable to fulfil. Schröer's work concerned mainly Goethe's artistic impulses, not his works of natural science, for which he had little affinity and which were a destined task of Rudolf Steiner. The presiding spirit of his teacher Schröer served Rudolf Steiner later also for the impulse leading to the presentation on the stage of the 'Oberufer Christmas Plays' which Schröer had published.

A quite different karmic note is struck by Rudolf Steiner's meeting with the herb gatherer: 'With him it was possible to speak about the spiritual world as with somebody of experience ... because he had a firm footing in the spiritual world it was possible—if one had powers of perception of one's own—to attain through him significant glimpses into that world'. While Rudolf Steiner otherwise—if seldom—in speaking about his experiences of the spiritual world would fall silent if he met with a lack of understanding, there was something familiar and reassuring about the herb gatherer and Rudolf Steiner must have experienced through this person something like the breath of a distant homeland. 'And gradually it seemed to me as if I were in the company of a soul from bygone ages who, untouched by civilization, science and modern views, brought me an instinctive knowledge of the past.'[155] This current of spiritual life is incorporated in different ways in the work of Rudolf Steiner: in lecture cycles about nature spirits, in the Mystery plays and in lectures in connection with the Christmas Conference of 1923.

The third motif of Rudolf Steiner's life during the first moon-node can be described as the Michaelic one. The building of the bridge between the physical and the spiritual world, to which he devoted his whole life, becomes visible here as the starting point of his biography. 'At that time it was all-important to me to find ways of expressing in clearly defined thoughts the living activity of the human spirit. My efforts in this direction in the sphere of scientific concepts had finally brought me to see that the activity of the human "I" is the only possible starting point for true knowledge. When the ego observes its own activity it has something spiritual immediately present in consciousness.' The original result which Rudolf Steiner achieved to enable the modern, thinking human being to understand the spiritual world was taken up at that time. 'And all the time I tried more and more deliberately to give *conceptual-form* to my direct *experience* of the spiritual world.'[155]

The ahrimanic spirits that unfold their activity out of the unconscious and confused state of man, are here confronted by the spirit which consciously takes the step within its ego that the Spirits of Darkness have to make in their battle against Michael. The latter have been removed from the spiritual world and into man and now threaten to cripple his thinking to such an extent that he is unable to perceive what sort of spirituality is entering into him. Thinking is thereby drawn down into a sphere in which it becomes completely passive and—removed from its source—is made an unconscious servant of the evil forces. In contrast to this, human thinking is filled through Rudolf Steiner—in the highest activity of the ego—with the impulse of spiritual beings transformed into the content of thought. Through that the aspiring, healing principle is given into the hand of man at the moment of his human-spiritual development, which is of such significance that it becomes the mirror for past and future events. This occurs when the spirit-filled thoughts are raised again to a beholding of the spiritual beings through the activity of the ego. Through Kaspar Hauser something should have taken place on the earth in the forties of the nineteenth century—when the battle of Michael against the Dragon began—corresponding to the activity at the end of the battle.

If one now progresses from the mirroring-point in the autumn of 1879 another moon-node further, one comes to the summer of 1898 (February 1861 + 37 years and 4 months). Through this ordering of time, which indicates a still deeper underlying secret, there arises the fact that the second moon-node of Rudolf Steiner is mirrored by the moment of his birth. This is not only an important moment in time but, at this point, an important spiritual event takes place in the biography. This indicates the impulse which was present immediately prior to Rudolf Steiner's birth. This supersensible impulse can be characterized as that of the highest Christian service. It consists of a decision to help mankind in the sense of Christ in the immediately ensuing incarnation. This prenatal decision has to be brought down to earth and established as conscious knowledge in the incarnated ego. The prenatal spiritual event mirrored at the beginning of the Michael Age in the decisive trials that Rudolf Steiner encountered before the turn of the century (1861–79–98) is changed by him into a deed which remains present in the spirituality of man and the earth. In the 26th Chapter of his autobiography Rudolf Steiner states: 'At that time my experience of Christianity underwent a severe test. This lasted from the time of my departure from Weimar, where I had completed my task, to the period when I wrote my book *Christianity as Mystical Fact*. Tests of this nature are obstacles placed in one's path by destiny (karma). They have to be overcome in the course of spiritual development.' The obstacles are primarily connected with the activity of the ahrimanic beings which have been transferred on to the earth and into man: 'I never for a moment fell a prey to influences from this realm in my world of ideas—not even unconsciously. For I took the greatest care that all my spiritual investigations were carried out in *clear, waking consciousness*. Consequently, all the more conscious was my inner struggle with the demonic powers which strove to develop scientific knowledge, but not into perception of spirit, but into a mechanical, materialistic way of thinking.' It is by no means a matter of course that the prenatal decision can be brought down into the conscious life of soul and thereby on to the earth undamaged and unreduced. 'I was obliged at that time to rescue my spiritual world-conception through inner battles.' This rescue came about in the end through the fact that Rudolf Steiner discovered and accepted the Christ-Impulse. 'My soul unfolded in me through having stood in the spirit before the Mystery of Golgotha in the most intimate and solemn feast of knowledge.'[156] Through overcoming the trials of soul which he underwent before the turn of the century, Rudolf Steiner gained the sure basis out of which, from the year 1899, as already discussed, until his death in March 1925, he worked in the sense of the Christ-Impulse, and was tirelessly and incessantly engaged therein. The Christ-Substance took possession of the 'I' which—dwelling in a body—was able to give help to mankind in unimaginable fullness of spirit and life.

1859–1879–1899

Immediately prior to Rudolf Steiner's birth there is a nodal point in human evolution about which one can say that it demands the incarnation of an individuality such as Rudolf Steiner. This nodal point is connected with the tasks of Rosicrucianism, which, through certain events from a particular time onwards, underwent a decisive change. Rudolf Steiner once wrote about this turn in the affairs of Rosicrucianism, in which he is himself involved, in the following way:

> Rosicrucianism was intended to be a strictly secret school for the preparation of those things which would become the public task of esotericism at the turn of the nineteenth century, when material science would have found a provisional solution to certain problems.
> These problems were described by Christian Rosenkreutz as:

1) The discovery of spectral analysis, which revealed the material constitution of the cosmos.
2) The introduction of material evolution into organic science.
3) The recognition of a differing state of consciousness from our normal one through the acceptance of hypnotism and suggestion.

Only when *this* material knowledge had reached fruition in science were certain Rosicrucian principles from esoteric science to be made public property.[157]

In respect of time and content the end of Kali Yuga is here implicitly characterized. But the year 1899 is related to the year 1859 according to the mirroring rule. Rudolf Steiner once spoke about this particular year in a striking way: 'The middle of the nineteenth century is just a nodal point in mankind's evolution. At the end of the fifties of the last century a whole row of human achievements coincided with one another which reveal through their interrelationships what is essential and still went unrecognized in man's evolution in the middle of the nineteenth century.' He then points to Fechner's published work: *Elements of Psychophysics* (according to other accounts first published in 1860) and says: 'A second thing which coincides, which takes place in the same year, is the development of spectral analysis by Kirchoff and Bunsen, whereby the unity of the universe is substantially demonstrated.'[158]

With that the first of the stipulations of Christian Rosenkreutz regarding the exoteric dissemination of spiritual knowledge was given in 1859. That is the moment in which the individuality of Rudolf Steiner was preparing to incarnate. The 'change of attitude towards knowledge' made it necessary to 'study in depth the mechanistic-physio-chemical system of the world'. The 'advancement is brought about by a knowledge of the inorganic world'. Necessary as this advance is on the one hand, so is it just as destructive on the other hand for all social life. 'This natural-scientific ideology makes people antisocial, it creates antisocial instincts.' This coming to terms with the natural scientific outlook is an essential impulse in the

life's work of Rudolf Steiner. 'We have to build up a spiritual
world for ourselves once again from within outwards. This is
the task that Anthroposophy sets itself, creating the basis for a
truly social framework for a new order of humanity. Certainly
it would be quite out of place to say that one should only
cultivate the inner man; that would be a kind of refined egoism. We have to speak today about building up outer con-
trivances afresh. But one always has to be aware of the fact
that the best contrived affairs will never be able to progress if
people do not develop the ability to recreate a spiritual world
from within outwards.'[158]

The mirroring rule can show us in two ways how Rudolf
Steiner's life is interwoven into the cosmic course of history
and what depends thereon, both in a temporal and a quali-
tative way; for the end of Kali Yuga, the beginning of the
Michael Age and the development of Christianity in spiritual
stages are events which rest on the establishing of history by
spiritual beings.

The death of Rudolf Steiner

The mirroring process in the deaths of Kaspar Hauser and
Rudolf Steiner is in this sense also an expression of a spiritual
struggle taking place in a more or less hidden way behind the
scenes of history, in which the opponents succeed in attacking
the exterior part, that is the physical body, in order to prevent
its *immediate* effectiveness on earth. It was in this sense that
Rudolf Steiner once spoke about Joan of Arc. 'The only thing
over which the enemies could exercise a certain control was her
physical body, which could be killed, whereby, however, her
spiritual influence became stronger. In each case it was a
sacrificial death, which was not the result of personal destiny,
but the carrying out of a higher mission.'[159]

If one now looks into the question as to what is directly
connected with Rudolf Steiner's death, the answer can only be:
it was the founding of the General Anthroposophical Society
in Dornach at Christmas 1923. Twenty one years after the

start of his spiritual activity within the Theosophical Society (1902) he resolves, one year after the burning of the Goetheanum (New Year's Eve, 1922), on a radically new approach to his work. After the founding of national societies in nearly all the countries of Europe, he himself takes over for the first time the chairmanship of the newly founded General Anthroposophical Society. Since the founding of the Anthroposophical Society in 1913 he had worked in it as its spiritual teacher. He held no office in it. He was not even a member of this society. The acceptance of chairmanship and the forming of an executive committee in Dornach around Rudolf Steiner signifies far more than constitutional changes. It is the result of the will, since the terrible destruction of the Goetheanum, to considerably strengthen the work on the physical plane, in order still to fulfil the tasks undertaken on behalf of mankind. This will is supported by the far-reaching opinion that the greatest imaginable misfortunes would come about if the possibilities inherent in the anthroposophical movement could not be brought more strongly to fruition.

The historical events that took place after Rudolf Steiner's death—particularly during the thirties—portray these misfortunes. With the death of Rudolf Steiner, which denotes a profound change in the relationship of the spiritual to the physical world, the misfortune becomes unavoidable, the catastrophe runs its course. Now the task remains of recognizing this clearly in order to gain the possibility of transforming the misfortune in the future.

At Christmas 1923 Rudolf Steiner formed the Foundation Stone meditation of the Anthroposophical Society which was to become the source from which unlimited spiritual life can flow today and in the future. This Foundation Stone meditation is to be looked upon as an act of the highest spiritual order, because through it socially creative forces are given into the hands of man in a concentrated form, which can lead to important changes on the physical plane. Therefore it is not to be wondered at that those in the background who did not want such a change should fight against Rudolf Steiner with all their might.

In the Foundation Stone meditation of Christmas 1923 Rudolf Steiner fused two streams of his spiritual activity, which had not previously been connected in this way. One is the foundation stone impulse in the narrower sense, which takes hold of the earth to transform it and is deeply connected with the building of the Goetheanum. The second is the impulse coming from the Threefold Movement which was emphatically pursued by Rudolf Steiner and then expressed again and again. What is meant here is the concept of three-fold man as well as the threefold social organism. Now it becomes clear that there are profound and decisive traces linking both these impulses to Kaspar Hauser.

The model building in Malsch

If one were to seek the origin of the foundation-laying impulse of the Goetheanum, one would be led, surprisingly enough, to Malsch, 16 kilometres southwards of Karlsruhe. It was there on the night of 5 to 6 April 1909, under the first full moon of spring, that Rudolf Steiner laid the foundation stone for the Rosicrucian Temple 'Francis of Assisi'. This Temple, which later became known as the 'Model Building in Malsch', is so small (2.5 × 3.5 metres), that it gives the impression of being the seed of a building. Actually it should also be as a seed in the earth, cut into the granite. For all its smallness the architectural, sculpted and painted form of the building displays the archetypal motives of Rosicrucianism. The building derives from the impulse which E.A.K. Stockmeyer received at the Theosophical Congress in Munich at Whitsuntide 1907 through the seals and pillars which Rudolf Steiner asked to have painted and drawn for the Assembly Hall there.[160] The will was kindled in Stockmeyer to discover and create the appropriate form in space for the pillars. To a question relating to this Rudolf Steiner drew

> with a few lines, how the seven pillars should run in two rows from west to east to enclose an elliptical interior and to support a vault in the shape of an ellipsoid with three axes,

of which the long one was oriented from west to east. The entrance was to be in the west and thence the two rows of pillars should start, beginning with the Saturn pillar. Behind the pillars there was to be a corridor, which was likewise to be roofed by ellipsoids with three axes (shell shaped). An elliptical wall was to enclose the whole structure on the outside. It had no windows. The seals were to be fixed to it, the first between the Saturn pillar and the Sun pillar, the second between the Sun pillar and the Moon pillar and so on, up to the seventh on the other side of the Venus pillar in the eastern recess, represented twice, right and left of the centre.

The room only had light from a single opening in the main vault, which was to be so arranged that at the spring equinox, towards nine o'clock in the morning, the sunlight would fall on a 'particular point' in the interior. The wall is to be painted red and the ceiling blue. The zodiac is to be painted on the inside of the main vault beginning with the Fishes in the west above the Saturn pillar.[161]

In this way the 'Model Building' was actually built 'in a thicket near the Forest House in Malsch'.

The vault, in the form of an ellipsoid with three axes, resting on twice seven pillars of an innovative design, is the architectural motif which Rudolf Steiner handed to me in the summer of 1908 in answer to my question. The theme of this design in the flow of its lines stands between the Greek Temple with its clear-cut straight lines and the domed building with its restless tendency towards the circular, which was first overcome by means of the cruciform plan. The Temple of Antiquity only knows two true dimensions. When one walks from the doorway towards the picture one does not actually move forwards, but one repeats the same conditions. It is the domed building which first makes the ancient Temple into a Christian building.[160]

The will to Christianize the earthly world which lies in artistic design is expressed in the archetypal picture of all the

foundation-stone-laying ceremonies performed by Rudolf
Steiner in his so heart-warming words at the laying of the first
Foundation Stone:

> Through pain our Mother Earth has become solidified. It is
> our mission to spiritualize her again, to redeem and to
> transform her into a spirit-filled work of art through the
> strength of our hands. May this stone be at the same time a
> first Foundation Stone for the redemption and transfor-
> mation of our Planet Earth and may the power of this stone
> undergo thousandfold increase. When we were still resting
> in the bosom of the Creator, surrounded by Divine Powers,
> the all-penetrating and all-embracing Father Spirit wove
> within us. But we were still without consciousness, not
> possessing independence. For that reason we descended into
> matter in order to learn here to have self-consciousness.
> Then evil came. Then came Death. But Christ was also
> active within matter and helped us to overcome death. And
> as we now die in Christ, so do we live. We shall overcome
> death and through our strong powers we shall deify and
> spiritualize matter. So shall the power of the Healing, Holy
> Spirit awaken within us.[160]

The ceremony of the laying of the Foundation Stone was
brought to an end with the Rosicrucian sayings as Rudolf
Steiner invoked 'the blessing of all the elevated and most
exalted beings of all the spiritual hierarchies connected with
the Earth evolution'.

What Rudolf Steiner could only express two and a half
years later in Karlsruhe about the knowledge of the phantom
(resurrection body) and its future evolution, was present here
as an active secret still hidden as though under a veil. It is by
the guidance of destiny, which can only strike us with
amazement, that Rudolf Steiner conducted his first Foundation Stone ceremony in an environmental and spiritual relationship to Kaspar Hauser, who had been called earlier to a
similar mission.

The impression of the inner relationship which Kaspar
Hauser bore to what Rudolf Steiner performed in Malsch is

greatly strengthened if we include the mysterious fact that we are here dealing with a Rosicrucian Temple in Malsch, the only one that still exists on earth. Already in the Karlsruhe lecture cycle, *From Jesus to Christ*, a close inner connection of Kaspar Hauser to Rosicrucianism is revealed in the above-given description, and his teacher Daumer is described by Rudolf Steiner as 'the last of the Rosicrucians'. Far further than this extend the statements which Count Polzer-Hoditz reported after his talk with Rudolf Steiner on 3 March 1925. There he says: 'The individuality which hides behind the Kaspar-Hauser-veil is a being which worked inspiringly into the Rosicrucian connections from the beginning, and then, on 29 September 1812, incarnated as the son of the Grand-Duke Karl of Baden and his wife Stéphanie de Beauharnais. Kaspar Hauser had an important mission of esoteric Christianity to fulfil.' (cf. p.281.)

This statement, which will be dealt with in more detail in Chapter 5, reveals yet another direct connection between Kaspar Hauser and Christian Rosenkreutz in addition to the one already mentioned in the first chapter. Therewith, however, the connection of the Rosicrucian temple to Kaspar Hauser himself is made plain.

Finally, there is still a third connection between Malsch and Kaspar Hauser. It has been reported by the Stockmeyer family that when Rudolf Steiner first set foot on ground in the vicinity of the Malsch building, he spoke about 'a consecrated sacred ground'. An ancient initiate, Aren, or Eren, worked here in bygone days. One is referred back to the time of the sinking of Atlantis. An arm of the sea covered the lower-lying plain where now the Rhine flows. Again one is emphatically referred to the secret background of what Rudolf Steiner does and says when one reads in the lecture he gave in Malsch, at the dedication ceremony of the 'Francis of Assisi Branch' on 6 April 1909, how he takes account of the life of this place and of this time and then, as something of a surprise, links it to, of all places, Atlantis. He describes how, during the last third of the Atlantean epoch, the great Initiate of the Sun-Oracle gathered a small group of people around him who were to bear the spiritual life of Atlantis into the post-Atlantean cultures. 'We, as theosophists, are in a position which we can only compare with that in which man found himself in ancient Atlantean times. And just as life has changed since that time, so will life alter again after a catastrophe at a time in the future.' It was expressly stated later: 'The features of Old Atlantis are being repeated.'[161]

At that time it was necessary for a small group of human beings, under the leadership of the Sun-Initiate, to prepare for and enable the Christ to incarnate in the fourth post-Atlantean epoch. In our time a similar group of people are called upon to learn to understand Christ, so that spiritual life is not lost to mankind in the technical life of the future.

Rudolf Steiner once described Kaspar Hauser as a 'straggler from Atlantis'.[162] Regardless of the thereby characterized exceptional circumstances, a direct connection with Atlantis is indicated. An individuality remains untouched by the whole of post-Atlantean cultural development in order to intervene at a decisive moment in human evolution in the sense of Rosicrucian Christianity. What the goals of this intervention were in detail has been explained many times.

We can find three essential ingredients in the building of the Rosicrucian Temple. In the founding itself is the substance of the resurrection, which redeems the earth. In the actual building, Rosicrucian wisdom becomes an artistically formed space. The environment conveys the contact with Atlantis, enduring throughout millennia. All these three elements are connected with Kaspar Hauser. The Rosicrucian Temple in Malsch looks unseeingly towards the north to the Castle in Karlsruhe where Kaspar Hauser was born. In the unuttered secret, through the course of historical events themselves, it is dedicated to the spirit, the Manes* of Kaspar Hauser.

The First Goetheanum in Dornach

When, on 20 September 1913, on the hill in Dornach, Rudolf Steiner laid the foundation stone for the 'Johannesbau' (John

Building—it was only called 'Goetheanum' from September 1918 onwards) the germ of the Malsch building had undergone a change and had been developed further. In this laying of the Foundation Stone ceremony the substance of Christianity had immediate precedence; the first steps towards the announcement of the Fifth Gospel were taken. One might also say that the laying of the Foundation Stone was itself the beginning of the Fifth Gospel. For the first time the Cosmic Lord's Prayer sounded on earth, 'the macrocosmic World-Prayer contained in the primordial Fifth Gospel which is connected with the Moon and Jupiter, even as the four Gospels are connected with the earth'.[163] This prayer, which is closely connected with Rudolf Steiner's spiritual mission, is the force of blessing for the emerging House of the Word, which is to ring out in the building as knowledge of the spiritual world. The Foundation Stone itself epitomizes the power of love in the two interlocking copper dodecahedra. It is the power of love which knowingly constructs the bridge between the two worlds. This building of the bridge—which Goethe recounts in his 'Fairy Tale'—brings the underground Temple to light. The building of the Goetheanum is the revelation of what is hidden, it is the result of the bridge building.

The Rosicrucian verses, spoken in Malsch and later in the laying of the Foundation Stone in 1923, form the germ which is the trinitarian point of growth embracing the whole of mankind, out of which the invisible, yet visible, building arises. When, after the building's destruction (New Year's Eve, 1922), Rudolf Steiner could say, in connection with the Christmas Foundation Meeting: 'The Goetheanum stands before our spiritual gaze,'[164] this points to the indestructible spiritual form that comes into view, but can also disappear again from the visible.

In Goethe's 'Fairy Tale' there is still another point of departure for the Dornach building. The building was there to serve for lectures and, above all, for the performance of the Mystery Dramas, of which the first, *The Portal of Initiation*, was originally staged in 1910 in Munich. This first Mystery

Play is consciously and directly linked to Goethe's 'Fairy
Tale'. The imaginations which Goethe received in 1794 from
the spiritual fount of the Rosicrucians in anticipation of the
Michael Age, are transformed by Rudolf Steiner into human
terms, the fairy tale figures turn into individual human beings
who experience their collective destiny on earth. The simplest
expression of this fact is in the giving of names to the characters in the final version, which Rudolf Steiner omitted to do
in the first draft.[165] The advance in development beyond
Goethe made by Rudolf Steiner is clearly expressed by this
relationship of the 'Fairy Tale' to the Mystery Drama. In this
advance is also present the mighty impulse to create a building
worthy and adequate for this purpose. Goethe's 'Fairy Tale',
in which the much-needed bridge between the sense world and
the supersensible is envisaged pictorially for the first time, is
like a spiritual seed waiting to develop within the hull of the
Dornach building. The name 'Goetheanum' is therefore a
spiritual reality.

The bridge principle is also visible in a simple way in the
basic concept of the First Goetheanum. The two pentagon-
dodecahedra of the Foundation Stone correspond with two
intersecting wooden cupolas in the building as such—an
expression of the interpenetrating worlds. The larger cupola
encompassed the auditorium, where the people congregated
who were receptive to the spirit. The smaller cupola covered
the stage, on which was performed that which artistically
conveyed to people a lively insight into the spiritual world.

The huge speaker's desk, carved in the shape of a larynx,
from which Rudolf Steiner spoke in this 'House of the Word',
stood significantly at the place where the two cupolas inter-
sected. It must not be forgotten that the Christ figure, the
representative of mankind, carved by Rudolf Steiner, depict-
ing Christ between Lucifer and Ahriman, was to have stood
under the small cupola in the long axis of the building. In
everything that a participant in the auditorium experienced
from the stage through the word or in art, he would have
perceived the Christ-Figure as though active from the background. What spiritual science intends and out of whatever

forces the bridge-building is performed, this was immediately
apparent and was presented in the Goetheanum for all to
experience.* After the fire Rudolf Steiner expressed this suc-
cinctly as follows: 'Basically the Goetheanum was built out of
love. Basically it perished under the sign of love ... While all
around hate was raging (1914–18) in Dornach love prevailed,
real love which was incorporated into the building. It was the
love which derives from the spirit.'[166]

The crucial year 1917—The impulse of the Threefold Commonwealth—1841–1879–1917

The second, powerfully active motif of the Christmas Meeting
of 1923, the Threefold Commonwealth impulse, was directly
proclaimed by Rudolf Steiner in the crucial year 1917, as the
basic knowledge of the wisdom of Michael. As quoted above,
Rudolf Steiner explained the mirroring-rule on 14 October
1917, according to which—from the year 1841 onwards—the
spiritual struggle of Michael against ahrimanic spirituality
became physical reality in 1917. One must take into account
the fact that in this year not only did the ahrimanic impulse
clearly establish itself on a historical level, but, above all,
Rudolf Steiner made the threefolding principle available to
man's knowledge and incorporated it into the living current of
earthly history as a direct expression of Michael's activity.

With that the impulse of threefoldness is to be thought of as
itself being threefold. In his book *Riddles of the Soul* Rudolf
Steiner—after 30 years of investigation, as he says elsewhere—
describes for the first time the nerves-and-senses system, the
rhythmic system and the metabolic-limb-system as the basis
for thinking, feeling and willing.[167] This threefoldness of
human nature as a given factor is joined by the threefolding of
the social organism, which can only be instituted intentionally
by mankind on the basis of a corresponding consciousness.
Some time later (1919) Rudolf Steiner describes in the lecture
cycle *The Mission of the Archangel Michael* the threefoldness
of man against the spiritual-cosmic background of the activity

of Lucifer, Ahriman and Christ. Here, for the first time, the Michaelic power of knowledge of this humanity-encompassing trinity becomes perceptible. This power can lead to what Rudolf Steiner, using the words of Nietzsche, calls 'The re-evaluation of all values'.

It is common to all these tri-unities that intrinsically different entities work together in a trinity. To get hold of, or to create, this trinity, demands an ever-renewed awareness of the differences. No pattern is provided, but instead there is an element which brings consciousness, arising when things are relevantly differentiated, restricted, polarized and united. In face of the reality man's thinking always threatens to fall asleep. The impulse of threefoldness is the spur to consciousness, the means of waking up to what is humanly appropriate, which is achieved when balance is restored between the extremes.

From the year 1917 onwards the opposing movement to the treble-threefold one which Rudolf Steiner represented became clearly established. Working from Central Europe Rudolf Steiner, through his threefold movement, openly reveals and activates the central impulse of the Michael Age issuing from the Rosicrucian stream. What Goethe and Schiller through their friendship were able to dimly apprehend of the threefold principle in imagination and thought, is now brought a definite step forward. The building of the bridge which they so longed for for the future is formulated by Rudolf Steiner in thoughts which make the threefolding of the physical-social life comprehensible and applicable. This spiritual penetration of the social organism which appeared in Central Europe is confronted by three spiritual movements that are actually opposed to human progress, two old ones which have been joined by another since the crucial year 1917 to form a highly dangerous co-operating triad. Rudolf Steiner speaks about these movements in a lecture on 13 June 1920. They are not outward movements, but depend upon special initiations:

The people I have often called the leaders in the Anglo-American movement have initiation knowledge, but certainly not for the benefit of humankind. Everything based on Jesuitism has initiation knowledge. And Leninism, too, has a strange kind of initiation science. It knows how to put things cleverly, using rational ideas produced in the head, and there is a definite reason for this. The cleverness of the human animal, the cleverness of human animal-nature, is coming to the fore in human evolution through Leninism. Everything arising from human instincts, human selfishness, comes to manifestation in Leninism and Trotskyism in a form that on the surface seems very intelligent. The animal wants to work its way to the fore, to be the most intelligent of animals. All the ahrimanic powers that aim to exclude the human element, to exclude everything that is specifically human, and all the aptitudes that exist within the animal kingdom—I have often stressed this—are to become the forces that determine humanity ... If you now take all the cleverness that exists within the whole animal kingdom, and imagine ahrimanic powers taking this up and making it come to life in human heads, in the heads of people who follow only their egotistical instincts, you can see that it may be true to say that Lenin, Trotsky and others are the tools of those ahrimanic powers. That is an ahrimanic initiation. It belongs to a different cosmic sphere than our own world does. It is, however, an initiation that also holds the potential for getting rid of human civilization on earth, getting rid of everything that has evolved by way of human civilization.

We are therefore dealing with three schools of initiation. Two are on the plane of human evolution and one is below that plane, though it is an initiation of tremendous will power, almost unlimited will power. The only thing that can bring order into all these developments, setting a goal that is worthy to be called human, is contained within genuine spiritual knowledge.[168]

What Rudolf Steiner expressed here can be put into a picture. The Christian initiation stream evolving in Central Europe is attacked by the three opposing streams from the west, the south and the east. The western and the southern streams have already been discussed in this book. The accession of the third stream must be seen in conjunction with the Michael battle of 1841.

The beast which was cast out of the spiritual world by the Michaelic powers now rages, out of the earthly sphere and out of man, against its conqueror. The three opposing streams can be understood in such a way that—as Rudolf Steiner indicated—thinking is attacked from the west, feeling from the south and the will from the east.

The western initiation brings thinking completely under the spell of what is physical and material. Thinking appears thereby to be an activity of the brain which is suited to grasping and regulating the affairs of the material world. The gaining of control over the physical world is regarded as the decisive task of this kind of initiation. In social life this current of initiation produces the mighty impulse of adapting commerce to the striving for profit, which is mainly brought about by the system of money and the interest accruing therefrom.

The southern, Jesuitical, current is a particular enemy of the free individuality that comes into independent contact with the spiritual world. The figure of Faust, as representing the modern striving after knowledge, is hated by adherents of this current. Man's feelings are awakened and cleansed by spiritual knowledge. The conscious way from head to heart leads to the individuality. As this is not desired, one addresses the feelings and will and thereby avoids the consciousness, as was described in detail above. Feelings and will can attain enormous strength, but they remain in semi-darkness, whereby a free relationship to the spiritual world resting on independent decision is made impossible. In the social sphere false authorities are set up, an outmoded hierarchy leads people by the nose without them becoming aware of the fact. One is spoonfed and is not treated equally as a human being. Ultimately one cannot become an individual with equal rights, because to be that presupposes the feeling that one is oneself a citizen of *both* worlds. The source of the life of rights, which is only to be found in the individual, is here dammed up.

In the eastern initiation current the will is set free, but human beings are governed by a completely ruthless tyranny. The place of the spirit is taken over by the beast. Man is no longer committed to truth, but succumbs to egoistic instincts.

These three spiritual currents, which naturally work with and in one another, encompass Central European spiritual life as in a gigantic pincer-movement. One can gain the impression of a dragon's jaws which—yawning wide—are about to swallow their sacrificial prey. In spite of all variations, these three initiation currents are united in their destructive intentions towards Anthroposophy.

The mirroring of the spiritual events of 1841 in the year 1917 leads to the fact that mankind in general is crossing the threshold of the spiritual world. The Michael-Being wants mankind to be able to take hold of the spiritual world. For that it is necessary for the previously leading and supporting historical powers to lose their effectiveness. This happens just in 1917. In the same way that the co-ordination of thinking, feeling and willing provided by the physical body is taken away from man at the threshold of the spiritual world, so at the passing of mankind as a whole over the threshold, the unity of the state is taken away from it. In his conscious appraisal of the threefold social organism Rudolf Steiner, active in Central Europe, grasped this approach to the threshold and made it possible for mankind to come to terms with the fact of the crossing of the threshold during spiritual development.

The centralized state has since become a vessel in the hands of dark, degrading powers. The fact of the threshold-crossing of mankind is revealed in historic dimensions in the perverse one-sidedness with which each of the three initiation currents contributes a part. What has to be consciously organized into a higher unity becomes a caricature, scattered and dispersed. The exponents of these one-sided movements are Wilson in the West and Lenin in the East. At the head of the southern current is the Papacy. In the centre the calamitous, all-embracing opposition-movement is already being prepared. One should try to keep all this in mind if one wishes to get an

inkling of the importance of the impulse towards the Threefold Social Organism which Rudolf Steiner advocated in
1917.

This Threefold Commonwealth impulse stands in historical
and karmic relationship to Kaspar Hauser. The historic connection consists of the fact that it was part of Kaspar Hauser's
mission to lead the human-spiritual powers of Goethe's time
over into a social form in a South German state. It would, of
course, be unhistorical to imagine that Kaspar Hauser could
have introduced the Threefold Social state. That was only
possible and necessary in that form after 1917. But it is quite
easy to imagine a form of society which is more akin to the
Threefold Social Order than the German Empire of 1917.
Above all we must take account of the fact that through
Kaspar Hauser a connection to the impulses of the German
Folk-spirit should and could have been created, which would
have provided a starting point for the further development of
spiritual impulses within the social life in place of the catastrophic spiritual vacuum.

The turning-point in 1918

This unrealized, thwarted historical possibility was changed in
the course of time into a significant incisive destiny. The forces
of history itself speak an eloquent language for those who can
hear it.

With the Threefold Social Order Rudolf Steiner turned first
of all to the governments of Vienna and Berlin with the
'Memoranda' of 1917. For Germany it was without doubt
Prince Max of Baden, later to be the last Imperial Chancellor
of the monarchy, who played the decisive role. Prince Max of
Baden, however, was descended from the Hochberg line of the
House of Zähringen, and only came onto the throne as a result
of the crime against Kaspar Hauser.

The grandfather of Prince Max of Baden, Leopold, the son
of the Imperial Countess of Hochberg, ascended the throne in
1830, still during the lifetime of Kaspar Hauser. There is no

doubt that Prince Max of Baden knew of Kaspar Hauser's destiny and regarded him as the legitimate heir to the throne. It was given into his hand not only to make amends for the crime committed by his family against Kaspar Hauser, but also within his power was a definite karma-redressing deed for the German Folk-destiny. Neither karmic connection of family or nation found their compensatory deed. He did not carry them out.

Rudolf Steiner spoke in Karlsruhe on 20 or 21 January 1918 with Prince Max of Baden.[169] The conversation was not only about the necessary reform of society in the sense of the Threefold Order, but the descendant from the 'Child of Europe's' family asked Rudolf Steiner to show him the way to an understanding of the European nations. Thereupon Rudolf Steiner made notes and additions for Prince Max of Baden in his own handwriting to the lecture-cycle *The Mission of Individual Folk-Souls* and sent it to him.

A second conversation between Prince Max of Baden and Rudolf Steiner, which took place in his Berlin apartments in 1918, is vouched for by reliable witnesses.[170] This second conversation must have been concerned with the fact that Rudolf Steiner prepared Prince Max of Baden—thought at that time to be the only possible Chancellor of the monarchy—for the spiritual deed which he saw to be so necessary at the time of the collapse of Germany.

This inference about the content of the conversation is arrived at through oral transmissions and, above all, through the fact that Rudolf Steiner pinned particular hopes on the chancellorship of the Prince. 'According to Hans Kühn, Rudolf Steiner expected "the new Imperial Chancellor to find the appropriate words, that is to have the courage, to proclaim straightaway to the German people in his inaugural speech, before the announced revolution took place, the idea of the Threefold Commonwealth, as proof of a profound change and wish for peace of the German nation". Rudolf Steiner was very anxious to learn about the text of the inaugural speech when he got hold of the newspaper. Never afterwards did I see Rudolf Steiner so shattered as by this disappointment, which signified the defeat and path of suffering for the German nation.'[169,171] The Prince was unable to carry out the task assigned to him by destiny. He subscribed far rather to the thoughts of Woodrow Wilson about 'the future happiness of nations'. Hardly noticed or acknowledged up till now, a decisive turning-point in German history passed by almost in secret. 'The beginning of the war had already demonstrated the nullity of German policy. It was again demonstrated in October 1918. So came that awful spiritual capitulation at the hands of a man on whom many in German lands had staked, as it were, their last hope.'[172] With this spiritual capitulation Prince Max of Baden places himself, unknowingly, among the ranks of Kaspar Hauser's enemies and the opponents of the spiritual evolution proceeding out of Central Europe.

In actual fact, a few days after this event, the man who is described in this book as the direct counterpart to Kaspar Hauser, namely Hitler, was beginning to emerge. This arises out of a kind of necessity from the unfulfilled deed of Prince Max of Baden, who could have made compensation for the people of Germany and introduced a new development. During the night of the 13 to 14 October 1918 Hitler suffered mustard gas poisoning at the Western Front (Ypres), which brought him to the brink of death and blinded him for several weeks. This poisoning brought about that sinister change in Hitler which made his human organism into the willing tool of an evil spiritual nature.

Further substantiation of this statement is necessary. To begin with it should be pointed out that, even in this terrible case, one has no right to pass a moral judgement on the individuality concerned. It would also be unnecessary because the question arises as to how far the person in question is to be considered in connection with the crime committed. Far rather we should take account of the important piece of spiritual-scientific knowledge by which we are told that the bodily and soul-spiritual development by no means necessarily run parallel with one another. This information is formulated by Rudolf Steiner in characteristic fashion in his lecture in Dornach on 7 October 1917, 'The Crumbling of the Earth and

the Souls and Bodies of Men'*: 'You can meet a human being
and also another and in the sense of the Augustinian doctrine
it could be said of the two human beings standing before you:
one is destined for good, the other for evil. But this refers only
to the outer bodily constitution, *not* to the individuality. In the
days of St Augustine the real individuality was never spoken
of. Suppose there are a number of human beings in front of us.
We might say—but this would have meaning only from the
modern age onwards, among the Greeks it would have had no
meaning—those human souls are the forgers of their own
destiny; there is no such thing as predestination. But those
souls are living in bodies, and it is these bodies that are destined for good or evil. During Earth-evolution it will be less
and less possible for the development of the soul to run parallel with that of the body. Why should it not be possible for
an individuality to incarnate in a body destined for evil on
account of its whole make-up? In spite of that the man himself
may be thoroughly good, because the individuality is no
longer closely and intimately connected with the body. This
again is not a comfortable truth but one with which it behoves
us to become familiar.'[173]

We get a little further if we apply this unpalatable knowledge
to Hitler, whose body really appears as though predestined to
evil in a unique historical fashion. This predestination, however, can only become effective if, on the other hand, a definite
deficiency enables it to be so. The Folk-destiny must be
regarded as a more highly organized whole. The connections,
therefore, are of a spiritually destined nature.

We must also bear in mind Rudolf Steiner's further statement that the spirit-soul element divides completely from the
body, that is to say it actually passes through death, but the
body lives on because the physical and etheric bodies do not
separate. Such a body as this then becomes a place of habitation for demonic-ahrimanic beings.*

It will, of course, be part of the task of future spiritual
research to discover what is the predisposition in the line of

---

Anthroposophical Quarterly, Spring 1974.

development of the individual to cause such a split. The profound change that took place at the beginning of Hitler's historic career can best be understood from his own description in his book *Mein Kampf*. Hitler writes about his experiences after 9 November 1918: 'The more I tried at that moment to understand the enormous event, the more my brow burned with shame at the indignation and disgrace. What did all the pain in my eyes matter in comparison with this misery? What followed was dreadful days and still worse nights—I knew that all was lost. Only fools—or liars and criminals—could hope for mercy from the enemy. Hate grew in me during these nights, hate against the perpetrators of this deed.'[174]

One must call to mind the historical situation in order to become clear about the distorted report. The fact of a military defeat of Germany was perceived by no other than Ludendorff himself. After 8 August 1918, the 'black day of German history' (Ludendorff), he urgently commanded the Imperial Government to start peace talks, which were actually capitulation negotiations. On 29 September 1918 he finally had to explain to the Imperial Government that the Armistice must be implemented immediately, as military defeat was inevitable. Upon that Prince Max of Baden became Imperial Chancellor on 3 October 1918 and had to carry out the military capitulation and after that the fatal spiritual one. The monarchy and its last doom-laden Chancellor had proved inadequate to take helpful and supportive steps for the future of the German nation in the sense of its further development. After that, of historical necessity, the revolution swept away all that had proved to be quite unfit for life. Hitler is unable to perceive this sequence of events; cause and effect were interchanged and the revolution was made to be the cause of the long-since accomplished military defeat. This is the beginning of Hitler's loss of a sense of reality which, of course, had already been prepared during his development and which acquired pathologically grotesque features at the end of his life. One has to say that instead of 'true perception' (*Wahr*nehmen) of the world of facts he perceived things falsely (*Falsch*nehmen). This 'taking-things-falsely', which consists of the ego's inability to connect outward reality with inner truth through the power of thought, leads to a 'false-setting-down' and a 'false-printing' of reality, the basis of which is a lie. What is alluded to here is graphically illustrated by the fact that Hitler temporarily lost his sight as a result of being gassed. What looked into the world out of those eyes after his recovery had a different glow. What looked into the world of men from them is the abyss of untruthfulness.

The same Ludendorff who himself had, after all, admitted the military defeat, soon afterwards blamed the defeat on the revolution in his own country and thereby created the unhappy legend of 'the stab in the back'. This personality, whose lies had worldwide consequences, becomes the main political backer of Hitler. Hitler and Ludendorff together undertake the putsch in Munich on 9 November 1923, to the 'martyrs' of which the book *Mein Kampf* is dedicated. These 'martyrs' later played a decisive ritualistic-propagandist role in the spreading of the National-Socialist movement.

What Hitler writes includes the assertion that there had never been a military defeat, whereby he would make out Ludendorff to be a liar. This senseless twisting of the truth breeds and nurtures hatred directed against the perpetrators of the deed of 9 November, whereby, as a result of the already existing mendacity, the identity of the perpetrators remains unclear. As the inner cohesion of thoughts has been broken, hate, as the original principle of the whole movement, has come home to roost in the 'Führer'.

It is very seldom in world history that 'hate', as the negation and destruction of mankind, has so clearly stood at the starting-point of a historical movement. In the present context this hate is embodied in the lust to destroy the Jews. 'Kaiser Wilhelm II was the first German Emperor to extend the hand of peace to the leaders of Marxism, without suspecting that there is no honour among rogues. While they were still holding the imperial hand in theirs, their other hand was already feeling for the dagger. There is no dealing with the Jews, but only the harsh "either—or". But I decided to be a politician.'[174]

The desultoriness, even the break in the thread of thoughts, quite apart from the errors of their content, can be sensed in this text. It is the ego, however, which links thought with thought according to the inner laws of thinking. The unthinking sequence passes through the following steps: Leaders of Marxism—rogues—the dagger-blow during reconciliation (a very sentimental sentence)—no dealing with the Jew (the levelling singular formulation 'with the Jew' is used)—harshness of decision—decision to become a politician. Only a philosophy of inhumanity might find an apparent logic in these words. What is actually presented with shattering candour is the implanting of a universal impulse directed towards the destruction of humanity, which is concealed behind the infamous words: 'But I decided to be a politician'. What was here planted as a seed has been conclusively revealed in historic reality.

The significance of such an important quotation can be exposed at a still deeper layer if one compares it with the words from St John's Gospel: 'I am the Way, the Truth and the Life'. What Hitler writes means in clear words: The Antichrist is hatred, lying and destruction. He took up office according to this principle and worked in this sense until his bitter, self-inflicted end.

The succeeding passage in the Gospel: 'No man cometh unto the Father, but by Me' may be transcribed freely in the following way, in order to make it plainer: No man can have access to the spiritual world in a humanly worthy manner except through the ego. In contrast to this the sentence quoted from Hitler can be explained thus: This body becomes a servant of the Antichrist which works best by means of politics, because truth has been driven out of politics.

What really happened to Hitler according to the account given here is supported by observation of the events of history. On 11, 12 and 13 October 1918 Rudolf Steiner speaks for the first time about Sorath, the Beast or Sun Demon as an intervening power in history connected with the impulse of Gondeshapur and the significance of the year 666 (cf. Chapter 3, p.191). Immediately before Sorath begins to work on a historical level in a person from Central Europe (Hitler), the knowledge of this being and its previous activity is given to

mankind by Rudolf Steiner. This again can be seen as a confirmation of the service for humanity that Rudolf Steiner
performs out of his spiritual reality. And just on the evening of
that karmically potent 13 October 1918, Rudolf Steiner speaks
again about the contrast between the Mystery of Golgotha
and the Sorath impulse of Gondeshapur. Then, however, he
turns to the greatest event of the twentieth century which
coincides with 1933, for which the opposing forces prepare the
decisive counterpart beginning in that same night with the
change brought about in Hitler. Rudolf Steiner says: 'We are
confronted today, in the first third of the twentieth century,
with the approach of an important event for humanity. All
upheavals and all catastrophes are nothing less than seismic
events which precede the great spiritual event of the twentieth
century. That is not an event that takes place in the physical
world, but one through which people will experience a kind of
illumination which will have happened before the first third of
the twentieth century closes. If the term is not misunderstood,
it can be called the reappearance of Christ Jesus. But Christ
Jesus will not appear in an outer body as at the time of the
Mystery of Golgotha, but as active within human beings, and
He will be perceived supersensibly: He will be present in His
etheric body. Whoever prepares himself for it can always
become aware of Him in visions, can continually receive
advice from Him, can, as it were, gain a direct personal relationship to Him. All that is impending in this way is comparable to what the Romans experienced before the time of
Augustus when the physically real Mystery of Golgotha was
approaching.'[175]

It is not only due to the astounding fact that Rudolf Steiner
could explain the spiritual happening immediately before the
great event took place, that we are able to see what kind of
change it was that Hitler underwent. This was made plain,
above all, through the effect it had. Three steps are clearly
discernible from Hitler's own account. To begin with, during
his activity as Education Officer, he made the, for him,
surprising discovery: 'I could lecture'.[176] What took place as a
result of this lecturing can be gathered from the success which

he describes as follows: 'Many hundreds, rather thousands, of comrades have been led back to their country and Fatherland through my lecturing. I 'nationalized' the armed forces and by this means was able to contribute to strengthening the general discipline.'[176]

In the triad: military tradition (comrades)—country and Fatherland (nationalizing)—discipline—it is easy to hear the opposite of that which the times are really seeking: community of mankind—getting hold of the individuality—serving human spiritual life.

The next step became visible at the time of 'the first Assembly which could be called a public one' in the presence of 111 people.[176] Again it is Hitler himself who gives what is the main message, which rightly needs to be heard in its context: 'I spoke for thirty minutes and what previously I had simply felt within me without having any knowledge of it, was now confirmed by reality: I was able to speak! After thirty minutes the people in the small room were electrified and the enthusiasm was expressed to begin with by the fact that the appeal to the generosity of those present resulted in a contribution of 300 Marks.' It reveals an amazingly relevant openness when 'electrification' is here spoken of.

The 'electrical effect' is mentioned above (p.185) as an expression of the connection of Ahriman and Sorath to the physical plane. It consists here of an effect on the human will, without this having passed through the human consciousness, either that of the speaker or of the listener.

The third step in the incorporation of what Hermann Kükelhaus in 1938 called the 'cosmic carcinoma' takes place at the 'first great national gathering of the unknown movement',[176] on 24 February 1920. Once more the decisive points by means of which an effect such as this is achieved are mentioned in the text. Furthermore, as will be seen later, starting point and goal are directed against the mass of the people which affects public opinion and is, in turn, influenced by it. Hitler writes: 'If, at the conclusion of this volume, I speak about this first great massed assembly of the movement, I do so because, with that, the Party burst the narrow framework of a small union and in its place, for the first time, decisively affected the mighty factor of our day, public opinion'.[176] Hitler turned to the 'mass' with 'his programme' in his next speech. It has to be recognized that in his account an effect is produced by him which finally brings antagonists and trouble-makers into agreement. Even if one were to assume that some opponents were kicked out of the meetings at the beginning, the about-turn in the sphere of the will in this decisive meeting was indicative of future progress. It is actually not a matter of establishing a conviction which every person can share, but of integrating people in a vague will which gains tremendous power through excluding the working of the ego, in other words through what it receives from the 'mass'. If one reads the text with this preparation one can only shudder at what takes place.

The opening ceremony was to take place at 7.30. At 7.15 I entered the Festival Hall of the Court Brewery in the 'Platzl' in Munich and my heart was ready to burst with pleasure. The huge room—for it still seemed huge to me at that time—was full to overflowing with people, row by row, a mass of nearly two thousand. And above all, it was those whom we wanted to reach. Well over half the Hall seemed to be taken up by Communists and Independents. Our first great proclamation was destined for an abrupt ending with them.

However, things turned out differently. After the first speaker had concluded, I took up the word. A few minutes later loud interruptions hailed down; hefty blows were exchanged in the Hall; a handful of faithful warriors and other supporters fought against the hooligans and managed after a while to restore a little peace. I was able to continue speaking. After half an hour the applause began to drown the screaming and bellowing. And now I got hold of the Programme and started to explain it for the first time. From one quarter of an hour to the next the loud interruptions were more and more suppressed by the shouted applause. And when I finally put the twenty-five theses point by point to the mass of people and asked them to give their verdict about them, they were accepted one after another amid ever growing jubilation, unanimously and again and again unanimously, and by the time the last thesis had found its way into the heart of the crowd, a room full of people stood before me bound together by a new conviction, a new belief, by a new will.[176]

By translating into the language of reality this description of the invasion of darkness out of which, with a kind of inevitability, all subsequent events take their start, one would expose it for what it is and would have to say something such as the following: Here an anti-human force is manifest, which therefore does not address itself to the single human being, but to the mass of mankind. Man's consciousness is not bound up thoughtfully and through its own decision with the single facts of life, but is befogged by empty, abstract programmes. Into this damped-down state of consciousness the Spirit of Darkness enters and extinguishes conscience and convictions. This dark spirit binds the people into a mass, which does not wish to know what is happening here and penetrates thinking, feeling and willing in a disorderly fashion. The mass, it is said, will be 'bound together by a new conviction, a new faith, a new will'. The word 'new' must be understood in this sense to be a process which in this form has actually not yet taken place within humanity. The breakthrough which was here achieved is experienced as such and thus described by Hitler: 'When, after nearly four hours, the room began to empty and the mass of people surged towards the exit, pushing and shoving in a slow stream, I knew that the principles of a movement among the German people was going forth, nevermore to be forgotten. A fire had been kindled, from the glow of which a sword would be forged which would win back freedom for Siegfried and life for the German nation.'[176]

The illusion which lies in such sentences is overcome when one sees that this fire will logically develop into a worldwide conflagration that is predestined to lead, not to the return of Siegfried, but to a Nibelungen-like destruction of the German nation. Nearly all the words here have the characteristically opposite meaning, so that life here really means death. Whoever reads the concluding sentences of this first part of the book *Mein Kampf* might be shocked to think that anyone could believe that this movement could bring about anything good. For the words 'marriage of revenge and lies' is openly used with reference to 9 November 1918. From this 'marriage', according to the law out of which they arose, the calamities of ruin proceeded, working on into the future. 'And I felt, beside the coming elation, the goddess of implacable revenge striding along for the perjury of 9 November 1918. Thus the Hall slowly emptied. The movement was launched.'[176]

One would have to measure what happens here against what came to light at the historical nodal points of 1933 and 1945. In Hitler's statements the luciferic and ahrimanic components can be sensed on all sides. But what is notable is that we get here what Rudolf Steiner—as already mentioned—calls the 'co-operation of Lucifer and Ahriman', which extinguishes and destroys what is of benefit to the individual. By the working together of the polar opposites, Lucifer and Ahriman,[177] an intensification is reached which exceeds by far the polarized effect and lays it open to being of service to the magical influence of Sorath. From the start Hitler exerts a force of intentional influence, which can properly only be understood as an occult-magical one in the sense of the Sun Demon. From that it becomes understandable that no human or, until now, historically applied antidote could be successful against it. That is the reason why, in reality, it is only from an initiate like Rudolf Steiner and those who congregate around him, freely and individually, that a compensating energy can proceed.

Of course, on the other hand, one can say that the real opposite force to the Christian-spiritual movement appeared in Hitler. From October/November 1918 onwards this took effect according to the law that a demon comes to power when the genius, the destined hour, is not taken hold of in freedom. Rudolf Steiner—as will be presently shown—has done everything to keep the balance and therewith has done an immense amount for the future, which cannot be lost. His helpful service, however, is from now onwards accompanied by the most violent opposing actions. In the background of history, extending into what is invisible and hidden, there is an enormous spiritual battle being waged. That which is outwardly visible is the symptomatic expression of this struggle.

To that belongs the fact that what comes about through Hitler from October 1918 onwards is expressed in a seven-year rhythm. After around 14 years the seizure of power takes place in 1933; after a bare 21 years the Second World War breaks out. And barely $6\frac{1}{2}$ years after this event of 1918 Rudolf Steiner is obliged to leave the physical plane. At Christmas 1924 Hitler is prematurely released from the Landsberg gaol, and just on 27 February 1925 of all days—Rudolf Steiner's last birthday—the NSDAP (National Socialist German Workers' Party) is re-founded in Munich where Rudolf Steiner had originally intended to build the 'Johannes' Building, the later Goetheanum. Whoever surveys the connection cannot regard this as an accident, as little as the fact that the burning of the Reichstag in 1933, which led to the Enabling Act and with it to Hitler's final sole command, took place on the same day.

It is remarkable also that the incorporation of this dangerous spirituality in Hitler happened after the completion of his thirtieth year and then persisted for $26\frac{1}{2}$ years. Both these ages are not without meaning. The Christ-activity in Jesus undergoes a great transformation in His thirtieth year and thus it is understandable that the anti-Christian principle also tries to achieve this period of time, as is also shown by Soloviev in the case of the incarnation of his Antichrist. In his lectures about the Buddha and the Bodhisattvas Rudolf Steiner points to the particular significance of the thirtieth year for higher spiritual activity.[178]

The period of 26 to 27 years is the one in which the physical-corporeal part of man still gives some support to the soul-spiritual development today. After that period an inner spiritual impulse is needed for his further progress. The active period for a spiritual being in Hitler hostile to mankind strangely enough just fills this length of time, whereby October and November of 1918 gain particular relevance. In this case such a moment would be like a neutral point for what follows, like a moment of birth. One would have to accept the peculiar concept of an entirely new organism having been brought about in a 30-year-old human being, even as regards the physical bodily nature. Does this have to be looked upon as a counter-picture to the phantom? Must we see in conjunction with this beginning the suicidal destruction of the body at the end?

Independently of these questions one can be sure that what works on into the far future as a result of what happened in 1945 was planned from the start by the powers here at work.

The Threefold Commonwealth year 1919

Since October/November of 1918 has now been recognized in world history as the point of entry for demonic forces, let us now turn our attention to Rudolf Steiner and what he was doing. When the ultimate failure of the ruling powers became clear, Rudolf Steiner immediately adapted himself to the new situation. From now on he saw that it was superfluous to talk further about the Threefold movement with government representatives.[179] He turned first of all to people close to him within the Anthroposophical Society, then to the German people and the civilized world with his Appeal (February 1919) and at the end of April 1919 with his book *The Threefold Commonwealth*.[180] The year 1919 can be understood as being the Threefold Commonwealth year in the sense that everything depended upon its first practical application. One gets the impression that Rudolf Steiner acted in the belief that this was the correct and decisive moment to act. In Württemberg, in Stuttgart, the first steps in this direction had actually been taken in the forming of works-committees in the associative amalgamation of businesses ('Kommende Tag' Ltd) for the financing of spiritual undertakings, and especially for the founding of the Free Waldorf School. Of all these only the school movement evolving out of the Free Waldorf School as a part of free spiritual life became a historical reality. At the beginning, owing to lack of understanding of the real social needs of the immediate present, about which Rudolf Steiner had repeatedly spoken from 1918 to 1920, and because of the growing opposition of those who ultimately wished to stick to the old order, the Threefold Commonwealth movement got stuck. Is 24 February 1920 an expression of the fact that insufficient people were able to waken up to the spiritual reality? Could the Threefold movement still become a reality after that day? When and by what means will human destiny present such an opportunity again, which will allow a social form to exist in respect of the crossing of the threshold by mankind? One can imagine the pain Rudolf Steiner experienced through the rejection of the Threefold Commonwealth if one knows that he foresaw the consequences which have since come about.

Without the slightest bitterness Rudolf Steiner turns to a different field for his spiritual work in the spring of 1920. The nine volumes of lectures which he gave up till Christmas 1921 were published under the expressive title 'Man in his relationship to the Cosmos'.[181] The question still remained, however, as to how the spiritual impulse contained in the sense of the Michael-Age in the Threefold Commonwealth movement could be saved from homelessness.

During the course of 1922 the development noticeably came to a head. Also the understanding which Rudolf Steiner was able to find among his friends only partly corresponded to what the matter demanded. Through that—as he himself once said in 1924—his impulses became blunted.[182] On the other hand a wide public looked towards Rudolf Steiner just at this time as once before in his life they had done at the turn of the century. During the series of public lectures which he gave in different German towns was one in Munich on 15 May 1922, at the end of which he was actively attacked by the 'Hitler-guards' and mortally endangered.[183] This motivated and planned attack on Rudolf Steiner, which brought to an end his public activity in Germany after the conclusion of the tour he was then engaged in, must be judged in the context here given as an expression of the growing inner opposition to his spiritual activity. The antagonism, based on the spirit, had become so strong that for the first time it could show itself openly and undisguisedly. Only a few people could discern the spirit of the times. For a knowledge of the true historical connections it must not be forgotten.

The Goetheanum fire

Owing to the curtailment of Rudolf Steiner's public activities the Threefold Commonwealth impulse was again pushed into the background. One of the reasons for this was the establishment of a new spiritual life, served by his lecturing. The growing danger in which Rudolf Steiner and his work stood was made manifest in the burning of the Goetheanum on New Year's Eve 1922. This burning—resulting from a world-historic Herostratus deed,[184] the background of which is not quite clear—can really be experienced as a symbol, shining into the far distance, to warn and rouse mankind to what they were about to lose.

The Goetheanum was built upon the foundation-stone of love, leading to the transformation and salvation of the earth. In the architecturally-formed curves of this edifice Rudolf Steiner had combined, in artistic, living form, what comes from the cosmos and what comes from the earth. The building was a physical structure imbued with the pulsating of an etheric organism, an etheric picture of all that lay at the heart of and filled earthly evolution. The etheric body of mankind as a whole was visible in this building. In the growing and becoming of this still-unfinished and not yet officially opened building was contained the whole formative power of Rudolf Steiner's individuality working from the spirit into the physical-etheric. Not only was an irreplaceable building, unique to human history, destroyed, but an evil, devastating blow had been dealt against Rudolf Steiner's etheric body, which was aimed at removing his activity from the earth. The spiritual-etheric form of the Goetheanum was transferred by the flames to the invisible surroundings of the earth—waiting there in hope for the time when it would reassert its right to live on earth.

Through the burning of the Goetheanum Rudolf Steiner's life was led, as it were, through death, but from destruction he wrested a new becoming, a resurrection.

After the Threefold Commonwealth impulse, the older Foundation Stone impulse of Malsch and Dornach also came into great danger. How should one deal with the fact that these impulses were not understood by people in an appropriate way? What can be undertaken to counter the growing spiritual Christ-enmity which seeks to drag mankind into the abyss in an ecstatic delusion?

The Christmas gathering 1923

In 1923 Rudolf Steiner set himself the task of trying to change this greatest of all misfortunes into good fortune. It was in this sense that he characterized the work of the spirits which support human progress. This work grows out of the Christ-Impulse, to the realization of which it belongs. In the founding of the General Anthroposophical Society by Rudolf Steiner in Dornach at Christmas 1923 is to be seen a deed by which he wanted to bring about the recompense. In face of the hostile will, which sought to hinder him in his future work, he first of all united the spiritual and administrative work of the Society and took the leadership into his own hands. In the Foundation Stone ceremony of the General Anthroposophical Society he renewed and transformed the laying of the Foundation Stone impulse with that of the Threefold Commonwealth; both were entrusted to the hearts of those who longed for Anthroposophy. The 'dodecahedral picture of love' was not sunk directly into the earth, but, for the salvation of the latter, it was sunk into the hearts of men. The Foundation Stone itself supports and takes hold of the threefold nature of man in his cosmic and earthly form. Its inspirational source, however, is the Mystery of Golgotha—as with the first Foundation Stone-laying in Malsch. This Foundation Stone was entrusted, by proxy for humanity in general, to a community which was to create the social structure as the healing impulse for the sick body of mankind.

Still during the Christmas gathering, just at the anniversary of the burning of the Goetheanum on 1 January 1924, Rudolf Steiner was confronted with a second terrible blow. During the social party in the big hall of the joiner's shop he was suddenly taken ill. 'Dr Steiner came swaying towards me, white as snow and groaning loudly,' reports Ilona Schubert.[185] 'We asked him what had happened and he said: "I have been poisoned".' Also to the question by Marie Steiner, his wife, who drew near: 'What is the matter?' he again answered: 'I have been poisoned—how are the other members of the Committee?' This following question shows that in the life-threatening situation in which he found himself it was not only for his personal friends that he worried, but he was afraid that an attempt had been made on the life of other members of the Committee. This fear was not confirmed. It would have sufficed for him alone to have been struck down. There can be no doubt about the happening as such, which has been reported in essentially the same way by various eye-witnesses.[186]

What happened to Rudolf Steiner, how it could have come about and what the background was for such an event is still a mystery and remains unexplained. Rudolf Steiner asked those who were direct witnesses not to speak about it. Historical conscience demands at the outset that one should not forget such an important occurrence as this, but try to find a solution to the riddle for the future. It is not only Rudolf Steiner's statement, but also his own attitude towards it and the succeeding treatment, which point unmistakably to an event which suddenly affected his organism from without. And there can be no doubt about it that this attack was intended to bring about Rudolf Steiner's death. The burning of the Goetheanum gnawed at his life-forces. One year later the physical basis of what activated him was to be destroyed. Quite rightly Rudolf Grosse writes of him that 'out of the limitless forces of his spirit' he was able to overcome the poisoning.[186] Rudolf

Steiner remained alive and accomplished his incalculable work by the realization of Schiller's phrase: 'It is the spirit which builds the body'. By means of this spirit-body Rudolf Steiner was able to work in 1924 with ever-decreasing and dwindling forces for another nine months. Then he was forced to lie down, and half a year later—on 30 March 1925—his contact with the physical body could no longer be maintained. With that he, who, through the Christmas gathering, had become the mouthpiece of the Gods—for the spiritual beings who provide the driving force for Anthroposophy allowed their powers and revelations to stream in abundance into the activity of Rudolf Steiner during 1924—had to fall silent. This was a unique manifestation of the Michaelic forces on earth and in human history. Rudolf Steiner was able to fulfil his destined task—the research and presentation of concrete karmic connections of individual biographies in succeeding lives on earth—in a way that had not been possible until then. This enabled a circle of people, prepared by a powerful spiritual impulse, to thoroughly accept spiritual existence. At the centre of the measureless, superhuman spiritual activity, controlled by Rudolf Steiner at every moment, was a healing impulse which was developed in special directions; in curative education, agriculture, medicine and also in the understanding of destiny. Seeds were sown for a distant future that are still awaiting germination. The powerful spiritual manifestations which became possible for the Michaelic beings as a result of Rudolf Steiner's free deed, posed a mighty question for his contemporaries: Will the powers of thoughtful and decisive understanding and the selfless willingness to make sacrifices be sufficient to preserve these spiritual revelations against the strongest demonic attacks? For, considering all that has been presented here, it is easy to see that the spirits opposed to mankind looked upon Rudolf Steiner's deed as a tremendous challenge. They wished to eliminate Rudolf Steiner—and were now confronted with the fact of a spiritual victory growing out of a resurrection.

A hotly contested position can plainly be seen. It results from the fact that through the founding of the General

Anthroposophical Society, Rudolf Steiner, as its authoritative leader, became much more involved in activity on the physical plane than before. This was now vigorously supported by the Michaelic beings and equally strongly opposed by the adversaries. This is the decisive question at the present time: Is it possible to work spiritually within the physical world? Rudolf Steiner once spoke about this in the following way: 'It was a very important decision, also in respect of the spiritual world, which I had to make at that time [Christmas gathering]. For it was a risk. A risk for the reason that, with the assumption of the outer leadership, it might equally well have happened that the revelations on the part of spiritual beings, upon whom we are thoroughly dependent when it comes to a matter of spreading Anthroposophy, might have become fewer by reason of the fact that I occupied myself with the outer administration of the Society. Today I can now look upon the tremendously important fact that this is not the case, but that on the contrary the spiritual impulse which must come down from the spiritual world if the anthroposophical movement is to flourish, has grown, so that our anthroposophical movement has become more and more esoteric since the Christmas gathering and it will continue thus. It is connected with the fact that certainly all—I mean from the spiritual side—very strong opposing forces, demonic forces, attack the anthroposophical movement. But it is very much to be hoped that the forces of the union which we were allowed to enter into with the good spiritual powers will enable us in future to conquer all the opposing forces on the spiritual level which make use of people on earth to achieve their aims.'[187]

Here the spiritual battleground of the Michael Age has been marked out. The forces of opposition make use of people for their purposes, by taking advantage of their lack of freedom, as was demonstrated in the case of the Hitler figure. The free deeds of people who carry out what is necessary are filled with the power of the Michaelic Time-Spirit. So everything depends upon the ego of man. For the impulse of the Christmas gathering in 1923 depended on the fact that it had to live among human beings on earth. That could not be

performed either by Rudolf Steiner or by spiritual beings. It
had become bound up in its work and destiny with a community of people on whose further development everything
now depended. Already on 18 January 1924 Rudolf Steiner
gave a warning, calling for people to awaken to their
responsibilities. 'If this Christmas gathering is just going to be
accepted in the way one so happily accepted earlier gatherings,
then it will slowly evaporate, it will lose its content and it
would have been better if it had not taken place. For what is
spiritual has the property of disappearing if it is not held fast—
not, of course, disappearing within the cosmos, but disappearing from the place where it had no longer been cared
for. It then seeks out other places in the cosmos. And for
something like our Christmas gathering one is not dependent
on what happens within the earthly kingdom. You should not
therefore imagine that what evaporates at the Christmas
gathering by not being put into practice will appear some-
where else on earth. That is not necessarily the case. It might
seek refuge in quite other worlds. Everything depends, therefore, on people finding the possibility of taking great care to
absorb its contents.'[188]

At the Christmas gathering Rudolf Steiner combined the
impulses of the laying of the Foundation Stone with that of the
Threefold Commonwealth, so that they were thereby transformed and ennobled. In this way they could be saved for
humanity. Rudolf Steiner had united his own life and destiny
with these forces and impulses, for which reason his existence
on the physical plane depended on seizing hold of the impulse
of the Christmas gathering. 'For something such as our
Christmas gathering one [that is to say, Rudolf Steiner him-
self] is not dependent on what is happening in the earthly
realm.'[188] The grasping of this impulse with thoughtful
understanding necessarily produces a homely, incarnating and
protective effect, whereas the lack of conscious awareness and
self-absorbed indolence made it difficult for Rudolf Steiner to
incarnate, made him ill and sapped his strength. Powerfully
attacked as he was by his enemies, his friends nevertheless did
not recognize the danger in which he hung, despite the ever-

repeated warnings, and did not extend to him the protection of their understanding, which alone would have kept him on the earth. Basically he had—like Kaspar Hauser—to go through the martyrdom which is produced by indolence of heart. (This is intended to be an historical statement about a tragedy, not arrogant accusation by someone born after the event.*)

Naturally one should not for one minute forget the tremendously brutal evil of suppression, through such reflections of awakening self-knowledge. The powers of this suppression-principle were—as already described—increased in Hitler to a previously non-existent form, because the magical, will-destroying forces of the Sun Demon worked into it in addition. We can be certain that Rudolf Steiner knew exactly what the effect of his death must be for humanity. From that the general sense of his statement made in 1925 during his last weeks and days becomes understandable: 'I shall have to get better again!' There is no rebellion in that against the destiny allotted to him, which he personally bore patiently, only the will, born out of knowledge, to deflect a catastrophe from mankind. When Rudolf Steiner left the physical plane on 30 March 1925, he did so leaving no instructions and without actually saying goodbye. Did he experience—as Christian Rosenkreutz did—as his greatest pain the fact that mankind finds it so difficult to accept the 'I am the Truth'? Did the view which was vouchsafed his soul of the immeasurable suffering which was to arise from the calamity cause him to fall silent with pity? Rudolf Steiner had to learn that the immediate bridge between the spiritual and physical worlds had broken because mankind was not worthy of it and was unable at the time to become ripe enough for this contact.

Since the end of Kali Yuga the spiritual world had spoken to mankind audibly and to an ever increasing degree through man's ego. This fact alone already shows the reality of the new Light Era. It is not the Gods who have forsaken men, but human beings did not wish to know anything about the Gods who were approaching them.

The sacrifices of Rudolf Steiner and Kaspar Hauser

Rudolf Steiner's sacrifice—like that of Kaspar Hauser—took the place of what mankind could have accomplished out of its own free will. Without wishing to belittle any individual who was living at that time, it must be stated that, with the death of Rudolf Steiner, the only person who could have countered the disastrous events of 1932/33 was taken from us. On several occasions during the last days of his life, Rudolf Steiner pointed to the consequences of not making use of the possibilities offered by the Age of Michael. 'Then karma [destiny] must take its course,' he said. Because Rudolf Steiner's work was rejected and driven from the physical plane, the necessary consequences of the destiny that was prepared by Kaspar Hauser, especially that of the years 1932/33 and 1944/45, had to be fulfilled. Rudolf Steiner had carefully taken into his hands and tried to carry out and transform the delicate web of destiny which connected him with the destiny of Kaspar Hauser. His last attempt at rescue, during the Christmas gathering, led him—in mirrored relationship to Kaspar Hauser—to a death of sacrifice. 'In a certain sense my last hope for the Society lies in the Christmas gathering' he writes in a letter of 1 December 1923.[189]

It is certain that for an initiate such as Rudolf Steiner death itself, as a saying goodbye to the earth, has a quite different meaning than for an ordinary mortal. But in this case we must draw attention above all to the importance for the earth and for mankind of a life that shared in essential cosmic events. It is true that an initiate can also work when free of the physical body, especially when people have become receptive to such influences through serious esoteric training. But from the fact that the opponents of human evolution, the enemies of Christ, have done everything they could to destroy the physical existence of Kaspar Hauser and Rudolf Steiner, it is obvious that the activity of such spirits on the physical plane is of paramount importance at the present moment in evolution.

When we speak here of the sacrificial death that these spirits underwent for mankind, even though this happened through man's wickedness, this means that, in a Christian sense, they were certainly unable to fulfil their task on the physical plane, but that in death their effectiveness was sealed and thereby raised to invincibility. Thus these spirits have achieved something for the Christian future of mankind that cannot be lost. It would therefore have been irrelevant to have spoken of the Christmas gathering having failed. Certainly there was much left uncompleted through the death of Rudolf Steiner. He himself speaks about the cosmic sanctuary which can be found by such an impulse. Does this not also mean that this impulse then works on out of the cosmos and that it depends on man to provide it with a home on the earth once more?

Everything that was to have been pointed out in this chapter can be summed up in a picture. Equidistant in time from the beginning of the Michael Age are the sacrificial deaths of Kaspar Hauser and Rudolf Steiner (1833—1879—1925). They relate to one another in their service to the one who stands at the middle point, visible and invisible, the human representative of the Christ-Impulse, Christian Rosenkreutz, with whom both are deeply connected. Behind the figure of Christian Rosenkreutz the Michael-Being can be felt, which in its Age wants to make the cosmic significance of Christ's earthly deeds recognizable and understandable to man. To prepare the way for people reactivated by Christ, Kaspar Hauser and Rudolf Steiner have both contributed with their lives and martyrdom.

5. Kaspar Hauser's Character

'He would have been a strange swindler:
For his destiny produced an echo, as
only a noble spirit can otherwise do.'

Sophie Hoechstetter
Das Kind von Europa, 1924
(The Child of Europe)

In this final chapter we shall summarize in a picture the essential points of the previous chapters. By this means it will become evident that Kaspar Hauser not only produced the effect of a noble and elevated spirit, but in himself a noble spirit was incarnate on the earth. The way to a remarkably clear and comprehensive picture of Kaspar Hauser's character is pointed out to us in the many scattered hints and statements of Rudolf Steiner, which at the same time enable us to answer in part the question that he put to Count Polzer-Hoditz on 3 March 1925. Rudolf Steiner spoke about the tasks that were of special importance for the future and he asked the final question: 'Where did Kaspar Hauser come from?' Towards a further solution to this question he made the following suggestion: 'One should not look to the death of Kaspar Hauser, but to his birth'. Then, in Rudolf Steiner's notes, there follows the most important piece of information about Kaspar Hauser: 'The individuality which hides behind the Kaspar Hauser-veil is a being which worked inspiringly into the Rosicrucian connection from the beginning, and then, on 29 September 1812, incarnated as the son of the Grand-Duke Karl of Baden and his wife Stephanie de Beauharnais. Kaspar Hauser had an important esoteric mission of Christianity to fulfil.' (See p.281.)

We should first keep in mind that Rudolf Steiner saw in Kaspar Hauser the heir to the throne of Baden, who—as can be gathered from all the surrounding circumstances—had incarnated in this family at a particular moment according to plan. This statement by Rudolf Steiner about Kaspar Hauser's descent coincides with the lifelong research of Hermann Pies. It must not be forgotten, however, that the riddle of Kaspar Hauser's identity had already been solved by von Feuerbach in his 'Memoires' (1832).

Because the identity of Kaspar Hauser, as the heir to the throne of Baden, had already been made clear to Rudolf Steiner, his question: 'Where did Kaspar Hauser come from?' obviously does not refer to his descent by birth, but to his spiritual origin. Possibly the question might also be applied to Kaspar Hauser's imprisonment, from which he was released into the world by an unknown hand. In his conversation with Count Polzer-Hoditz, Rudolf Steiner makes the decisive statement that Kaspar Hauser is a being who worked inspiringly in a Rosicrucian connection from the very beginning. Through this statement Rudolf Steiner himself points to a time far beyond the birth. If one compares this remark with others that he made about Kaspar Hauser, one finds, surprisingly enough, that they clarify each other.

In chronological order Rudolf Steiner first points to the fact that in Kaspar Hauser we are dealing with a 'straggler from Atlantis'. The meaning of this statement can only be that Kaspar Hauser has not incarnated again as a human being on the earth since the time of Atlantis. This interpretation of Rudolf Steiner's words is confirmed by the report of a conversation that Countess Keyserlingk had with him in June 1924. Rudolf Steiner said in answer to a question as to a previous incarnation of Kaspar Hauser: 'He had not been able to find either a previous or a succeeding incarnation'.[190] This is signified lastly by the further statement that we are here dealing with a higher being who has a special earth-mission.[190] The underlying fact caused Rudolf Steiner, in September 1924, to describe Kaspar Hauser as an 'angel'.

If one follows up the question of Kaspar Hauser's lack of incarnations since Atlantis, Rudolf Steiner's reference to an 'angelic being' takes us further. An angel is a spiritual being, the lowest part of whose nature consists of an etheric body and whose highest member is the Holy Spirit, whereby a constant conscious contact is maintained with the spiritual world.* An organization such as this can also occur in an initiate, as for instance in Buddha. These high initiates are no longer obliged to incarnate, but if they consciously decide to do so, they thereby share helpfully in the destiny of their human brothers and sisters.

What is special, perhaps unique, in the character of Kaspar Hauser is that, in order to help mankind, he has held himself back from an incarnation since Atlantis; he has renounced incarnating out of a sense of spiritual sacrifice. This sacrifice, which was the unusual gift of a highly-developed individuality, was the outcome of a great amount of unselfishness which is a profound characteristic of Kaspar Hauser. All who met Kaspar Hauser with an open mind got this impression of pristine unselfishness.

Looked at from another point of view one can say that, in wisely planned anticipation of Christ's incarnation and the task of connecting the Christ Impulse with future human history on earth, a highly-developed individual had been selected by the leaders of mankind as they existed in the Atlantean Sun-Oracle[191] to forego his incarnation and to remain in the etheric environs of the earth. Understood in this way Kaspar Hauser was found to be a worthy servant of the sacred history of mankind, a fact which shines through the picture he presents on earth as also does the high degree of his unselfishness.

The question must now be asked: How did Kaspar Hauser, who had not been incarnated since Atlantis, acquire the Christ-Impulse for himself, when Rudolf Steiner emphasizes on several occasions that the understanding of the Christ-Impulse can only be acquired on the physical plane since the time of the Mystery of Golgotha.[192] If one looks into Atlantean antiquity one can only visualize and describe him as a 'Sun-Human-Being'[191] who has attained a knowledge of the Sun-Spirit, the Christ. Thus it becomes understandable that he appears from the start in the Rosicrucian current, because Rosicrucianism is to be regarded as the continuation of the Sun-Oracle.

The riddle as to how Kaspar Hauser came to accept the Mystery of Golgotha without having incarnated since Atlantis can be solved if one takes into consideration his special connection with Christian Rosenkreutz. In chapter 1 both Kaspar Hauser and Christian Rosenkreutz were recognized as being companions of Christ (see p.64). One would think that the Kaspar Hauser individuality lived in such an intimate brotherly companionship with Christian Rosenkreutz that he shared in what the latter had experienced and suffered in imitation of Christ.[193] The sentence which Rudolf Steiner uttered with a certain amount of reservation that 'next to Christian Rosenkreutz, Kaspar Hauser was the one who experienced the sufferings of Christ most acutely', is not to be understood as a mere comparison, but as the expression of a direct kinship-of-being of these two individualities.

The impression made by this kinship can become more profound and concrete if one takes it in conjunction with the following saying of Rudolf Steiner: 'This Being had worked as the inspirer of the Rosicrucian connections from the very start', and with other statements of a similar kind. Through that it also becomes possible to understand this particular acceptance of the Christ-Impulse by Kaspar Hauser. When speaking about the beginnings of Rosicrucianism this can only refer to the first initiation of Christian Rosenkreutz. 'In the narrow sense the Rosicrucian movement began in the thirteenth century', it is stated in a lecture by Rudolf Steiner on 27 September 1911 in Neuchâtel. 'We must look for the starting point of a new culture in the middle of the thirteenth century.'[194]

According to a statement of Rudolf Steiner, the individuality of Kaspar Hauser must have been closely connected with this starting-point. A closer study actually leads to the discovery that the widely separated statements of Rudolf Steiner derive from an overall picture. At that time—so says Rudolf Steiner—twelve outstanding individuals came together as the representatives of the whole sevenfold Atlantean civilization and the (up till now) five post-Atlantean cultural epochs. In these twelve men, who were permeated with the Christ-Impulse, there lived in the form of a College all the

knowledge and wisdom of human history. At the same time
there worked within this circle the twelve world-views of spirit-
directions as the sum total of the twelvefold truth given by the
macrocosm.

The reference to the fact that the thirteenth, who was later
to be called Christian Rosenkreutz, was a very frail child in his
incarnation in the thirteenth century—that is to say his
material corporeality offered the minimal amount of resistance to what came from the spirit, so that the education
which was given him by the twelve worked right down into the
physical body—must be seen in conjunction with the fact that
he was the first to gain complete mastery over a physical body
renewed by Christ. 'In the merging of the wisdom of the
twelve, the spiritual powers of the thirteenth extend infinitely.'

Finally there came a time when the thirteenth refused all
nourishment and pined away. An event that could happen
only once in history now took place. It was an event that can
happen when the macrocosmic forces work together for the
sake of the fruits which such an event is to bring about.
After some days the body of the thirteenth became quite
transparent and he lay for days as if dead. At certain definite
times the twelve gathered around him and in these moments
all their knowledge and wisdom streamed from their lips. In
short formulae that were like devout prayers, they let their
wisdom flow to the thirteenth while he lay there as if dead.
The twelve in a circle around the thirteenth—that is the
truest way to picture them. The process ended when the soul
of the thirteenth awakened as an entirely new soul, having
undergone a great transformation. Something like a new
birth of the twelvefold wisdom had taken place within the
thirteenth. The twelve themselves were now able to learn
from the disciple something altogether new. But even the
body—the wholly transparent body—was now vitalized in a
way that cannot be compared with anything else. The
thirteenth was able to speak of new experiences and the
twelve realized that one of these experiences had been a
repetition of St Paul's vision at the gate of Damascus. In the

course of a few weeks the thirteenth now gave forth again all the wisdom he had received from the twelve, but in a new form. It was as though this new form had been given by Christ Himself.[194]

At this original initiation of Christian Rosenkreutz the position of the hierophant had been assumed by the circle of the twelve. The initiator, who lived in this circle of the twelve as a uniting force, is the Christ Himself, who makes the fruits of the deed of Resurrection on Golgotha available to the one who is to become the leader of true Christianity. The physical body, which has been led over into death in order to meet the Christ, becomes divested of the effects of materiality, of weight and of impenetrability and opacity. Through the experience of the Resurrection during initiation, not only a transformation of spirit and soul takes place, but above all a vivification of the body, so that 'this vitalization of the wholly transparent body cannot be compared with anything else'. With that Rudolf Steiner touches on the deeper secrets of Christ's deed; a few days later he speaks in detail about it in his lecture-cycle in Karlsruhe *From Jesus to Christ* (see Chapter 3).

After the death of the thirteenth the twelve 'dedicated themselves to the task of recording in imaginations—for that is how it must have been—what the thirteenth had revealed to them.'[194]

Of more importance than the fact that this resulted in the publication of *The Secret Symbols of the Rosicrucians* (1785–88) and later Blavatsky's *Isis Unveiled* (1877), is the explanation that Rudolf Steiner gave for it: 'The occult process must be imagined in such a way that the fruit of the initiation of the thirteenth has been preserved within the spiritual atmosphere of the earth as the remains of the etheric body. These remains worked as an inspiration upon the twelve and also upon their pupils, so that the Rosicrucian stream of occultism could go forth from them.'[194]

We are now confronted by the fact that the Rosicrucian inspirations, which are here the basis of the imaginations, emanate from the after-death preserved etheric body of

Christian Rosenkreutz, whereas, according to the quoted statement of 1925, Kaspar Hauser has worked inspiringly from the start into the Rosicrucian connection. Both statements speak in a similar way about the original Rosicrucian inspiration, yet there seems to be a contradiction here, because in the one case it is the remains of the etheric body of Christian Rosenkreutz and in the other the being of Kaspar Hauser which is said to be the inspirer.

The seeming contradiction is solved if one takes into account the peculiar constitution of Kaspar Hauser's being, which—as already explained—encompasses an etheric body as its lowest member. Thus Kaspar Hauser, as an individuality living in the spirit, was in a position to take hold of and fill from within the etheric body that Christian Rosenkreutz had led through initiation. He thus came into contact with the Christ-Impulse dwelling therein. It was from this etheric body, spiritually filled with the essence of Kaspar Hauser, that the inspirations went forth which could be received by particularly advanced Rosicrucians. About this more advanced way of teaching in an initiation-school Rudolf Steiner said, in respect of Buddha's teaching out of his spirit-body: 'In schools of this kind there are teachers who teach in the physical body; but for the more advanced pupils it is also possible to receive lessons from a teacher who teaches only in his etheric body.'[195]

The whole process is here understood to mean that Kaspar Hauser is that being who protects and looks after the etheric body of Christian Rosenkreutz when the latter deserts it. Through that a particularly close connection is established between Christian Rosenkreutz and Kaspar Hauser. With regard to the earth-experiences during incarnations there exists on the other hand a distinct polarity. According to Rudolf Steiner, Christian Rosenkreutz is an individuality who goes through a far greater number of incarnations than is normal, whereby one can surmise that it has to do with a 100-year rhythm.[196] This is also the deeper cause of the 100-year rule of the Rosicrucians, which Rudolf Steiner said is a necessary protection against inner and outer attacks.[194]

Christian Rosenkreutz prepared himself through many

incarnations to take up his physical-spiritual body renewed by Christ's resurrection in his original initiation in the thirteenth century. In his next incarnation, which began about the middle of the fourteenth century and lasted more than 100 years, his initiation experiences were renewed and thereby strengthened. The spiritual experience of St Paul at Damascus, which Christian Rosenkreutz underwent spiritually in his previous life, was now repeated during an oriental journey to Damascus, the physical scene of this event. Yet, during this incarnation, which took place about 200 years after the first initiation, Christian Rosenkreutz was initiated still more deeply, so that at the time of the consciousness soul, which has pre-eminently to deal with evil, he can become the true leader of Christianity. Rudolf Steiner writes about this in September 1907: 'Within this whole stream, the initiation of *Mani*, who also initiated Christian Rosenkreutz in 1495, is considered to be of a "higher degree", it consists of the true understanding of the nature of evil.'[157] Thereby Christian Rosenkreutz reached the stage in which, through him, initiation could proceed.[197]

To sum up, Christian Rosenkreutz can justly be called 'the Master of the real physical body', over which he has acquired such sovereignty, in imitation of Christ, that he is able to dispose as he likes with incarnation, but also work in such a way on the physical plane as befits an incarnated human ego.

This individuality stood, and still stands—with others—alongside the individuality of Kaspar Hauser, to whom he is the polar opposite during his incarnation. This polarity is a co-operation in a higher sense; the enhancement which comes about lies in the service which each renders to the Third, which is Christ.

The point of time in which this long-standing polarity ceased, owing to Kaspar Hauser's incarnation, is revealed as a decisive and well-planned moment which is connected with the further development of the work of the Rosicrucians. This work of the Rosicrucians is directed towards making the etheric body of Christian Rosenkreutz, and therewith the influence which it disseminates, ever stronger and stronger.*

'Everything that is made known as true Theosophy

(Anthroposophy) is strengthened by the etheric body of Christian Rosenkreutz; and those who proclaim the message of true Theosophy let themselves be overshadowed by this etheric body which can work upon them when Christian Rosenkreutz is actually incarnated, and also when he is not.'[194] The procedure is to be seen as an increasing circulation in which the selfless sacrificial deeds of the Rosicrucians work, as it were, from below upwards and the spiritual forces of intuition, inspiration and imagination stream down graciously from above, where they react fruitfully and inspiringly upon the work of man. The whole activity of the Rosicrucians—and with that also the initiation of Christian Rosenkreutz him-self—was directed towards the goal of preparing for the greatest event of the twentieth century, the reappearance of Christ in the etheric realm.

> Devotion to the most powerful etheric body of Christian Rosenkreutz will be able to bring the new clairvoyance and lofty spiritual forces to manifestation; but this will be possible only for those who truly follow the schooling given by Christian Rosenkreutz. Until now, esoteric Rosicrucian preparation was necessary for this; but it is the mission of the twentieth century to allow this etheric body to become so powerful that it will also work exoterically. To those who are influenced by it the experience of Paul at the gate of Damascus may be vouchsafed. Up to now this etheric body has worked only into the Rosicrucian School; during the twentieth century more and more human beings will be able to receive this influence and thereby to witness the appearance of Christ in the etheric body. It is the work of the Rosicrucians which makes it possible to experience the manifestation of Christ in the ether-world. The number of those capable of beholding this manifestation will steadily increase. This new revelation must be traced back to the work of the twelve and the thirteenth in the thirteenth and fourteenth centuries.[194]

Kaspar Hauser is not only connected with this goal of Rosicrucian striving through acting as the inspirer within the

Rosicrucian stream; the inner task which was allotted him was to prepare already in the nineteenth century for a healthful outcome of this spiritual event of the twentieth century. As a being who was able, in a unique way, to inhabit the etheric body which came into existence through the initiation of Christian Rosenkreutz, he was called upon to make it possible for people to become aware of the reappearing Christ through a healthy etheric clairvoyance. This has been alluded to from a different point of view in the third chapter of this book, where the years 1812 and 1911/12 and especially the years 1833 and 1933 are discussed. Here is revealed how this task is connected with the character and development of Kaspar Hauser, which encompasses the whole historical process.

As an inspiring force in the Rosicrucian stream, Kaspar Hauser is at the same time the uniting, socializing factor. All who truly participate in the common source of inspiration are an objective part of it. Thus Kaspar Hauser worked in the Rosicrucian circle as a mercurial element, dissolving what was circumscribed and isolated and combining it in a higher unity and a common activity. Rudolf Steiner once explained that the action of mercury in nature corresponds to the activity of love in the human soul.[194] This, however, was and is—as will be confirmed at the end of this book—the mercurial element belonging to Kaspar Hauser, in the way in which he brought it to expression in his life—particularly in contradistinction to the Mars-like Napoleon.[198]

If—in conformity with Rudolf Steiner's statement—one regards Kaspar Hauser as the inspiring influence from the beginning of Rosicrucianism, then he is—with the exception of Christian Rosenkreutz himself—the first Rosicrucian to unite with the etheric body of Christian Rosenkreutz in the spiritual world. If one sees it in this light, then another very enigmatic remark is explained, which Rudolf Steiner made in connection with Daumer, when he called him the last of the Rosicrucians.[199] The 'first' meets the 'last' Rosicrucian because, through the activity of the 'first', a kind of termination, a definite turn in the activity of the Rosicrucians, was to have been achieved. With Kaspar Hauser's incarnation and his planned participation in history, the previously largely hidden preparatory work for the future, carried out by the Rosicrucians, came to an end. A period of development has ended and, in this sense, therefore, Daumer was the 'last' of the Rosicrucians.

In the first phase, at the beginning of the seventeenth century, Rosicrucianism tried to intervene directly in the process of history and in the social structure. Towards the end of the sixteenth century Christian Rosenkreutz called together that great occult conference, at which the leading individualities of mankind joined together in order to prevent the falling apart of humanity into 'practical people' and 'mystics'. One can be sure that the Kaspar Hauser individuality was also present in this circle of people. Rudolf Steiner emphasizes especially that it was not only those who were incarnated on earth who took part, but all those individualities who were in the spiritual world.[200]

The decisive deed in the overcoming of the approaching crisis for mankind was performed on Mars by Buddha, who, in the service of Christian Rosenkreutz, deflected its course through a cosmic sacrifice in 1604. Through that it became possible for the first time to unite Rosicrucian esoteric development with 'every kind of life-situation and occupation'. The important thing about Rosicrucianism is that 'it does not tear a person away from the activity which his earthly destiny demands of him'.[200] Through the Buddha-sacrifice on Mars in 1604 the cosmic basis was prepared for the creative activity which was to have been introduced in the nineteenth century by Kaspar Hauser and was actually largely accomplished by Rudolf Steiner. But already then, at the beginning of the seventeenth century, a little of this change was directly visible. This future impulse was living in the appearance of Demetrius. Above all, however, Rosicrucianism was expressed historically for the first time by the publication of *The Chemical Wedding of Christian Rosenkreutz* by Johann Valentin Andrae, Anno 1459 and by other Rosicrucian writings.*

Before the outbreak of the French Revolution, Christian Rosenkreutz himself was at work in the figure of the 'Comte de St Germain' to prevent the Revolution and to put a healthy development in its place. Was this to prevent the arrival of Napoleon on the scene and to prepare for Kaspar Hauser's incarnation? The conflicting role of Napoleon in connection with Kaspar Hauser has already been discussed (see p.147 et seq.).

It is plain that the intervention of Count St Germain had no outward success. The next step in the development of Rosicrucianism was now to be the one in which the individuality of Kaspar Hauser, wisely retained in the spiritual world as a precaution, was to be placed upon the physical plane in order to work historically from an important station in life. This change of policy of the Rosicrucians was necessary in order to prepare mankind for the approaching Michael Age and the impending end of Kali Yuga. The task and importance which was assigned to Kaspar Hauser in this capacity was discussed in Chapter 3. The change of policy here mentioned was actually first put into practice by Rudolf Steiner.

If previously it had been our aim to collect together all the facts that could give a clear explanation of Kaspar Hauser's spiritual origin, we shall now attempt to show how the characteristic features of the spiritual origin of this highly developed individuality are revealed in his earth-life.

If one starts first of all with the activity of Kaspar Hauser during the Atlantean civilization, one is struck straight away with the fact of his birthplace, Karlsruhe, which is situated in the immediate vicinity of Malsch. Here the physical contact with Atlantis makes itself felt and one can become conscious of the fact that obviously there was a profound need for the birth of this being to be linked, as with a fine thread, to Atlantis. The model building in Malsch, which is physically connected with Atlantis and etherically with the Rosicrucian-Impulse, is regarded in Chapter 4 as a memorial to Kaspar Hauser. The Atlantean and Christian components are fused together in the building and its surroundings.

One can gain further insight into the immediate impact of Kaspar Hauser if one discovers an Atlantean and a Christian layer in his personality. One comes across the former when one calls to mind his pre-intellectual, sheer unbelievable power of memory, about which Rudolf Steiner speaks in his lecture of 17 June 1908. The latter, Kaspar Hauser's Christian layer, is met with in remarkable differentiation. We only have to bring to mind how in this pure Christianized individuality a very strong attraction to the 'phantom', the 'New Adam'[201] was active. One can see this confirmed not only in Kaspar Hauser's diet and care during his imprisonment, but also in his unusual sense-qualities, as an expression of his renewed physical body and in his inconceivable life-forces.

Kaspar Hauser's arrival in Nuremberg in 1828 reveals a further Christian feature: his appearance is characterized by complete innocence and purity of heart. Independently of one another both Daumer and Tucher recognized and described him as the 'paradisaical archetypal man' (Daumer), or as 'the first man from Paradise before the Fall' (Tucher). Feuerbach saw in him 'a living rebuttal of the doctrine of original sin'.[202] An expression of what moved his contemporaries to these utterances was the intense sympathy which Kaspar Hauser showed towards animals and people. 'He could not be induced to hit anyone, even in fun, that was far too painful for him, too,' reports Daumer. His sympathy also extended to his gaoler[203] and at his death he lived with forgiveness for his murderer.*

These pure childlike forces in Kaspar Hauser were the real reason for his having been called 'the Child of Europe'. The angelic childlikeness of Kaspar Hauser brings us closer in mind to the Nathanic Jesus-Being. A warm-hearted person such as the prison warder Hiltel, with whom he at first lived, was deeply affected by this direct human touch. 'His innocence was so patent that he would swear to it, even though God Himself averred the opposite,' Hiltel said later.[13] What had taken place in this devout human being to make him use such an expression to convey his deepest conviction of an impression he had gained as a human being? The connection with the Nathanic Jesus-Being, however, goes far beyond a mere feeling of closeness. This Nathanic Jesus-Being, a still more highly organized individuality, was held back from incarnating since

Lemurian times (before the Fall of Man) at the wise discretion
of the Leaders of Humanity. This discarnate angelic being was
ensouled by Christ with His redemptive work proceeding from
the Mystery of Golgotha for the sake of mankind.[204]

Something similar took place in the being of Kaspar Hauser, who was also held back in the supersensible world by the
Leadership of Humanity before Atlantis fell into decadence
and destruction.* He was to appear on the earth after the
Mystery of Golgotha—which already lay in the plan for
humanity—to prepare an important turning-point in mankind's history. This turning-point in history was the appearance of Christ in the etheric world, the greatest event of the
twentieth century. The inspirer of the Rosicrucian movement
had incarnated a hundred years earlier. Taking into consideration all that was discussed in Chapter 3, his task of
preparing for the Christ-Event consisted of arranging situations in life and awakening spiritual powers so that the
greatest possible number of people would be enabled to
understand and take up the progressive unfolding of the
Christ-Impulse. The words of Christ: 'My Kingdom is not of
this World' remain true; the meaning of the incarnation of an
ego disappears, however, if the Kingdom of the Christ-Spirit is
unable to work deeper and deeper into the earthly world, in
order ultimately to enlighten and irradiate it completely.

Kaspar Hauser was killed in 1833, exactly 100 years before
the start of the Etheric Christ-Revelation. In this connection
we have to remember the strange fact which Rudolf Steiner
also mentioned in his two lectures about Kaspar Hauser.
Jakob Wassermann writes in his novel about the burial of
Kaspar Hauser on 20 December 1833: 'It was in the afternoon
and the sky was a cloudless blue. The whole town was astir. A
famous contemporary who called Kaspar Hauser "the Child
of Europe" reports that it was at the time when both moon
and sun were in the sky together, the former in the east and the
latter in the west, and both shone with the same pale lustre.'[44]
Rudolf Steiner draws attention to the fact[205] that in earlier
times people used to observe the celestial constellations and
weather conditions at the time of important events and keep

them in mind. A harmonizing of the cosmic and atmospheric conditions with the events of destiny that befall an individual presumes that the individual has a connection with what is cosmic, that it has grown into what is cosmic. An individual such as this does not carry out his own will, but serves the divine will.

The sacrificial death of Kaspar Hauser must be seen in this cosmic light, without which—as Rudolf Steiner says on another occasion—'the contact between the earth and the spiritual world would have been completely severed'.[49] The very immensity of the task that Kaspar Hauser undertook and wished to accomplish and which he now relinquishes to destiny, was able to achieve its goal in sacrifice for mankind. Through Kaspar Hauser's sacrificial death and through the coming of Anthroposophy the spiritual possibility for the future of mankind has been preserved, in spite of all opposition. For this to be taken hold of and realized depends not least upon whether the character, task and destiny of Kaspar Hauser is recognized for what it is.

At this point it becomes possible to illuminate and understand the methods employed by the enemies of Kaspar Hauser from a different point of view to that put forward in Chapter 1. The crime against Kaspar Hauser presupposes a knowledge of the time and place of his appearance. The opponents knew whence Kaspar Hauser came and they had knowledge of the task he was to fulfil in a Christian sense for the evolution of the earth. We can now understand the treatment which Kaspar Hauser received in prison as an attempt to produce only the Atlantean characteristics of his nature. The attempt was made to forcibly hold him back in a former distant state of life and consciousness, so that he would be prevented from recapturing and becoming conscious of what he had absorbed in his soul of the Christ-Impulse. His treatment was arranged so that he would be pushed back into a pre-Christian period of development. Nothing Christian should be kindled within him, only what was very ancient should appear in him. The opponents of Kaspar Hauser actually succeeded in transferring him into such a state of consciousness as existed before the development of the ego—the child was prevented from standing upright and was not allowed to experience either day or night, and never to see either sun or moon or stars. This holding him back in the dusk and the darkness, this limitation of the sense of sight, which is intimately connected with the awakening of sensual awareness and intellectual development, reminds us of the dim and misty fog-blurred vision of the Atlanteans.

Rudolf Steiner points to this ancient state of consciousness in his lecture of 17 June 1908, in which he speaks significantly of Kaspar Hauser. The present-day state of consciousness has developed out of a 'different, very ancient state of consciousness, in which man did not come into direct contact with sense objects as he does today, but instead was connected with spiritual facts and beings'.[206]

The terrible experiment to hold back Kaspar Hauser in the forces of his previous incarnation was carried out with the intention of making his particular task of unfolding spiritually-motivated conditions of life and the conscious development of the Christ-Impulse unworkable.

When Kaspar Hauser was thrust out into the world by his enemies in 1828, he gave the impression—as far as the radical changes in the conditions of human development allowed—of a 'straggler from Atlantis', whereby, certainly, the level of development of the individuality has to be taken into account.

One certainly must not conclude from this that the intentions of the opponents succeeded. It was just because of the way he was treated that he was led in childish ecstasy—at the threshold of consciousness—into the depths of human sorrow in which he could re-experience the way of suffering and death of Christ. Thus after his release into the world, the primordial faculties of Atlantis were exhibited in him, but, with the awakening of his individuality, future qualities came to expression in the all-embracing compassion of which he was capable; the Christian-Impulse rose out of the depths of experience and, finally—as Rudolf Steiner expresses it—'the knowledge of reincarnation and karma'.

The opponents' venture developed more and more into a

fiasco the longer Kaspar Hauser lived. It can be described as a tragic paradox that the martyrdom which was further prepared for him resulted in his becoming more deeply connected with the Christ-Impulse in an incarnation on earth. What worked decisively into this development was the sincere belief of Pastor Fuhrmann in the resurrection.

The path of suffering which Kaspar Hauser had to tread until the time of his death is marked out in four stations: 1. The assassination attempt in October 1829, which put him in fear of death; 2. The seduction and confusion occasioned by Lord Stanhope; 3. The anguish and restriction of his schooling and life with his teacher, Meyer; 4. Wounding and death.

From every stage of this path of suffering Kaspar Hauser wrested something positive, a perfecting of his being, whereby one must certainly take into account his youthfulness and his severely hindered development. The experiencing of the murderous force led him to complete non-violence, to a horror of weapons and every sort of violent behaviour. In face of Lord Stanhope's artful seduction, which he was unable to see through, he preserved his trust in other people through his benevolence and good-humour. Nothing worse could have befallen him than to be placed at the mercy of the teacher Meyer and by Lord Stanhope of all people. He bore it with resignation towards his destiny, patiently, tolerantly and ultimately thankfully. In dying he could sum up what he had become through suffering. He was blessed with the closeness of Christ of Whom he had become aware.

It is to be presumed that the opponents knew something of the all-embracing significance of his martyrdom. Only thus can be explained the agitative activity of Lord Stanhope after Kaspar Hauser's death. It is as though a radiant vision shining into the future were to be covered over with grime and darkened.[207]

Concluding word

The individuality living in Kaspar Hauser has been distinguished by its service to the Christ-Impulse throughout the whole of known history. It reveals the degree of its own development by this selfless service. That is why it was chosen long ago by the Leadership of Humanity to intervene decisively in the course of events on a unique historical occasion. It was thwarted by the united forces of evil which gain power over the material body on earth. Through Kaspar Hauser's individuality having sacrificed everything it had in the service of humanity, it converted the necessary outward defeat into a victory for the spirit. Service, in the imitation of Christ, became enhanced to a deed of sacrifice of cosmic importance for the earth, by which contact with the spiritual world (the bridge) could be maintained. Kaspar Hauser provided fruitful supersensible influences, which live in the forces of Christianity for present and future times. Kaspar Hauser is a Christian figure, not only because he was the inspirer of Rosicrucianism, but because he also lives in the circle of those people whose intention it is to lead mankind in the future to an understanding of Christ.

As far back into the past as we have to probe to gain an understanding of Kaspar Hauser's nature, so far must we also look into the future to get a glimpse of his importance. What this being has achieved for future times in the supersensible world by his incarnation, destiny and sacrificial death, must be distinguished from what was unsuccessful on the physical plane through hindrances to his original task or, as the case may be, what was put in its place—as was discussed in Chapter 3. If one keeps both these domains in mind, the conflicting picture it presents can be understood in the light of the Faust words: 'The night seems deeper now to press upon me, but in my inmost spirit all is light' (Bayard Taylor translation, *Faust* II, Act V, Scene V).

Does anything exist which can illuminate the nature of Kaspar Hauser as if by a light? This can be found in his strange connection to the metal quicksilver. 'Quicksilver is the metal which exerts the strongest influence on Kaspar Hauser,' Daumer reports.[208] The childlike sense that feels joyously drawn towards the impression made by the shining mobility of a globule of mercury also reveals the secret of the being in which both Atlantean and Christian elements are living. In the effects that this metal belonging to the planet Mercury had on him is something of the forces of the world that confirms the being of Kaspar Hauser. In the substance quicksilver can be found the seal to Kaspar Hauser's nature if the metal's secrets are laid bare in the way which Rudolf Steiner once described: 'When human beings become ever more spiritualized, quicksilver (mercury) will also become solid. At one time gold and silver formed drops, just as water does now. The fact that mercury is still fluid is connected with the whole process of earth evolution. It will become solid when the Messenger of the Gods, Mercury, has fulfilled his mission. In the middle of the Atlantean root race quicksilver was brought down from Mercury in etheric form. Had we not had quicksilver we should not have had the Christ-Principle. In the drops of quicksilver we have to see what was incorporated in the middle of the Atlantean epoch.'[209]

The combination of Atlantean and Christian elements in Kaspar Hauser appears in a higher light through this Mercury task. In the sequence of the great evolutionary epochs the middle of Atlantis is also the central point of earth evolution. At that time it was necessary to implant the Christ-Power etherically into the earth, by which it could be redeemed and the soul of man could be released through spiritualization. The liquid state of the metal quicksilver points to what is direct, immediate and living in this process. The future, far distant approaching solidification of quicksilver will indicate that this process has come to an end. The being of Kaspar Hauser is bound in devotion to the origin and goal of the Mercury-Service for Christ. The Mercury activity of the Christ-Principle during the Atlantean evolution is not contrary to the incarnation of Christ and the Mystery of Golgotha; the latter events have their unique significance in the creation of the resurrection-body, the restoration of the spiritual-physical phantom. The redemption of the earth and the redemption of mankind as a merged process demands many stages. The deed of Christ here referred to has to be seen in relationship to the beginning and end of earth evolution. In his *Theosophy of the*

Rosicrucian Rudolf Steiner gives a piece of information which can help our understanding further.

In the first half of earth existence, the influence of the planet Mars is the ruling factor, and the influence of the planet Mercury in the second half. Mars has given iron to the earth and the Mercury influence manifests on the earth in such a way that it makes the human soul more and more free, more and more independent. In occultism, therefore, we speak of the Mars half of earth evolution and the Mercury half. Whereas the other names describe a whole planet, earth evolution is spoken of as Mars-Mercury.[210]

It is to this second half of earth evolution, the activity of the planet Mercury, that Kaspar Hauser's soul-spiritual work is directed. The Mercury Spirit, which was served by the being of Kaspar Hauser, acted from the middle of Atlantis on into the nineteenth century, in order to bring about that liberation and loosening of the inner structure of as many people as possible, so that they would be enabled to raise themselves up to an experience of the etheric Christ after the first third of the twentieth century had passed. The current of the Rosicrucian work, in which Kaspar Hauser worked inspiratively, had worked for hundreds of years to prepare mankind for the event of Christ's appearance in the etheric world. With that, however, the Christ-serving spirit of Mercury is only beginning its activity. A far future lies before it which stretches even to the end of the world. It is for this future that Kaspar Hauser lives. It is discernible in three currents which work for and with the Christ. The first of these turns towards the earth, takes hold of it and seeks to redeem it, as was visible in the laying of the Foundation Stone for the Rosicrucian Temple 'Francis of Assisi' in Malsch. The second seeks to free mankind from the fetters of what is material and heavy. Through it the physical and etheric bodies of man become so transformed that he can become a worthy citizen of the spiritual world. In the place of the Mars Spirit, which lives by the power of the sword, the Mercury Spirit which brings peace in a helpful way takes an ever greater part in evolution. The greatest gift of the Mercury

Spirit, however, is the benefit it brings to mankind: 'What quality of soul works in the way that quicksilver or mercury works in outer nature? The medieval Rosicrucian knew that the corresponding quality of soul is *love* in all its forms.[211]

Kaspar Hauser's sacrifice, which preserved the contact for mankind between the earth and the spiritual world, grew out of the source of love in the soul. As a Mercury-messenger Kaspar Hauser serves the Christ and leads mankind into the future as one of its guiding spirits.

Appendix I

Summary of references by Rudolf Steiner relating to Kaspar Hauser

Dated reference

1. 1905/6   Conversation with Frau Rissmann in Nuremberg—provided by Rudolf Rissmann.
   Karl Heyer, *Kaspar Hauser und das Schicksal Mitteleuropas (Kaspar Hauser and the destiny of Central Europe)*.

2. 1908   Lecture of 17 June in Nuremberg.

3. 1916   November in Dornach—notes by Count Ludwig Polzer-Hoditz.

4. 1923   Lecture of 23 March in Dornach.

5. 1924   Countess Johanna Keyserlingk, *Zwölf Tage in Koberwitz (Twelve days in Koberwitz)*.
   Karl Heyer, *Kaspar Hauser und das Schicksal Mitteleuropas*.

6. 1925   3 March in Dornach—notes by Count Ludwig Polzer-Hoditz.

7. 1925   3 March in Dornach—notes by Count Ludwig Polzer-Hoditz.

Undated references

8. Karl Heyer, *Kaspar Hauser und das Schicksal Mitteleuropas*.
9. Karl Heyer, *Kaspar Hauser und das Schicksal Mitteleuropas*.

Unconfirmed

10. Reincarnation.
11. 'Angel'.

Quotation from Jakob Wassermann, *Caspar Hauser*.

1 Rudolf Rissmann, 'Rudolf Steiner at the beginning of the century'

'Some years previously Rudolf Steiner said to my mother that Kaspar Hauser was a "stray Atlantean". My mother often told me this as we passed by Daumer's house.'

Karl Heyer, *Kaspar Hauser und das Schicksal Mitteleuropas*

'According to a well-authenticated source Kaspar Hauser was described by Rudolf Steiner as a *"stray Atlantean"*. That happened in about 1905/6 in reply to a question by a Nuremberg citizen, whose parents were close friends of Professor Daumer. In Rudolf Steiner's reply—apart from what it otherwise conveys—is at least the assumption that Kaspar Hauser displayed characteristics akin to those of the Atlanteans. That also includes his strong faculty of memory.'

2 Rudolf Steiner, lecture of 17 June 1908 in Nuremberg

'Whoever observes the world from a more or less practical point of view today is still able to recognize that what is said by spiritual science is not a mere figment of imagination. If that were the case, one could then say that human beings who are retarded at the present day owing to some chance happening would be least affected in their memory. One would also have to show that if the attempt were made to train the intellect of such a person who had been artificially held back in his development, his memory would suffer as a consequence. Here in this very town a characteristic case of this kind can be observed.

'This case, so enigmatic for many people, of a person who was brought to this city in such a mysterious fashion and who met his death in an equally mysterious way in Ansbach and about whom a writer, indicating the enigma of his life, says that he was carried to his grave as the sun was sinking on the one horizon and the moon was rising on the other; this case was observed closely by Professor Daumer, who cannot be praised highly enough. You know that I am referring to Kaspar Hauser. If you ignore all the pros and cons which have been raised in connection with this case; if you only consider those facts which have been established beyond doubt, you will be aware of the fact that this foundling, who simply appeared on the streets one day, who, because no one knew whence he had come, unable to read or count when he was discovered, was called "the Child of Europe".

'At the age of 20 this youth possessed nothing derived from the intellect, but, strangely enough, he had a wonderful memory. When his education was begun, when logic was implanted in his soul, his memory disappeared. This change in his consciousness was connected with something else. He possessed an inconceivably pure and natural sense for truth and it was just in respect of this sense for truth that he became ever more confused. The more he was allowed to nibble at intellectuality, the more his sense for truth receded.

'There would be much to study by immersing ourselves in this artificially retarded soul. The tradition which is current among the people in general, but is rejected by erudite folk, that Kaspar Hauser could exert a remarkable influence on rabid animals while he was in a state of complete ignorance and unaware that there were also other beings different from himself, is an acceptable fact to those who base their views on spiritual science. Wild animals cowered and became quite tame. Something exuded from him that caused such a wild animal, which attacked all other animals, to become calm. As was said earlier: on account of a case such as this which can be understood by spiritual science, we are able to penetrate deeply into the soul of this remarkable—and for many inscrutable—personality, and such a case may be envisaged by us that shows how everything which cannot be explained in everyday life can be traced by spiritual science to spiritual facts. It is clear that such spiritual facts cannot be gained by means of speculation, but only through spiritual observation, nevertheless they are understandable to comprehensive and logical thinking.'
(Public lecture in connection with the cycle of lectures about the Apocalypse of St John, GA 104.)

3 Notes by Count Ludwig Polzer-Hoditz. November 1916

'Those circles which conceal everything and today still try to conceal what happened in connection with Kaspar Hauser's destiny, are those members of western Lodges and Jesuits who have worked together in their leading organizations for more than 150 years, but demonstrably since January 1802. The latter, therefore, do not want to have exposed what they have staged as an experiment, as an elaborate attempt to separate the individual in question from his mission and to hold him in a twilight zone, not completely spirit and not altogether a man on earth, but diverted from his mission and kept as though in spiritual exile; that is to say, to build a body, but not be able to take hold of it as an individual ego. This experiment, however, did not succeed and that is the reason why Kaspar Hauser had to die. The people concerned were forced to experience that their experiment achieved just that which they had tried to avoid: the awakening of the individuality, yes, even that he became conscious of reincarnation and karma. But that was just what should not have been. South Germany should have become the new Grail-Castle of the new Knights of the Grail and the cradle of future events. The spiritual ground had been well prepared by all those personalities whom we know of as Goethe, Schiller, Hölderlin, Herder and others. Kaspar Hauser was to have gathered around him, as it were, all that existed in this spiritual ground thus prepared. But that was not wanted by those circles (the western Lodges and the Jesuits). They could not tolerate a centre that was awakening to consciousness if they were not to relinquish their power and designs for power. A spirit such as Goethe's frightened them. Napoleon forced them to unite and form a league for the aspired-to world domination in the sphere of ideology and commerce. Napoleon had already thwarted their effort; it was he who fundamentally forced the two currents into union. From that time onwards the tasks allotted to each were clearly circumscribed. But for that their clearly defined goal of world domination became all the more effective. The ideological and spiritual affairs were given exclusively into the hands of the Jesuits; the commercial ones into the hands of the Anglo-American Lodges of the West. These plans, however, will lead to ever more tragic catastrophes, because none of them take human development into account. What was intended to happen through Kaspar Hauser was overthrown by mankind. On these "planned" ruins the black-and-white principle gained ascendancy. The black-and-white principle, however, is something constructed, something exclusive. This is also the tragedy of Bismarck himself, who was quite well able to con-struct the model for a Federal State, the constructive idea of a true Central Federation, but could not supply the supporting idea, that which would have made a state construction of this kind appear necessary and justified. It was that which Bismarck was seeking in Frankfurt, too, the Goethean spirit, that which could have devel-oped in the region of southern Germany through Kaspar Hauser but did not come about. It was in Frankfurt, actually, where Bismarck encountered the principle of black-and-white and all that then bound him to the King of Prussia. It was from then on that the era of the lawyer began, but politics is not a legal problem.'

4 Rudolf Steiner, lecture of 23 March 1923 in Dornach

'In this second post-Atlantean epoch—strange though it may seem, it was so—great importance was attached to whether a human being was born during fine weather, whether he was born by night or by day, during winter or in summer. There was nothing resembling intellectual reasoning but people had the feeling: whatever heavenly constellation is approved by the Gods, whether fine weather or blizzard, whether day or night, when they send a human being down to the earth, this constellation gives expression to their thoughts, to their Divine Thoughts. And if a child is born perhaps during a thunderstorm or during some other unusual weather conditions, that was regarded by the laity as the expression of the Divine Thought allocated to the child.

'This was so among the laity. Among the members of the priest-hood, who in turn were dependent on the Mysteries and kept the official register, so to speak, of the births—but this is not to be understood in the modern bureaucratic sense—these aspects of weather, time of day, season of the year and so forth, indicated under what conditions the Divine Thought was allocated to a human being. This was in the second post-Atlantean epoch, the Ancient Persian epoch.

'Very little of this has persisted into our time. Nowadays some-thing extremely boring is suggested if it is said that a person talks about the weather. It is considered derogatory to say of anyone nowadays that he is a bore, he can talk of nothing but the weather. In the days of Ancient Persia such a remark would not have been understood; it was someone who had nothing interesting to say about the weather who would have been regarded as extremely boring! And in point of fact it is true that we have lifted ourselves right out of the natural environment if no connection can be felt between human life and meteorological phenomena. In the Ancient Persian epoch an intense feeling of participation in the cosmic environment expressed itself in the fact that people thought of events—and the birth of a human being was an important event—in connection with what was taking place in the universe.

'It would be a definite advance if people—they need not merely talk about the weather being good or bad, for that is very abstract—if people were again to reach the stage of not forgetting, when they are relating some incident, to say what kind of weather was experienced, what natural phenomena were connected with it.

'It is extremely interesting when, here or there, striking phenom-ena are still mentioned, as, for instance, was the case in connection with the death of Kaspar Hauser. Because it was a striking phenomenon, mention is made of the fact that the sun was setting on the one side while the moon was rising on the other, and so forth. And so we can come to understand human nature as it was in the second post-Atlantean epoch.' (*Driving force of Spiritual powers in World History.*)

5 Countess Johanna Keyserlingk, *Zwölf Tage in Koberwitz, 1924*

'Another statement which later occupied my mind a great deal was the following: Herr Winkler had asked Rudolf Steiner if he could tell him anything about the previous incarnation of Caspar Hauser. Rudolf Steiner gave the answer on the following day. He had made spiritual investigations at Caspar Hauser's birthplace and at the place where he was murdered, but he had not been able to find either a previous or a subsequent incarnation. In this case we are dealing with a higher being, who had a special mission on the Earth.'
To this—seemingly identical:

Karl Heyer, *Kaspar Hauser und das Schicksal Mitteleuropas*

'To this is added a further very important statement by Rudolf Steiner, the authenticity of which is beyond doubt according to all information at my disposal; namely: In the year 1924 Rudolf Steiner was approached by someone who asked him about the destiny of Kaspar Hauser and was given the answer by Rudolf Steiner—on the next day—*that he had not been able to discover a previous incarnation of Kaspar Hauser.*'

6 Notes by Count Ludwig Polzer-Hoditz, 3 March 1925 in Dornach

'But always remember this: the Jesuits have deprived humanity of religiosity, of devotion; they are identical with the power of the Roman state. The battle—that is to say the sin against the Holy Spirit—is the power by which they enforce their supremacy. It is the only sin about which the scriptures say it cannot be forgiven. Yet, still the spirit cannot be entirely eradicated, but only a few people will carry it over into the future . . . the battle directed against the spirit has always and will always lie at the back of all outward events.'

7 Notes by Count Ludwig Polzer-Hoditz, 3 March 1925 in Dornach

'Then we spoke about the aims of Catholic and western Lodges and with deep seriousness Rudolf Steiner stressed the fact that there are three tasks to be solved of especial importance for the future:

1. The question about the two Johns.
2. The identity of Demetrius.
3. The origin of Kaspar Hauser.

In all these problems it is especially significant that one's gaze is not directed towards the death of the subject, but towards the birth. Whence did they come and what was their task? The individuality that hid behind the veil of Kaspar Hauser is a being which has worked inspiringly into the Rosicrucian connection from the very start and then was incarnated on 29 September 1812 as the son of the Grand Duke Karl of Baden and his wife Stephanie de Beauharnais. Kaspar Hauser had an important mission of esoteric Christianity to fulfil. It is immaterial who Demetrius was, who Kaspar Hauser was, because a question of this sort diverts attention away from the actual happening. It is not a question of who Demetrius was, who Kaspar Hauser was, but of what was to have been achieved by them. One should occupy oneself with the question as to what was to have been brought about through them, for by such a direction of investigation we shall always gain the key to an understanding of many problems.'

8 Karl Heyer, *Kaspar Hauser und das Schicksal Mitteleuropas*

'Of especial importance is what Fuhrmann reported about the way Kaspar Hauser accepted the mystery of the doctrine of forgiveness and other such doctrines (in contrast to what Feuerbach expected): "It is just in this connection that Kaspar Hauser expressed the greatest, the most elevated, feeling, it was just in this that he showed an emotion and zeal which moved all who saw him—as it did me—to astonishment and wonder. His tears flowed copiously by the recounting of the story of Jesus, his words and gestures expressed the deepest reverence, the holiest admiration for the suffering of the Saviour" ...

'These last reports by Pastor Fuhrmann are in agreement with an alleged statement of Rudolf Steiner which we would otherwise have left unmentioned because it has not been definitely confirmed, had not the statements of Pastor Fuhrmann appeared to uphold it from a certain point of view. Rudolf Steiner is reported to have said: Alongside Christian Rosenkreutz, Kaspar Hauser is the one who had the greatest understanding for the suffering of Christ.'

9 Karl Heyer, *Kaspar Hauser und das Schicksal Mitteleuropas*

'The dimensions in which Rudolf Steiner envisaged the figure of
Kaspar Hauser is expressed in his (well-authenticated) remark: "If
Kaspar Hauser had not lived and died as he did, then the contact
between the earth and the heavenly world would have been completely severed." It is a word which reveals further grand prospects,
hinting at a positive reverse argument to what happened to Kaspar
Hauser. It makes us think of the greatest event of earth evolution
when we compare it with this small event.'

There are two statements by Rudolf Steiner that have not been
confirmed up till now, the contents of which, however, can be held to
be reliable:

10 Reincarnation

If Kaspar Hauser had been murdered as a child, he would have been
able to reincarnate rapidly. The perpetrators acted in accordance
with a knowledge of this fact. It is *one* of the reasons for the treatment to which they subjected him.

The content of this statement is supported by similar references
which he made. In this connection he once revealed to a Munich
couple the surprising fact that a very young baby they had lost
would be reincarnated in their family within a year. The basic
underlying anthropological law about this states that a child entering life with a web of destiny covering a whole long lifetime on earth
is able to build a new second body if the first one is destroyed or
proves to be unable to survive. The second body does not necessarily
have to develop within the same family.

11 'Angel'

In the circle of the priests of the Christian Community Rudolf
Steiner is said to have reported in connection with the Theological
Course in Dornach in September 1924 that Kaspar Hauser was an
angelic being. It has been explained in Chapter 5 how this remark is
to be understood.

12 The citation in Wassermann's novel to which Rudolf Steiner
refers in both his lectures about Kaspar Hauser (17 June 1908 and 23
March 1923) is as follows:

'He was buried two days later. It was the afternoon and the sky was a cloudless blue. The whole town [Ansbach] was stirring. A famous contemporary who called Caspar Hauser "The Child of Europe" relates that on that occasion both moon and sun were in the sky at the same time, the former in the East, the latter in the West, and that both heavenly bodies gleamed with the same pale light.'

Karl Heyer comments on this citation:

'If the "famous contemporary" introduced by Wassermann really existed or was a poetic invention of his, and who that person might be, I was unable to ascertain. According to my enquiries it would seem that the latter is the more likely conclusion. That particular constellation of sun and moon at the time of the burial could in any case not have been visible, for the funeral took place on the morning of 20 December (that is to say not two, but three days after Kaspar Hauser's death on 17 December). That has been expressly confirmed in a report of the Town Magistrate of Ansbach, 22 December 1933.

Further to that, however, as I have been assured; neither sun nor moon could have had the indicated position either on the day of the fatal wounding (14 December) or on the death day (17 December) or at any time during the days of the funeral, because it was only on 26 December that full moon took place.

The question then is certainly of no special significance if the position of the heavenly bodies is only a poetic invention of Wassermann in order to "indicate" the "Mystery" of Kaspar Hauser's life. But against this conclusion there stands a statement from a lecture by Rudolf Steiner. Thus there remains a question which the astronomers or the astrosophists can try to solve out of the background of Anthroposophy.'

Appendix II

Open questions of Kaspar Hauser investigation

Twentieth-century research into the Kaspar Hauser question has resulted in reliable results in the case of his identity, the exchange of babies and his murder. These are described in particular by Pies in his book *Kaspar Hauser—eine Dokumentation* (1966). Three other lines of enquiry have not, however, led to equally clear results:

1. The dynastic crime
2. The imprisonment
3. The occult background.

The dynastic crime as such can be accepted with certainty. This is chiefly confirmed by the attitude of many of the members of the House of Baden. Thus it is rightly assumed that Sophie of Sweden— the wife of Leopold, the son of the Grand Duchess of Hochberg, who came to the throne in 1830—knew of the crime against Kaspar Hauser and became an accomplice in his murder in 1833. When Sophie told this to Leopold at Christmas 1833 it resulted in the break-up of their marriage. Leopold, who had apparently been unaware of the fact up till then, turned to drink. Louis II, the son of Leopold and Sophie, became insane as a result of the crime and was obliged to quit the throne because of it. Luise of Prussia, the wife of the Grand Duke Frederick (the brother of the unhappy Louis II), who had reigned since 1856, used all the means at her disposal to get hold of all the incriminating documents which certainly existed at that time, in order to destroy them. This was especially successful in the case of Henriette von Feuerbach. In 1875 she induced the German Emperor Wilhelm I to publish the document concerning the birth and death of the heir apparent in September/October 1812. That has already been reported in Chapter 1 of the present work. Also the actions of the Baden police after the death of Hennenhofer, who was certainly involved in the case, is a sure admission of guilt for every unprejudiced mind: Hennenhofer's rooms were immediately cleared out completely after his death.

Many details of the dynastic crime have previously remained unclear. One thing is certain, however, that the Grand Duchess of Hochberg was definitely involved in the exchange of babies, or had even been the perpetrator herself. What happened next remains obscure. The dynastic crime always demanded the ultimate elimination of Kaspar Hauser, for every later appearance of the legitimate heir to the throne would have destroyed any prospects of succession to the throne by the sons of the Grand Duchess of Hochberg. Therefore one reason for the murder of Kaspar Hauser—as already explained—is to be sought on the dynastic level. In 1833 the possibility was still there that Kaspar Hauser would have been recognized as being the legal heir to the throne.

That would have been quite conceivable because the identity of Kaspar Hauser as the heir apparent to the throne of Baden had been made clear to Queen Karoline of Bavaria, the aunt of Kaspar Hauser, in the 'Memoirs' of Feurbach in 1832. The intention of these 'Memoirs', which were strictly confidential at that time, was to restore Kaspar Hauser to the throne, according to his hereditary right, through his highly placed relatives. Did the fear of the inevitably great public upheaval that would have ensued deter those in the know from doing anything about it?

Decisive questions remain concerning the Grand Duchess of Hochberg—how much did she actually know? Did she give away the baby in return for a promise that her sons would inherit the throne? To whom did she give it? In that case her complicity would have been serious, but limited. Her sons appear not to have known anything about the crime during her lifetime. They had to put their pathologically extravagant mother under guardianship. She died in 1820 from a serious illness. Did she know when she died that the abducted child was still alive? Many questions still exist which will never be answered on a documented historical basis, because the documents have been systematically destroyed. It is therefore very unlikely that documents will still be found in future which will throw light on these circumstances, as, in addition to that, the archives of the House of Baden were completely destroyed by the burning of the Karlsruhe Castle in September 1944. At best traces or indications might have been discovered there which had escaped the previous selective destruction.

In his book *Kaspar Hauser, kein Rätsel unserer Zeit* (1978), Kurt Kramer attempted to present the dynastic crime as a political one. After that cliques arose in Baden as well as in Bavaria which knew the truth of the matter and wanted to get one better over each other. What sort of people were they and what advantage did they hope to gain? Is it really justified to think that such a large number of people knew of an unparalleled crime against a child—and did not say anything? By that they necessarily made themselves accomplices. But if one really accepts that fact they could never tell what they knew, because they would thereby have exposed themselves to being participants. In that way they would have helped to put Kaspar Hauser on the throne, but would thereby have landed themselves in prison. One can see that such observations can neither be confirmed nor logically substantiated.

The question of the imprisonment and incarceration of Kaspar Hauser has not been so well explained as the dynastic crime. The imprisonment itself, however, must be accepted. It is borne out by a multitude of psychic and physical observations of Kaspar Hauser which do not allow of any other interpretation. The whole impression he made when he first appeared confirms the belief in a prolonged confinement. Apart from that nearly everything is uncertain. One presumes that before his imprisonment he had been with Frau von Dalbonne in Beugen-on-the-Rhine. A coat of arms [drawn] by Kaspar Hauser has a surprising similarity to the coat of arms in Beugen Castle (Pies, *Dokumentation*)—it is a suggestion, a possibility! After that the course which Kaspar Hauser took is lost in complete darkness, if we wish to rely on actual confirmed evidence. Even Fritz Klee who succeeded in uncovering the history of the exchange of children was not successful in elucidating this mystery, in spite of intensive endeavour. The final station in Kaspar Hauser's path of suffering seems to have been Castle Pilsach, according to the conclusion of Clara Hofer in 1924. From there it would have been possible to convey Kaspar Hauser to Nuremberg at Whitsuntide 1828. It is perhaps possible that Kaspar Hauser was subjected to hypnotic manipulation for this journey, but it is probable that during the transportation—as was also the case during his imprisonment for the purpose of attending to his occasional bodily needs—he was anaesthetized with opium. In all these things, however, there is no sure basis for a conclusion.

The desire to overcome this remaining uncertainty has led both Grunelius-Schacht and Kramer to deny the incarceration completely and to postulate a transition from a more or less normal life to a life in the world at large as being brought about by hypnotic means. The final unacceptability of this belief will be explained here in spite of the fact that there is no shred of evidence to support the idea of a 'normal' life situation.

The hypnotism-theory is put forward by Kramer without his

being able to make it in any way convincing that a hypnotic block lasting for so long and being so effective is at all possible. Through the impractical and unconsidered relationship of Kramer to occult matters another danger to Kaspar Hauser is presented: he is made into a medium controlled by hypnotism. This is only made possible because hypnotism is overvalued and misunderstood. For his supporting evidence Kramer quotes du Prel's work *Riddles of Man* (1892). 'Let us imagine the following case: A sailor on a ship in the Mediterranean is put to sleep by hypnotic means and receives the suggestion that he should continue to sleep until the evening, but then to wake up without having retained any recollection of his past life. After this suggestion has been firmly implanted into the sailor's mind he is transferred to a small boat and put ashore on a little island, but the ship departs under full sail. After waking up this sailor would be exactly like a new-born human being with the sole exception that he has entered life as a mature reasoning being; he would begin his life as a man. He would ponder to no purpose as to who he was and how he had arrived in these completely unknown natural surroundings. Without any memory of his past he would be filled with such astonishment and awe at himself and at the place where he awoke that he could easily become lost in thought about it.' To begin with Kramer overlooks the fact that this is a hypothetical explanation only, but in no sense a description of an actual happening. Furthermore, Kramer can produce not a single example to illustrate such an event. As far as I know no case which is remotely similar has ever been reported. Even if one were to presume that the case described had actually taken place, one would have to understand it exactly in order to realize that nothing would thereby be explained in connection with the case of Kaspar Hauser, for, by means of hypnotism, something can be extracted from the sailor (the recollection of his name and the whole of his past), but nothing can be given to him. Through hypnotism, for instance, no new faculties can be lent to him. 'He would begin life as a man.' Hypnotism does not create a new existence, does not engender a new being. Feuerbach describes what was experienced by everybody who observed Kaspar Hauser at the beginning: 'His whole being and conduct revealed a child in him of scarcely two or three years in the body of a youth.'

Kaspar Hauser showed at his appearance an inconceivable childishness, purity and innocence and was possessed of unique sense faculties and memory. Can such a memory be produced by means of hypnotism? Can somebody be enabled to see in the dark by means of hypnotism? It must be remembered that neither hypothetical explanations nor actual experiences in the field of hypnotism can lead to the conclusion that a completely new state can be created in a human being by hypnotism. One must assume that, on the one hand, Kaspar Hauser had preserved his childlike condition and on the other had lived as a perfectly normal child. It is clear that such assumption creates an insoluble contradiction in itself.

Further to that we must remember that the years of suffering endured by Kaspar Hauser in prison is supported above all by *physical* observation. In irresponsible selection Kramer omits everything that does not fit in with his hypothesis. He mentions, it is true, the anomaly of Kaspar Hauser's knees, diagnosed by Dr Preu, but he argues that this was not mentioned again at the autopsy (why should it be, after all?). He forgets completely to make the phenomenon understandable by any thoughts on the subject. He could have discovered the description in the autopsy report of the changes that had taken place in the brain and liver, described by the doctors as the result of years of imprisonment with little chance of movement and a one-sided nourishment.

The theory of hypnotism must be finally abandoned if we are to understand Kaspar Hauser's character. The fact of years of imprisonment on a diet of bread and water is supported by the circumstance that it was only with the greatest difficulty that Daumer could wean Kaspar Hauser from his accustomed form of nourishment. The disbelief supported by the natural-scientific view that a one-sided diet of this kind could not be continued for years on end, led Kramer on the one hand to deny the imprisonment altogether and on the other to proclaim that Kaspar Hauser was a medium: 'Nevertheless, the idea of incarceration in a cell is nonsense—and that from a scientifically trained doctor who ought to know that nobody in the whole world would be able to survive an imprisonment in the dark with bread and water for such a long time. The town's official medical authority, Dr Preu, along with his privately practising colleague Dr Osterhausen, seem not to have heard of scurvy or vitamin deficiency.'

The explanation for the fact, not denied by Kramer, that Kaspar Hauser himself chose only to consume bread and water, is further supported by the suggestion (respectively autosuggestion) of a medium: 'Daumer is mistaken, however, if he thinks that his bread-and-water-Kaspar is a unique phenomenon. Kaspar Hauser was

exceptional, also as a medium, he was especially sensitive, hyper-
sensitive and extraordinarily somnambulistically disposed—a freak
of nature—but he was in no way unique, as we shall see. There have
been and are mediums who at times, and for a certain length of time,
make do with a reduced diet, or impose one on themselves.' (Kramer).

Kramer does not notice the grotesque illogicality of his
arguments: first he maintains that a person cannot live without a
'normal' diet, then he suddenly creates the suggestion, i.e. autosuggestion. Through that there is really no solution to the riddle,
only the attempt to disprove the fact of Kaspar Hauser's suffering in
prison by means of materialistic dietary superstitions. In the course
of time people have tried to deny everything to Kaspar Hauser: now
finally Kramer tries to deprive him of his suffering also.

Kaspar Hauser's exceptional sense qualities and his occasional
supersensible abilities of awareness are used by Kramer to make him
appear to be a medium and the plaything of all kinds of confused
influences without any kind of proper investigation. We know what
that means: he is not an individual who has been repressed, he is *just*
a medium. This way of solving riddles really consists of destroying
what is enigmatic about them.

The imprisonment of Kaspar Hauser, which must be regarded as a
fact, poses a special problem with respect to the dynastic crime. In
Chapter 1 it has been pointed out that there is a certain contradiction in this. The dynastic crime called for the death of the subject,
the occult manipulations demanded the life of imprisonment. It is
questionable if there is any connection between the two. The planned treatment meted out to Kaspar Hauser excludes the dynastic
crime for the time of its occurrence, which at the most demands
concealment, though this is hard to imagine.

To begin with we shall have to content ourselves with the truly
unsatisfactory situation that nothing of any certainty can be known
about the course of the imprisonment and incarceration of Kaspar
Hauser. In this realm, too, no further discoveries are to be expected.
Ultimately only future spiritual investigation will be able to throw
light on the details of Kaspar Hauser's path of suffering. Such
spiritual revelations, however, are only possible through the will of
the spiritual world itself and the ability of a human being to get hold
of these revelations and to understand and express them correctly.

That also applies to the disclosure of the occult background in
particular cases. From the outset it would be a hopeless task to

obtain documentary and historic evidence about the occult perpetrators in the background. At the best only traces could be found of
their real whereabouts. The idea of the occult must be understood in
this felonious sense to mean that the perpetrators direct their
attention from the start towards leaving no concrete traces behind
them. Contact with outer events is maintained by means of inter-
mediaries, who distract attention from what is happening. Lord
Stanhope was certainly an intermediary of this kind in his dealings
with the western Lodges. It must remain open as to what other
connections he still had, but it is a significant fact that Wassermann
portrays him as having a connection with the Jesuits. According to
Wassermann, Lord Stanhope is informed about his mission by letter
from the 'Grey One'. The instinct of the poet here divines the truth—
but this cannot be historically documented. If, however, such an
incriminating document were known to exist in the estate of Lord
Stanhope—which has not come about and is highly improbable—
one would only get one step further and would not arrive at the heart
of the matter. One could only obtain spiritual certainty in judging
these things if one were to allow the facts which they reveal openly to
speak objectively to us.

Notes (numbered)

GA = Rudolf Steiner Gesamtausgabe, the collected works of Rudolf Steiner in the original German, published by Rudolf Steiner Verlag, Dornach, Switzerland

RSP = Rudolf Steiner Press, London

AP = Anthroposophic Press, New York

1. Johann Wolfgang von Goethe, *Sprüche in Prosa.*
2. Georg Friedrich Daumer, *Mitteilungen über Kaspar Hauser, Enthüllungen über Kaspar Hauser, Kaspar Hauser.*

   Anselm Ritter von Feuerbach, *Kaspar Hauser—Beispiele eines Verbrechens am Seelenleben des Menschen* [Examples of a crime against the soul-life of man].

   Heinrich Fuhrmann, *Kaspar Hauser's Konfirmationsfeier am 20 Mai 1833. Kaspar Hauser—Beobachtet und dargestellt in der letzten Zeit seines Lebens.* [Kaspar Hauser's confirmation ceremony on 20 May 1833. Kaspar Hauser—observed and described during the last part of his life.] Trauerrede, bei der am 20 Dezember 1833 erfolgten Beerdigung des am 14 desselben Monats meuchlings ermordeten Kaspar Hauser gehalten und nur auf vielseitiges Verlangen herausgegeben. [Funeral sermon given on 20 December 1833 on the occasion of the burial of the treacherously murdered Kaspar Hauser on the 14th of the same month and only published at the request of many people.]
3. Jakob Wassermann, *Caspar Hauser oder die Trägheit des Herzens* [Caspar Hauser or the indolence of the heart].

   Hermann Pies, *Kaspar Hauser—Eine Dokumentation.* [Hermann Pies, Kaspar Hauser—a documentation (containing a proof of the previous publications by Pies and the whole of the pertinent literature)].

   Karl Heyer, *Kaspar Hauser und das Schicksal Mittel-Europas im 19 Jahrhundert* [Kaspar Hauser and the destiny of Central Europe in the Nineteenth Century].
4. Julius Meyer, *Authentische Mitteilungen über Kaspar Hauser* [Authentic records of Kaspar Hauser].
5. Daumer, 1873, p.xxii et seq.

6. Daumer, 1873, p.xxiii.
7. Daumer, 1873, p.37.
8. At present Pies is preparing a new edition of the whole of his investigation in 3 large volumes.
9. Feuerbach according to Pies, *Die Wahrheit über Kaspar Hauser's Auftauchen und erste Nürnberger Zeit* [The truth about Kaspar Hauser's appearance and first days in Nuremberg].
10. Further information on this subject can be found in Pies, *Kaspar Hauser—Eine Dokumentation* in the chapter: 'Kaspar Hauser's legitimacy to the throne of Baden'.
11. Heyer, *Kaspar Hauser*.
12. Anselm von Feuerbach, *Merkwürdige Verbrechen* [Remarkable crimes]. This book also contains the already mentioned Memoirs.
13. Pies, *Dokumentation*, p.20.
14. Pies, *Dokumentation*, p.18.
15. Pies, *Dokumentation*, p.19.
16. Pies, *Dokumentation*, p.24.
17. Pies, *Die Wahrheit über Kaspar Hausers Auftauchen* [The truth about Kaspar Hauser's emergence], p.140 et seq.
18. Pies, *Die Wahrheit über Kaspar Hausers Auftauchen*, p.144.
19. Pies, *Die Wahrheit über Kaspar Hausers Auftauchen*, p.157. The whole legal judgement is printed on pp. 145–157.
20. Pies, *Dokumentation*, p.161.
21. Pies, *Dokumentation*, p.31.
22. Pies, *Dokumentation*, p.160.
23. Daumer according to Pies, *Dokumentation*, pp.43 et seq.
24. Daumer, 1873 pp. 457 et seq.
25. Feuerbach according to Pies, *Die Wahrheit über Kaspar Hausers Auftauchen*, pp.57 et seq.
26. Feuerbach according to Pies, *Die Wahrheit über Kaspar Hausers Auftauchen*, pp.53 et seq.
27. Feuerbach, *Merkwürdige Verbrechen* [Remarkable crimes], p.240.
28. Feuerbach, *Merkwürdige Verbrechen* [Remarkable crimes], p.225.
29. Tucher according to Pies, *Die Wahrheit über Kaspar Hausers Auftauchen*, pp.63 et seq.
30. Feuerbach, *Merkwürdige Verbrechen* [Remarkable crimes], p.230 et seq.

31. Rudolf Steiner, *Philosophy of Spiritual Activity* (RSP, 1992): 'The World as Percept'.
32. Feuerbach, *Merkwürdige Verbrechen* [Remarkable crimes], p.243.
33. Pies, *Dokumentation*, p.76.
34. Fuhrmann [Funeral sermon].
35. Tucher according to Pies, *Dokumentation*, p.97.
36. Daumer, 1873, p.254 et seq.
37. Feuerbach, *Merkwürdige Verbrechen* [Remarkable crimes], p.252.
38. Fuhrmann [Funeral sermon].
39. Insertion by the author.
40. Fuhrman according to Pies, *Dokumentation*, p.110.
41. Wassermann, *Caspar Hauser*, p.315.
42. Fuhrmann [Funeral sermon].
43. Daumer, 1873, p.246.
44. Wassermann, *Caspar Hauser*, p.316 (p.463 in the English).
45. Fuhrmann [Funeral sermon].
46. Friedrich Rittelmeyer, *Rudolf Steiner Enters my Life*.
47. See: Heyer, *Kaspar Hauser*, p.51.
48. cf. Rudolf Steiner, *Human Values in Education* (RSP, 1971), Arnheim, 18 July, 1924. GA 310.
49. Rudolf Steiner in: Heyer, *Kaspar Hauser*, p. 287.
50. Pies, *Die Wahrheit über Kaspar Hausers Auftauchen*, p.10.
51. Merker, *Kaspar Hauser—Nicht unwahrscheinlich ein Betrüger* [not unlikely an impostor].
52. Verhör Kaspar Hausers vom 6 November 1829 [Kaspar Hauser's Trial on 6 November, 1829]. Printed in Pies, *Dokumentation*, p.175.
53. *In Memoriam Adolf Bartning, Altes und Neues zur Kaspar Hauser Frage*, p.74 [Old and New Indications about the Kaspar Hauser Question].
54. Heyer, *Kaspar Hauser*, p.90.
55. See: Rudolf Steiner, *Study of Man* (RSP, 1966), Stuttgart, 22 August 1919. GA 293.
56. Gospel according to St Luke 9:33.
57. Daumer, 1873, p.2 et seq.
58. Quotation from Reinhart Buchwald, Schiller, Volume 2, pp.381, 382.
59. Goethe, *Faust* II, Act I. A gloomy gallery.
60. Rudolf Steiner, *Wahrspruchworte*. GA 40.

61. cf. Rudolf Steiner, *Old and New Methods of Initiation* (RSP, 1991), Dornach, 26 February 1922, GA 210.

62. Rudolf Steiner, *Anthroposophical Leading Thoughts* (RSP, 1973), XLV 3. 'In the time that went before his working upon earth, Michael had to witness with anxiety and suffering the evolution of mankind ...' (21 December 1924.)

63. Rudolf Steiner, Dornach, 19 February 1922 (see Note 61).

64. Rudolf Steiner, Dornach, 26 February 1922 (see Note 61).

65. Gospel according to St Matthew 18:3.

66. Rudolf Steiner, *Et Incarnatus est* (Mercury Press, 1983), Basle, 23 December 1917.

67. Gospel According to St John 8:32.

68. Friedrich Schiller in his poem *Resignation*.

69. Rudolf Steiner, *Fall of the Spirits of Darkness* (RSP, 1993), 14 October 1917.

70. Rudolf Steiner, *The Threefold Commonwealth*, Chapter I. (Updated edition: *Towards Social Renewal*, RSP, 1977.)

71. Heyer, *Kaspar Hauser*, Chapter 'Heimatlose seelen' [homeless souls].

72. Rudolf Steiner, 'Die geistige Signatur der Gegenwart' (1888); in *Methodische Grundlagen der Anthroposophie 1884–1901*, GA 30. Also *The Cosmic New Year* (Anthroposophical Publishing Co., 1932), 1 January 1920.

73. Rudolf Steiner, *Towards Social Renewal* (op. cit.) (Supplement).

74. cf. Rudolf Steiner, *The Mission of the Archangel Michael* (AP, 1961).

75. Rudolf Steiner, *The Course of My Life* (AP, 1951), Chapters 7 and 26.

76. Rudolf Steiner, *From Jesus to Christ* (RSP, 1991).

77. Rudolf Steiner, 'Ascension and Pentecost', Dornach, 7 May 1923, in *Festivals and their Meaning* (RSP, 1996).

78. Rudolf Steiner, *Knowledge of Higher Worlds: How is it Achieved?* (RSP, 1969).

79. Rudolf Steiner, *From Jesus to Christ* (op. cit.), Karlsruhe, 5 October 1911.

80. Rudolf Steiner, *Foundations of Esotericism* (RSP, 1982), Berlin, 17 October 1905.

81. Rudolf Steiner, *Knowledge of Higher Worlds* (op. cit.).

82. See Note 57 and Appendix I, Numbers 3, 6 and 7.

83. Rudolf Steiner, *Karma of Untruthfulness*, Vols. I and II (RSP,

1988 and 1992), GA 173 and 174. And Rudolf Steiner, *Heilfaktoren für den sozialen Organismus*, Dornach, 3 July 1920 [Healing processes for the social organism], lecture about Jesuitism and Freemasonry, GA 198.

84. cf. Wassermann, *Caspar Hauser*, Chapter: 'An interrupted performance'.
85. Rudolf Steiner, *Polarities in the Evolution of Mankind* (RSP, 1987), lecture of 13 June 1920.
86. Rudolf Steiner, *Occult Science—an Outline* (RSP, 1984), Chapter: 'The Evolution of the World and Man'.
87. see: Rudolf Steiner, *From Jesus to Christ* (op. cit.), lecture of 10 October 1911.
88. Rudolf Steiner, *From Jesus to Christ* (op. cit.), lecture of 11 October 1911.
89. Rudolf Steiner, *From Jesus to Christ* (op. cit.), lecture of 14 October 1911.
90. See Rudolf Steiner, 'Progress in the knowledge of the Christ,' Paris, 27 May 1914 (GA 152) and *The Four Sacrifices of Christ* (AP, 1981), 1 June 1914.
91. Emil Funk/Joachim Schultz, *Zeitgeheimnisse im Christus-Leben* [Secrets of Time in the Life of Christ].
92. Rudolf Steiner, *Easter and Pentecost*, lecture of 7 May 1923 (see Note 77).
93. Heyer, *Kaspar Hauser*, p.36 et seq.
94. Daumer, 1873, p.139 et seq.
95. Pies, *Dokumentation*, p.175.
96. See in this connection: *Beiträge zur Rudolf Steiner Gesamtausgabe* [Contributions to the collected edition of Rudolf Steiner's works]. Notes by Rudolf Steiner on the Science of the Senses. Number 34, p.16 'The 12-fold Ego'.
97. See Rudolf Steiner's lecture: 'Man's Twelve Senses in their Relation to Imagination, Inspiration. Intuition', Dornach, 8 August 1920, in *Spiritual Science as a Foundation for Social Forms* (AP, 1986).
98. Daumer, 1873, p.172 et seq.
99. Heyer, *Kaspar Hauser*, p.43 includes accounts by Daumer and Rucher.
100. Rudolf Steiner, 'The Work of the Ego in Childhood—A contribution towards an understanding of Christ', Zürich, 25 February 1911. *Anthroposophical Quarterly* 21:4.
101. Pies, *Dokumentation*, p.223 et seq.

102. Daumer treats of this in his work of 1873 under the title: *Biespiele eines ärzlich bezeugten Hauserschen Wunders unleugbarer Art* ['Examples of a medically certified "Hauser Miracle" of an undeniable kind'].

103. Lecture by Rudolf Steiner on 17 June 1908 in Nuremberg in *The Apocalypse of St John* (RSP, 1985), GA 104. Heyer discusses Rudolf Steiner's statement on p.13 et seq, of his book.

104. Rudolf Steiner, *The Spiritual Guidance of Humanity* (AP, 1992), GA 15.

105. Emil Funk, *Der Kalendar von 1912/13*. And *Beiträge zur Rudolf Steiner Gesamtausgabe*, Numbers 37/38 (see also Note 96 above).

106. Rudolf Steiner, *Study of Man* (op. cit.), 1 September 1919. GA 293.

107. Rudolf Steiner, Articles about the Threefold Social Organism and Current Affairs 1915–1921, GA 24: *The Renewal of the Social Organism* (AP, 1985).

108. G.Glöckler, 'Zur Frage der Kernergie.' *Mitteilungen aus der Anthroposophischen Arbeit in Deutschland*, Michaelmas 1977. [The Question about Atomic Power, News about the Anthroposophical Work in Germany.]

109. Rudolf Steiner, *Foundations of Esotericism* (op. cit.), Berlin, 5 October 1905.

110. Rudolf Steiner, *The Deed of Christ and the Opposing Spiritual Powers* (AP, 1976), Berlin, 22 March 1909.

111. Rudolf Steiner, *Theosophy of the Rosicrucian* (RSP, 1981), Munich, 6 June 1907.

112. Johannes Tautz, *Der Eingriff des Widersachers, Fragen zum okkulten Aspekt des Nationalsozialismus*. [The intervention of the Adversary, Questions about the occult aspect of National Socialism.]

113. Mephistopheles in *Faust* II, Act 5, Sepulture, verse 11690 et seq.

114. Alexander Solzhenitsyn, Open letter to the Soviet Leadership.

115. Rudolf Steiner, *Geisteswissenschaft und soziale Frage* [Spiritual Science and the Social Question], Three Essays 1905/06, Dornach, 1977.

116. Quotations from Rudolf Steiner, Articles about the Threefold Social Organism and Current Affairs 1915–21. See note 107.

117. Albrecht Haushofer, *Moabite Sonnets*, Berlin 1946. Haushofer was murdered in Berlin, 23 April 1945.

118. Jacques Lusseyran, *Das wiedergefundene Licht* [English edition: *And There Was Light*, Floris Books 1993]. Chapter, 'Life and Death'.

119. Goethe, *Faust* I, Before the City Gate, verse 1136 et seq.

120. Heyer, *Kaspar Hauser*, p.94 et seq.

121. See in connection with this: Heyer, *Kaspar Hauser*, p.197 et seq. And—by the same author—*Die Französische Revolution und Napoelon*, p.328 et seq.

122. Rudolf Steiner, *From Buddha to Christ* (AP, 1978), lecture V, Neuchâtel, 18 December 1912.

123. Rudolf Steiner, *The Cosmic New Year* (op. cit.), Stuttgart, 1 January 1920.

124. See Chapter 2, 'Kaspar Hauser and the German Folk-spirit', p.74.

125. Both quotes from Rudolf Steiner/Marie Steiner-von Sivers, *Correspondence and Documents 1901–25* (RSP, 1988).

126. From *In memoriam Adolf Bartning, Altes und Neues zur Kaspar Hauser Frage* [Old and New aspects of the Kaspar Hauser Question]. The letter was addressed to her nephew Anselm Feuerbach.

127. Rudolf Steiner, Karlsruhe, 25 January 1910. See: *The Reappearance of Christ in the Etheric* (AP, 1983).

128. Rudolf Steiner, Stuttgart, 6 March 1910. Ibid.

129. Hermann Kükelhaus . . . *ein Narr der Held*, Zürich, 1964, p.9 [a fool the hero].

130. Rudolf Steiner, *The Ahrimanic Deception* (AP, 1985), Zürich, 27 October 1919.

131. Rudolf Steiner, *Influences of Lucifer and Ahriman* (AP, 1993), Dornach, 2 November 1919.

132. Rudolf Steiner, *Influences of Lucifer and Ahriman* (ibid.), Berne, 4 November 1919.

133. Ira Levin, *Rosemary's Baby*, p.145.

134. Ira Levin, *Rosemary's Baby*, p.149.

135. Ira Levin, *Rosemary's Baby*, p.199.

136. Rudolf Steiner, *Karmic Relationships* (RSP, 1989), Vol. VI, Arnheim, 19 July 1924.

137. Rudolf Steiner, *Karmic Relationships* (ibid.), Vol. VI, Arnheim, 19 July 1924.

138. See Vladimir Soloviev, *The Antichrist*.

139. Rudolf Steiner, *The Problem of Faust*, Faust's visit to the Mothers, Vol. II. Lecture from 2 November 1917 in Dornach, GA 273.

140. See in connection with this Rudolf Steiner, 'Der Zugang zum Christentum durch die Geisteswissenschaft' [The approach to Christianity by way of Spiritual Science]. Lecture from 27 April 1907 in Berlin, GA 96.
141. Rudolf Steiner, *The Apocalypse of St. John* (op. cit.), Nuremberg, 29 June 1908, GA 104.
142. Rudolf Steiner, *Spiritual Science as a Foundation for Social Forms* (op. cit.), GA 199.
143. Rudolf Steiner, *Three Streams in the Evolution of Mankind* (RSP, 1985). Lecture from 11 October 1918, GA 184.
144. Rudolf Steiner, *Three Streams in the Evolution of Mankind* (ibid.). Lectures of 11 and 12 October 1918. Rudolf Steiner, 'How do I find the Christ', published in *Evil* (RSP, 1997).
145. Rudolf Steiner, 'How do I find the Christ?' (ibid.), Zürich, 16 October 1918.
146. Rudolf Steiner, *Three Streams in the Evolution of Mankind* (op. cit.). Lecture from 12 October 1918.
147. For further details see Rudolf Steiner's lecture as above, note 146.
148. Rudolf Steiner, *Ancient Myths* (AP, 1994), Dornach, 26 December 1917, GA 180.
149. Rudolf Steiner, *The Wrong and Right Use of Esoteric Knowledge* (RSP, 1966), Dornach, 18 November 1917, GA 178.
150. Rudolf Steiner, *The Etherization of the Blood* (RSP, 1985), Basle 1 October 1911.
151. See Rudolf Steiner, *Goethe as the Founder of a New Science of Aesthetics* (Anthroposophical Pub. Co., London, 1922), GA 30.
152. See in connection with this *The Mission of the Archangel Michael* (op. cit.). Lecture 1, 21 November 1919.
153. Rudolf Steiner, *The Fall of the Spirits of Darkness* (op. cit.), Dornach, 14 October 1917.
154. Quotation from above, note 153, Dornach, 27 October 1917.
155. Rudolf Steiner, *The Course of My Life* (op. cit.).
156. Ibid.
157. Rudolf Steiner/Marie Steiner-von Sivers, *Correspondence and Documents 1901–25* (op. cit.).
158. Rudolf Steiner, *Geisteswissenschaftliche Behandlung sozialer und pädagogischer Fragen* [Spiritual-scientific way of dealing with social and pedagogical questions], Stuttgart, 6 July 1919, GA 192.

159. Rudolf Steiner, *The Destinies of Individuals and Nations* (RSP, 1986), Berlin, 19 January 1915.
160. Rudolf Steiner, *Bilder okkulter Siegel und Säulen* [Occult Seals and Columns], GA 284/285, pp. 113–22. E.A. Karl Stockmeyer, *The Model Building in Malsch*.
161. Rudolf Steiner, *The Principle of Spiritual Economy* (AP, 1986), 6 April 1909.
162. Heyer, *Kaspar Hauser*, p.21.
163. Rudolf Steiner, *Guidance in Esoteric Training* (RSP, 1994). Address on the occasion of the laying of the Foundation Stone of the Goetheanum on 20 September, 1913.
164. Rudolf Steiner, *The Christmas Conference for the Foundation of the General Anthroposophical Society 1923/24* (AP, 1990).
165. See Rudolf Steiner, *Entwürfe, fragmente und Paralipomena zu den vier Mysteriendramen*, GA 44 [sketches, fragments, paralipomena to the four Mystery Dramas].
166. Rudolf Steiner, *Awakening to Community* (AP, 1974), Stuttgart, 23 January 1923.
167. Rudolf Steiner, *The Case for Anthroposophy* (RSP, 1970).
168. Rudolf Steiner, *Polarities in the Evolution of Mankind* (RSP, 1987), Stuttgart, 13 June 1920.
169. See in connection with this: Hella Wiesberger, 'Rudolf Steiner's öffentliches Wirken für die Dreigliederung des sozialen Organismus. Eine Chronik'; in *Nachrichten der Rudolf Steiner Nachlassverwaltung*, No. 24/25 Easter 1969. [Rudolf Steiner's public endeavour on behalf of the Threefold Commonwealth. A Chronicle. Contained in 'News from the Trustees of Rudolf Steiner's Estate'.]
170. The exact date of this conversation could not be ascertained.
171. Hans Kühn, *Dreigliederungs-Zeit* [The time of the Threefold movement].
172. Rudolf Steiner, *Towards Social Renewal* (op. cit.).
173. Rudolf Steiner, 'The Crumbling of the Earth and the Souls and Bodies of Men.' *Anthroposophical Quarterly* 19:1. Dornach, 7 October 1917.
174. Hitler, *Mein Kampf*, Munich, 1934.
175. Rudolf Steiner, *Three Streams in the Evolution of Mankind* (op. cit.), Dornach, 13 October 1918.
176. Quotations from Hitler, *Mein Kampf*.
177. Rudolf Steiner, *The Cosmic New Year* (op. cit.), Stuttgart, 1 January 1920.

178. Rudolf Steiner, *From Buddha to Christ* (op. cit.), Milan, 21 September 1911, 'Buddha and Christ. The Sphere of the Bodhisattvas'.

179. See in this connection: Emil Leinhas, *Aus der Arbeit mit Rudolf Steiner* [From the work with Rudolf Steiner].

180. Rudolf Steiner, *Towards Social Renewal* (op. cit.).

181. Rudolf Steiner, *Man: Hieroglyph of the Universe* (RSP, 1972), GA 201. *The Bridge between Universal Spirituality and the Physical Constitution of Man* (AP, 1979), GA 202. Die Verantworkung des Menschen für die Weltentwickelung [The Responsibility of Man for World Evolution], GA 203. *Materialism and the Task of Anthroposophy* (AP, 1987), GA 204. *Menschenwerden, Weltenseele und Weltengeist* [Man's coming into existence, World-Soul and World-Spirit] parts I and II, GA 206. *Cosmosophy*, parts I (AP, 1985) and II, GA 207 and 208. *Nordische und Mitteleuropäische Geist-impulse* [Northern and Central European Spiritual Impulses], GA 209.

182. Rudolf Steiner, *The Constitution of the School of Spiritual Science 1924/25* (RSP, 1980), Dornach, 18 January 1924, GA 260a. See also: Friedrich Rittelmeyer, *Rudolf Steiner Enters My Life*. And Emil Leinhas, *Aus der Arbeit mit Rudolf Steiner*.

183. Leinhas, see note 179.

184. Rudolf Steiner, *World History in the Light of Anthroposophy* (RSP, 1977), Dornach, 31 December 1923.

185. Ilona Schubert, *Reminiscences of Rudolf Steiner and Marie Steiner-von Sivers*, London 1991.

186. See also Rudolf Grosse, *Die Weihnachtstagung als Zeitenwende* [The Christmas Gathering as a turning-point in time].

187. Rudolf Steiner, 'The Constitution of the General Anthroposophical Society and of the Free High School for Spiritual Science', Paris, 23 May 1924.

188. Rudolf Steiner, as above, Dornach, 18 January 1924.

189. Rudolf Steiner/Marie Steiner-von Sivers, *Correspondence and Documents 1901–25* (op. cit.).

190. *Koberwitz 1924*, published by Count Adalbert von Keyserlingk, part I. Countess Johanna von Keyserlingk [Twelve Days together with Rudolf Steiner].

191. cf. Rudolf Steiner, *Occult Science—an Outline* (op. cit.), Chapter 'Man and the Evolution of the World', GA 13.

192. See for example the lecture from 21 September 1911 in Milan: *From Buddha to Christ* (op. cit.).

193. Heyer, *Kaspar Hauser*, p.51.
194. Rudolf Steiner, 'Rosicrucian Christianity', Neuchâtel, 27 September 1911. *Esoteric Christianity and the Mission of Christian Rosenkreutz* (RSP, 1984).
195. Rudolf Steiner, *From Buddha to Christ* (op. cit.), Neuchâtel, 18 December 1912.
196. For instance: 'Already in the fourteenth century the individuality of the thirteenth had reincarnated'. Lecture from 27 September 1911 in Neuchâtel (see note 194).
197. Rudolf Steiner, Lecture from 15 December 1907 in Düsseldorf. GA 98.
198. See Heyer, *Kaspar Hauser*, p.94 et seq.
199. See Heyer, *Kaspar Hauser*, p.23.
200. Quote from Rudolf Steiner, *From Buddha to Christ* (op. cit.), Neuchâtel, 18 December 1912.
201. cf. Chapter 3 and Rudolf Steiner, *From Jesus to Christ* (op. cit.), Karlsruhe, 14 October 1911.
202. Heyer, *Kaspar Hauser*, pp. 75–79.
203. Contained in Pies, *Kaspar Hauser*, Stuttgart, 1925, p.179. Or Heyer, *Kaspar Hauser*, p.78.
204. Rudolf Steiner, 'Preliminary stages leading to the Mystery of Golgotha', GA 152.
205. Rudolf Steiner, *The Driving Force of Spiritual Powers in World History* (AP, 1972), Dornach, 23 March 1923, GA 222.
206. Rudolf Steiner, *The Apocalypse of St. John* (op. cit.), Nuremberg, 17 June 1908. GA 104.
207. See in this connection Pies, *Die Wahrheit über Kaspar Hausers erste Zeit* [The truth concerning Kaspar Hauser's first days], pp.175–223. Section concerning Lord Stanhope.
208. Pies, *Kaspar Hauser*, Eye-witness accounts and personal recollections I, p.242.
209. Rudolf Steiner, *Foundations of Esotericism* (op. cit.), Berlin, 28 October 1905, GA 93a.
210. Rudolf Steiner, *The Theosophy of the Rosicrucians* (op. cit.), Munich, 31 May 1907, GA 99.
211. Rudolf Steiner, 'Rosicrucian Christianity II', Neuchâtel, 28 September 1911. (See note 194.)

Notes (refer to page numbers)

(Marked with * in text)

6. 'The figure of Kaspar Hauser was a decisive event in my youth, almost a vision since the awakening of consciousness.' Quoted from the essay by Jakob Wassermann: 'My personal experiences with regard to the "Caspar Hauser novel".'

18. This is where Pies has to admit that Meyer left out just the most important last sentence in his 'Authentische Mitteilungen' [authentic records].

57. Rudolf Steiner mentions this constellation described by Wassermann in his two lectures about Kaspar Hauser (see Appendix I, Numbers 2, 4 and 12).

62. Rudolf Steiner referred to the existence of such background events and figures—without mentioning Kaspar Hauser—in 1916 and 1917 in *Karma of Untruthfulness*, vols. 1 and 2 (RSP, 1988 and 1992).

72. It is in this sense that the Dutch painter, Hieronymous Bosch, portrayed those who had died or who were not yet born as black and living people as white. (See: *The Pictorial Language of Hieronymous Bosch* by Clément A.Wertheim Aymès.)

75. The records of Rudolf Steiner's conversations included in the estate of Count Polzer-Hoditz are published here for the first time. They have been made available to the author of the present work on account of his studies of Kaspar Hauser. They did not form the starting point for this work, but fit naturally into the whole (see Appendix I, Number 3). Further points from these records will be explained at the appropriate place.

76. The words: 'on the true ground of the German nation', which might understandably sound ominous to those born later, should not be a cause of irritation. Daumer was neither a nationalist not a materialist. He was actually referring to the spiritual ground of the German nation.

80. The fifth post-Atlantean cultural epoch (AD 1413–3573—the middle of which is AD 2493)—will still last for about 1500 years. The development of the German nation shows a rhythmical increase (respectively decrease) in the strength exerted by the German Folk-spirit. During the time of the migration of the

people—from about the seventh century onwards—the German people separated from the other Germanic peoples. This was when the German language first came into existence. Around the year 1200 the courtly language of the Hohenstaufen dynasty was blossoming. The fourth phase of this rhythm will come in the twenty-fifth century in close proximity to the middle of the fifth cultural epoch (AD 2493). One must think in such temporal terms when speaking about the development of nations and when one is concerned about the existing situation, which at present shows no hope of a solution.

83. According to a remark by Rudolf Steiner, Charles IV of Bohemia was the last initiate on the German throne. A lasting monument to his connection with the Grail-Kingship is to be seen in his castle of Karlstein. Furthermore, Charles IV carried out his occult impulses in secret as befitted the time.

83. The inner current of the Grail-Community was continued later by the Order of the Knights Templar which was then taken over in secret by the Rosicrucians when the latter Order was destroyed. (See Rudolf Steiner *The Temple Legend*, RSP, 1997, lecture from 22 May 1905, GA 93.)

92. A reference to the 33-year rhythm is to be found in the *Soul Calendar* of 1912 by the wording: 'The year 1879 after the birth of the Ego'.

101. Kaspar Hauser lived in the Castle at Karlsruhe from 29 September till 15 October 1812. The lecture cycle *From Jesus to Christ* was given between 4 and 15 October 1911.

118. 'This person, with his natural and direct purity and unself-consciousness, presented a perfect picture of the first man in Paradise before the Fall, just as I found and described him.' (Noted by Baron von Tucher in 1828, as quoted by Daumer in his *Kaspar Hauser*, published Regensburg 1873.) 'The cold, hard-hearted isolation of human selfhood and circumspection, this true "Fall of Man", had not yet taken place in this human being. A paradisaical archetype of mankind stood before us in a moral sense, an adorable miracle in the midst of an utterly depraved world of mankind submerged in an abyss of selfishness and evil.' (Daumer, *Enthüllungen über Kaspar Hauser*.) [Revelations about Kaspar Hauser.]

119. A definite connection between the phantom-body and a change of diet is evident in the case of stigmatization. In his lecture cycle *From Jesus to Christ* (RSP, 1991) Rudolf Steiner says:

'Through the mystic feeling of Christian initiation we really penetrate as far as the physical body; then appear the stigmata, the places of the bleeding wounds of Christ Jesus'. (Lecture from 14 October 1911.)

It is known already—even though this is sometimes questioned—that in a stigmatized person the phenomenon of more or less doing without food is present. In the best known case of stigmatization in our time, Theresa von Konnesreuth completely abstained from physical nourishment for some decades (see Luise Rinser, *Die Wahrheit über Konnesreuth* [The truth about Konnesreuth]). This phenomenon is understandable if one calls to mind that the phantom-body is of a physical-spiritual nature, and through that the relationship of the human being to the material world of physical substance undergoes a profound change.

125. The calamitous outcome of the direct connection between the Germans and the Russians (especially for the latter) was expressed in a lecture given by Rudolf Steiner in Berlin, 17 January 1915. (*The Destinies of Individuals and Nations*, RSP, 1987.)

127. The same statement by Rudolf Steiner is also to be found in the following connection: On 8 June 1918 Rudolf Steiner was staying with Count Polzer-Hoditz in Tannbach near Gutau in the 'Lower Mill' quarter. On visiting a radioactive spring in the vicinity Rudolf Steiner mentioned in the course of conversation that radioactivity has only been present in the Earth since the Mystery of Golgotha. (*Erinnerungen an den grossen Lehrer Dr Rudolf Steiner. Lebensrückschau eines Österreichers* von Ludwig Graf Polzer-Hoditz, Prag 1837. ['Memories of the great teacher Dr Rudolf Steiner. Review of the Life of an Austrian' by Count Ludwig Polzer-Hoditz]). cf. also article by Walter Cloos in *Die Kommenden*, 10 January 1979: 'Was ist die natürliche Radioaktivität in Wirklichkeit? [What actually is natural radioactivity?]).

141. What effect might the 1945 atomic bomb explosion have on the earth-organism? Two questions can be raised in this connection. Firstly, one may ask if the earth organism as a whole—along with unquestionably-existing other rhythms—evinces a 33-year rhythm too. The following thoughts call for us to look more closely into this. For a start, the historical development of man is closely linked to the earth, so that the latter can take

part in the historical rhythm; apart from that the living earth organism is the Body of Christ and thus it seems justified to take account of the rhythm created by the incarnated Sun-Spirit within this body.

Secondly, one has, of course, to ask how the effects will become apparent. Basically we have to point out that, because of the increasing materialism and egoism of man, the earth organism reacts, among other things, with earthquakes (see in this respect the three lectures by Rudolf Steiner: 1. 'The Interior of the Earth and Volcanic Eruptions', 16 April 1906, GA 96; 2. 'Das Innere der Erde' [The interior of the Earth], 21 April 1906, GA 97; 3. *The Deed of Christ and the Opposing Spiritual Powers*, AP, 1976, 1 January 1909, GA 107). One can understand in a figurative sense that the Body of Christ trembles at the growing amorality of mankind. The law of compensation in human destiny, mentioned above, takes effect here too. The sufferings of the mainly innocent victims, who have no direct connection with the causes, provide compensation for mankind in general. In connection with man's place of habitation, earthquakes are in any case a cause of great distress.

According to statements by Rudolf Steiner we should expect more earthquakes in future. Earthquake research does not confirm these statements at present. It must however be taken into account that the criteria for assessment are not yet settled. Does it depend upon the universal frequency and intensity of the earthquakes—according to a still unknown and changing rhythm? Or on the sequence of earthquakes at a particular place? Rudolf Steiner's Vesuvius example in his lecture of 16 April 1906 seems to imply this. Does it depend upon the numbers of casualties or on the occurrence of earthquakes in hitherto protected areas? In that connection mild quakes were experienced in Berlin during the last years—a fact which experts would have thought to have been impossible 20 years ago. A large number of questions are presented here which await future research.

150. What is here elaborated by Rudolf Steiner is, in my opinion, meant to signify the constructiveness and exclusiveness of the black-and-white principle. Something is constructed which, for its part, excludes some other possibility. The rise of Prussia to become a world power and the later founding of the German

Empire excluded any other kind of development taking place in Central Europe.

179. 'When the world revolts, as it does today, it is the heavens which are revolting, that is to say, that part of the heavens which is retained in the human soul and which does not then appear in its true form, but as its opposite, which appears in battles and blood instead of in imaginations. It is no wonder, therefore, that those people who take part in work which is so destructive for the social order, actually gain the impression that they are doing something beneficial. For what do they feel within themselves? They feel that heaven resides within them; but it is only a caricatured form within their soul. The truths which we should comprehend today are of such earnestness as that!' (Rudolf Steiner, *Spiritual Science as a Foundation for Social Forms*, AP, 1986, lecture of 11 September 1920. GA 199.)

183. The idea that there are causes which lie in the future and pre-determine the present is something of great importance for all studies of karma. It is basically elaborated by Rudolf Steiner in *Manifestations of Karma* (RSP, 1995), Hamburg 19 and 20 May 1910 (GA 120). One can also arrive at this thought by acquiring a more profound understanding of the concept of time—as Rudolf Steiner once briefly described it in the case of his own development: 'During this period—and this is already due to external spiritual influences—I gained complete understanding of the concept of time. This knowledge was in no way connected with my studies and was guided totally by the spiritual life. I understood that there is a regressing evolution, the occult-astral, which interferes with the progressing one. This knowledge is the pre-condition of spiritual clairvoyance.' (Rudolf Steiner, Marie Steiner-von Sivers, *Correspondence and Documents 1901–25*, RSP, 1988, GA 262).

190. It refers to the *Swastika*, not to the sign of Sorath given by Rudolf Steiner in the two previously mentioned lectures.

190. Twice 666 is 1332. A Sorath-effect is expressed immediately prior to this date in the battle of Philip le Bel against the Order of the Templars (1307–14). (cf. Rudolf Steiner, *Inner Impulses of Evolution*, AP, 1984, lecture 6, 25 September 1916 and 'The Templars', Dornach, 2 October 1916. GA 171.)

195. 'It was laid down that all discoveries made by them must remain a secret among the Rosicrucians for a hundred years. Only after a hundred years might these Rosicrucian revelations

be given to the world; only after they had been worked upon for a hundred years was it permissible to speak of them in an appropriate way. Thus from the seventeenth until the eighteenth century, the knowledge was in preparation which came to expression in the year 1785 in the work "The Secret Figures of the Rosicrucians".

'Now it is also very important for us to know that the Rosicrucian inspiration in every century was given in such a way that the actual bearer of it was never outwardly designated as such. Only the very highest initiates knew who he was. Today, for example, it is only permissible to speak in the external world of happenings which took place a hundred years ago, for that is the period which must have elapsed before it is lawful to speak of them openly. The temptation to pay fanatical veneration to an authority drawn into the sphere of the personal—than which there is nothing worse—is too great for human beings to resist. It is too immediate. The maintenance of silence is a necessary precaution not only against the external temptations of ambition and pride, which it might be possible to ward off, but above all against the occult, astral attacks which would all the time be directed against such an individuality. Hence the condition that such matters may be spoken of only after a hundred years have passed is a necessary one.' (Rudolf Steiner, *Esoteric Christianity and the Mission of Christian Rosenkreutz*, RSP, 1984, GA 130. Lecture given in Neuchâtel, 27 September 1911.)

On the hundreth anniversary of Kleist's longing, which could only have been satisfied by spiritual science, Steiner mentions in his lecture that it was 'an unusual dispensation of karma' that he should come to speak about what would have satisfied Kleist's longing for spiritual science exactly 100 years after the latter's tragic death. One gains the impression from this that something in the nature of a healing takes place in Kleist's karma. (See Rudolf Steiner, *The Inner Realities of Evolution*, RSP, 1953, Berlin, 21 November 1911.)

In Berlin, on 23 April 1912, Rudolf Steiner drew attention to the meaning and significance of the span of 100 years in Rosicrucianism. Indeed it is a venerable rule in Rosicrucianism that a teacher of a Rosicrucian Order is never outwardly proclaimed as such by his contemporaries; the fact that he *is* such a teacher may not be spoken of until 100 years after his death—not before—because only so can the *impersonal* element be preserved in a genuine spiritual movement. (*Earthly and Cosmic Man*, Rudolf Steiner Pub. Co., 1948, lecture IV, GA 133.)

198. We must consider the fact that Daumer and Kaspar Hauser bear the same age relationships to one another. Daumer was born in 1800, that is 12 years before Kaspar Hauser. He was 28 years old when Kaspar Hauser was given into his care—and 33 years old when Kaspar Hauser was murdered at the age of 21. In the 33-year life of Jesus Christ this age relationship is expressed by the great change brought about at the age of 12 by the union of the two Jesus children.

204. This is another case in which precisely 99 years ensue.

206. At the outbreak of war in 1914 the then Grand Duchess of Baden is said to have remarked: 'That is revenge for the crime committed against Kaspar Hauser!'

222. With the word 'Manes' one has to understand 'Manas', the spirit-self, the being of man which, after death, spreads out over the planets and zodiac to form a multiplicity of beings. Rudolf Steiner once gave the following explanation for 'Manes' (*Study of Man*, RSP, 1966, Stuttgart, 4th lecture, 25 August 1919):

'First there is, in embryonic form, what we call the spirit-self. We cannot include the spirit-self among the constituents or members of human nature when we are speaking of the present-day man; but there is a clear consciousness of the spirit-self in people who are able to see into the spiritual. You know that the whole oriental consciousness, in so far as it is educated consciousness, calls this spirit-self *Manas*, and that *Manas* is always spoken of in the oriental spiritual teaching as indwelling in man. But among western peoples, too, even if they are not exactly "learned", there is a clear consciousness of this spirit-self. And I say deliberately: that this clear consciousness exists; for among the people, at least before they had completely absorbed the materialistic point of view, that part of man which remains over after death was called the *Manes*: people said that after death there remains over the *Manes*—*Manas* is the same as *Manes*. I say that the people have a clear consciousness of this, for the people in this case use the plural, the *Manes*. We who from a scientific standpoint connect the spirit-self more with man before death, use the singular form 'the spirit-self'. The people who speak of the spirit-self more realistically from a naïve knowledge use the plural form because at the moment in which a man passes through the gate of death, he is received by a plurality of spiritual beings. I have already pointed this out in another connection: we each have a spirit who leads us personally, belonging to the hierarchy of the angels; over them we have the spirits belonging to the hierarchy of the archangels, who enter a man immediately he passes through the gate of death, so that he then exists in a certain way in the plural, because many archangels have entered into his being. The people feel this very clearly because they know that after death man perceives himself (to a greater or lesser degree) as a plurality, in contrast to his appearance in this life which is a unity. Thus the *Manes* live on in the naïve folk consciousness as the plural aspect of the spirit-self, of *Manas*.'

225. It should be mentioned that the first Goetheanum was never officially opened or dedicated—but it was already in use. The official opening was postponed by Rudolf Steiner owing to the fact that the statue of the 'Representative of Man' had not yet been completed. For this reason it had not yet been installed in the place intended for it and therefore it escaped the fire.

233. 'The complication arising out of human nature is made particularly acute by the fact that—as I have explained from a different point of view—the human being as such reaches the age of 27, that is to say, only develops by the course of nature to the age of 27. What then occurs does not happen of its own accord, as in ancient times, but must be sought after. So it is today, that young people go through a period of development up till their 27th year, during which time the human elements aggregate of their own accord. A person expects to receive them from life until his 27th year. Then, when his 27th year arrives, life does not supply him with anything further. He also does not contribute anything of his own. From then on his life begins to grow hollow and empty and everything becomes dreary if he does not rouse himself to take up the life of the spirit which, as I have said, pours over him like a wave. The crisis—which actually occurs in every human life at around the 27th year and lasts until about the 35th year—comes to expression through characteristic events at the present time, for everything that lives in the general nature of mankind comes to expression very strongly in isolated phenomena. Thus, for

instance, a leading and highly regarded personality—though there was not much that this personality led—was confronted at a certain moment with a very important decision. But at the same time as this decision had to be made, something else happened to this personality. He had been incarnated previously in the ninth century AD and had been a kind of black magician living in a place in southern Europe. That worked into the present incarnation of this personality in such a way that when this important event occurred he actually died, that is to say the body was deserted by the soul which had reincarnated into it. But the personality lived on and was nevertheless still there to all outward appearances. Just imagine what opportunities that gave to all kinds of ahrimanic spirits and individualities to continue to live on in such a dead human being! That is one among such cases as are provided by the complications of modern life. Such things as this play into the deeds of mankind today, play into the destinies of human beings. One cannot gain an insight into what happens in such a case today without having at least an inkling of such incisive events as those which I have just mentioned. I have often stressed the fact—and there are people here today to whom I have stressed it: one cannot judge the things leading up to the catastrophe of the First World War as one formerly used to judge history, because on all sides windows have been opened through which ahrimanic beings enter. And because spiritual causes of the most dubious and unusual kind have played their part in the events of July 1914, one is unable to speak about the historical causes of this World War catastrophe without considering the spiritual factors involved.' (Rudolf Steiner, Dornach, 6 April 1919. GA 190.)

251. A specially powerful argument in this direction is to be found in the lecture given in Dornach, 17 April 1921, in which a possible loss of his life is referred to: 'For us, what matters is the strength to stand firmly on the ground of what we recognize as right. Yes, nothing will be left undone to undermine this ground; of this you can be sure. I had to bring this up once more, particularly in connection with the considerations concerning the course taken by European civilization; for it is necessary that at least the intention develops to place oneself firmly on the ground we must recognize as the right one. It is also necessary that among ourselves we do not give ourselves

up to popular illusions concerning the various attacks. Their aim is to undermine the ground we stand on. It is up to us to work as much as is humanly possible, and then, if the ground under us should become undermined and we do slide down into the chasm, our efforts will nevertheless have been such that they will find their spiritual path through the world. For what appears now are the last convulsions of a dying world. But even if it is in its last throes of death, this world can still strike out like a raving maniac, and one can lose one's life due to this frantic lashing out. This is why we must at least recognize what kind of impulses give rise to this mad lashing out. Nothing can be achieved by what is timid; we must appeal to what is bold. Let us try to measure up to such an appeal!' (*Materialism and the Task of Anthroposophy*, AP, 1987, lecture 6, GA 204).

256. The seven-membered being of an angel comprises etheric body, astral body, ego, spirit-self, life-spirit, spirit-man, Holy Spirit. Through participation in the Holy Spirit the angel becomes a 'Messenger of God'. (See in this connection: Rudolf Steiner, *The Theosophy of the Rosicrucians*, RSP, 1966, Munich, 2 June 1907.)

261. One has to distinguish to some extent between this work of the Rosicrucians and what Christian Rosenkreutz himself does. The work of Christian Rosenkreutz consists now and throughout many further incarnations in the future of developing and forming the resurrection body itself, whereby he is serving a distant goal of mankind. (See lecture by Rudolf Steiner in Neuchâtel, 18 December 1912: *From Buddha to Christ*, AP, 1978.)

264. 'The Chemical Wedding' was composed and distributed in handwritten form in 1604 and printed in 1616. The Rosicrucian writings appeared in Kassel 1614/1615. A historical effect was prevented at that time owing to the 30 Years War. The martial events hid the spiritual figure which wanted to make its appearance.

266. 'Kaspar Hauser's genuine show of concern for others could be quite touching through some of the expressions he used. Daumer, for instance, gives an example of this in the following sayings of his from October 1828: "He does not like to think about the time he was imprisoned because he can imagine the fear that his captor must have experienced. The latter must

have constantly wished for his death, which did not come about, and thus he believed that the unknown person must have lived in the greatest anxiety until he got rid of him, a fact which was painful to him when he thought about it." Daumer remarks about this: 'Such expressions had not come to Kaspar Hauser through his education or any sort of acquired culture, nor was it the outcome of any sort of religious influence, they came to him purely and independently in all their originality out of the unclouded human nature, which life in the world caused him to fall away from." ' (From *Kaspar Hauser* by Heyer.)

267. Rudolf Steiner's saying about 'the straggler from Atlantis' should not lead one to think of it as something unintended, accidental or without plan.

Selected Bibliography

Bock, Emil, *Wiederholte Erdenleben. Die Wiederverkörperungsidee in der deutschen Geistesgeschichte*. 6th edition 1975. [Repeated earth lives. The idea of reincarnation in the spiritual history of Germany.] Short reference in connection with Daumer.

Feuerbach, *Kaspar Hauser oder Beispiel eines Verbrechens am Seclenlesen eines Menschen*, Munich 1963.

Grunelius-Schacht, Sonja von, *Caspar Hauser, Mon Cher—der namenlose Prinz*. Stuttgart, 1975.

Heyer, Karl, *Kaspar Hauser und das Schicksal Mitteleuropas im 19 Jahrhundert* [Kaspar Hauser and the destiny of Central Europe in the Nineteenth Century]. Stuttgart (Kressbroun) 1958.

König, Karl, *Mignon—Versuch einer Geschichte der Heilpädagogik. Der Beitrag der Geisteswissenschaft zur Erweiterung der Heilkunst*. Vol.I, Dornach 1950. [Attempt to write the history of Curative Education. The Contribution of Spiritual Science to extending the Art of Healing.]

Kramer, Kurt, *Kaspar Hauser—Kein Rätsel unserer Zeit*, Ansbach 1978. *'Ich möchte ein solcher werden wie...'* Material zur Sprachlosigkeit des Kaspar Hauser*. Publ. Jochen Hörisch. Suhrkamp Taschenbuch—Wissenschaft 283. Frankfurt am Main, 1979. [Kaspar Hauser—no riddle of our time. *'I want to become like ...* Source material about Kaspar Hauser's lack of speech.]

Krell-Werth, Emma, Ruf des Pirol [The Song of the Golden Oriol— Poems about Kaspar Hauser]. Dornach 1976.

Kunze, Wilhelm, *Mythos, Gestalt und Schicksal von Kaspar Hauser*. Nuremberg-Leipzig 1931. [Myth, personality and destiny of Kaspar Hauser.]

Lampe, Bernd, *Kaspar Hauser in Treblinka*. Play, Stuttgart 1979.

Maikowski, René, *Auf der Suche nach dem lebendigen Geist*. Freiburg 1971. [In search of the living Spirit.]

Pietzner, Carlo, *... und aus der Nacht: Kaspar*. A play in seven scenes. MS printed 1975. [... and out of the night.]

Schuster, Volkfried, *Niklaus von Flüe—Monroe-Doktrin—Kaspar Hauser*. Dornach 1978. *Kaspar Hauser in der Universalität der Geschichte*. See also article with similar title in *Das Goetheanum*, year 1979, Numbers 18 and 19. [Kaspar Hauser in the universality of history.]

Steffen, Albert, *Krisis, Kartharsis, Therapie* (Chapter: 'Das Kaspar Hauser Problem'. Dornach 1944).

Wohlbold, Hans, 'Kaspar Hauser'. *Anthroposophie* XIV 4/5 Jan/Feb 1932.

Wohlbold, Hans, 'Das eigentliche Problem Kaspar Hauser'. *Blätter für Anthroposophie.* VI, 2 February 1954.

For a complete catalogue of publications, write to:

TEMPLE LODGE PUBLISHING
51 Queen Caroline Street
London W6 9QL